Great Commanders

EDITED BY JAMES GRANT WILSON

GENERAL GREENE

ARMY AND NAVY EDITION

Great Commanders
★ ★ ★ ★

General Greene

Francis Vinton Greene

HERITAGE BOOKS
2006

HERITAGE BOOKS
AN IMPRINT OF HERITAGE BOOKS, INC.

Books, CDs, and more—Worldwide

For our listing of thousands of titles see our website
at
www.HeritageBooks.com

A Facsimile Reprint
Published 2006 by
HERITAGE BOOKS, INC.
Publishing Division
65 East Main Street
Westminster, Maryland 21157-5026

Copyright © 1893 D. Appleton and Company
New York

— Publisher's Notice —
In reprints such as this, it is often not possible to remove blemishes from the original. We feel the contents of this book warrant its reissue despite these blemishes and hope you will agree and read it with pleasure.

International Standard Book Number: 978-0-7884-2255-3

CONTENTS.

CHAPTER	PAGE
I.—ANTECEDENTS AND EDUCATION, 1742–1770 . .	1
II.—EARLY LIFE IN RHODE ISLAND, 1770–1775 .	10
III.—BOSTON AND LONG ISLAND, 1775–1776 . . .	23
IV.—FORT WASHINGTON, 1776	43
V.—THE JERSEYS, 1776–1777	60
VI.—THE BRANDYWINE AND GERMANTOWN, 1777 . .	76
VII.—APPOINTED QUARTERMASTER GENERAL — VALLEY FORGE—MONMOUTH AND NEWPORT, 1777–1778 .	94
VIII.—QUARTERMASTER GENERAL — SPRINGFIELD, 1778–1780	118
IX.—RESIGNS AS QUARTERMASTER GENERAL—WEST POINT, 1780	141
X.—TAKES COMMAND OF THE SOUTHERN ARMY, 1780 .	161
XI.—THE RETREAT TO THE DAN AND THE BATTLE OF GUILFORD COURT HOUSE, 1781	191
XII.—THE BATTLE OF HOBKIRK'S HILL AND THE SIEGE OF NINETY-SIX, 1781	228
XIII.—THE BATTLE OF EUTAW SPRINGS AND THE CLOSE OF THE SOUTHERN CAMPAIGN, 1781–1783 . .	263
XIV.—CLOSING YEARS AND DEATH, 1783–1786 . .	303
INDEX	321

LIST OF ILLUSTRATIONS.

                                                    FACING PAGE

Portrait of Nathanael Greene   . . .   *Frontispiece*
    From the painting by Charles Wilson Peale.

The Engagement at Harlem Heights 48
    From The Campaign of 1776 around New York, by Henry P. Johnston, published by the Long Island Historical Society.

Fort Washington 58
    From The Campaign of 1776 around New York, by Henry P. Johnston, published by the Long Island Historical Society.

Operations at Newport 116
    From Marshall's Life of Washington.

Theater of Operations in the Southern Campaign . . 190

The Battle of Guilford Court House 226
    From Johnson's Life of Greene.

The Battle of Hobkirk's Hill 242
    From Johnson's Life of Greene.

The Siege of Ninety-Six 258
    From Johnson's Life of Greene.

The Battle of Eutaw Springs 276
    From Johnson's Life of Greene.

LIST OF AUTHORITIES CONSULTED.

Life of Nathanael Greene, by George Washington Greene, 3 vols., 1871.
Life of Greene, by William Johnson, 2 vols., 1822.
Life of Nathanael Greene, by Charles Caldwell, 1819.
Life of Nathanael Greene, by W. G. Simms, 1849.
Life and Writings of George Washington, by Jared Sparks, 12 vols., 1858.
Correspondence of the American Revolution, by Jared Sparks, 4 vols., 1853.
Life of Washington, by John Marshall, 2 vols., 1832.
Life of Washington, by Washington Irving, 5 vols., 1859.
Memoirs of the War in the Southern Department, by General Henry Lee, 1813.
Campaign of 1781 in the Carolinas, by Henry Lee, third edition, 1824.
Battles of the United States, by Henry B. Dawson, 2 vols, 1858.
Field Book of the Revolution, by Benson J. Lossing, 1859.
Battles of the American Revolution, by Henry B. Carrington, 1876.
Campaign of 1776 around New York, by Henry P. Johnston, published by the Long Island Historical Society, 1878.
Life of Steuben, by Friedrich Kapp, 1859.
Life of General Kalb, by Friedrich Kapp, 1884.
Life of Knox, by Francis S. Drake, 1873.
Treason of Charles Lee, by George H. Moore, 1860.
History of the Independence of the United States, by William Gordon, 4 vols., 1788.
History of the American Revolution, by David Ramsay, 3 vols., 1793.
Journals of the American Congress, 1774-1788, 4 vols., 1823.
The Clinton-Cornwallis Controversy, by Benjamin F. Stevens, 2 vols., 1888.
History of the Campaigns of 1780 and 1781, by Lieutenant-Colonel Tarleton, 1787.
History of the American War, by C. Stedman, 2 vols., 1794.
Anecdotes of the Revolutionary War, by Alexander Garden, 1822.

GENERAL GREENE.

CHAPTER I.

ANTECEDENTS AND EDUCATION.

NATHANAEL GREENE was born in 1742, "on the 27th day of the fifth month," according to the entry in his father's diary. The Gregorian Calendar was not adopted in England or its colonies until ten years later, and March was then considered the first month. His birth was therefore on August 7, 1742. He was of the fourth generation of the descendants of John Greene, surgeon, of Salisbury, England, whose ancestors had lived for several generations in Dorsetshire, and are referred to in the parish records of births, marriages, and deaths, as gentlemen and landed proprietors. John Greene sailed from Hampton in the ship James, on April 5, 1635, and landed at Boston sixty days later. Like many others, he had left England in order to make his home in a land where he could worship God according to his own conscience; but he soon discovered that the theocratic government of Massachusetts Bay was more intolerable than that of the land he had left. He therefore followed Roger Williams into the wilderness, and aided him to found the colony of Rhode Island. The services of this little community in establishing civil and religious liberty have not received in public estimation the credit to which they are entitled. The colony was so small that it was overlooked among its more powerful neighbors, but "tall oaks from little acorns grow." The opinions of Roger Williams were shared by such an infinitesimal minority of mankind, two hundred and fifty years ago, that it was necessary that they should first be put into practice by a small community; and it is the glory of Rhode Island that the opinions of this handful of settlers on Narragansett Bay should now be the foundation principle of government among more than one hundred millions of English-speaking people scattered over the four quarters of the globe.

The principles on which Roger Williams founded his colony were: the right of every man to worship God according to the dictates of his own conscience; the right of the people to choose their own public officials of all classes; and the right of property—which last is upheld by all governments, but was carried so far by Williams that he denied the authority of any one to give or receive original titles to land in America without the consent of the Indians as primary owners. These rights were fully and completely secured by the charter for Providence Plantations which Williams secured from the Earl of Warwick and his associates under the Protector in 1643, and in that which Clarke secured from Charles II in 1663 for Rhode Island and Providence Plantations. The latter charter gave such complete civil and religious liberty, that, when the colonies revolted in 1776, and the others formed their State constitutions, it was only necessary in Rhode Island to pass

ANTECEDENTS AND EDUCATION.

an act of the Assembly substituting allegiance to the colony for allegiance to the King. No other change was necessary in its fundamental law, and under this charter its affairs were successfully administered, until 1843.

With Williams and Clarke and Gorton, John Greene helped to found this colony. He was in the first company to follow Williams from Salem, and he arrived at Providence in the spring of 1636, bringing with him his wife and five children—four sons and an infant daughter. Williams had bought his land at Providence from the Indian chiefs who owned it, and he conveyed it for a consideration of £30 to his "loving friends and neighbors," twelve in number, among whom was John Greene. Five years later John Greene, in company with a few others from Providence and a few from Newport, purchased from the Indians a tract on the west side of Narragansett Bay, about four miles wide and twenty miles long, which was at first called Shawomet, but afterward named Warwick in gratitude for the kindness shown them by the Earl of Warwick, then Governor-in-Chief and Lord High Admiral of the Colonies. Here John Greene passed the remainder of his days, and here his descendants were born. He received his full share of persecution from Massachusetts. When in 1637 he returned to Salem to sell his house, he was arrested and thrown into jail for having spoken disrespectfully of the magistrates, and having charged them with " usurping the power of Christ over men's consciences." In 1643, when Massachusetts attempted to claim jurisdiction over Shawomet, and seized Gorton and his neighbors and carried them to Boston for trial, Greene was obliged to escape across the bay to Newport with his sick wife, who died a few weeks afterward. In the following year, with Gorton and Holden, he was sent to England to lay their grievances before the Earl of Warwick's Committee, and from him they secured a decision in their favor, which, though appealed by Massachusetts, was never materially reversed. He died in 1659, his last public service being as one of a committee of ten selected in 1647 to organize the colony under the charter of 1643. His son was one of the ten "Assistants" to the Governor named for the first year in the charter of 1663.

His descendants multiplied rapidly in Warwick; they married young, lived long, and reared large families. Each generation in succession furnished men prominent in the community—governors, deputy governors, secretaries of the colony, and delegates to the General Assembly. Nathanael Greene was of the fourth generation of these descendants. He was the fifth of a family of nine children—two by a first marriage and seven by a second. His father, also named Nathanael, was a Quaker preacher of the most vigorous as well as the most narrow-minded and superstitious type. His son described him in after years as "a man of great piety, of an excellent understanding, and governed in his conduct by humanity and kind benevolence, but his mind was overshadowed with prejudice against literary accomplishments." He was also a large landed proprietor, and the owner of a forge, grist mill, flour mill, and saw mill, as well as a store for the sale of general merchandise. The forge and mills had been established by his father Jabez, and at his death the property passed equally to his six sons without being divided,

ANTECEDENTS AND EDUCATION.

and the business was continued by them. It was situated on Potowomut, a peninsula on the west side of Narragansett Bay just south of Warwick. In 1741 a second forge was established by the brothers at Coventry, about ten miles northwest of Potowomut, and the two establishments continued in operation till the close of the century. The property at both places gradually passed into the hands of Nathanael the preacher, and all of his eight sons were put to work in the forges or mills at an early age. At his death, in 1771, his sons inherited the property and continued the business jointly under the name of Jacob Greene & Co., but Nathanael Greene never paid any attention to it after he joined the army in 1775. Its value, exclusive of real estate, was appraised in 1743 at £8,055, with £2,408 of uncollected debts—a considerable sum in those days. The principal product of the forges was anchors, and these, together with the flour made at the mills, were transferred across the bay in sloops to Newport, bringing back return cargoes of ore and black sand from Pennsylvania, and wheat and coal from Virginia.

At the age of thirty Nathanael Greene wrote sadly to one of his intimate friends: " I lament the want of liberal education. . . . I was educated a Quaker, and among the most superstitious sort; and that of itself is enough to cramp the best of geniuses, much more mine." Certainly his disposition and temperament and sympathies were very different from those of his father. The latter was vigorous of mind and body, but extremely narrow and prejudiced. He believed that no books were worthy of study but the Bible, was opposed to war and strife, abhorred worldly amusements. The son, on the other hand, had an active and alert mind, a happy disposition, and a strong, well-formed body. He craved knowledge from his childhood, possessed a sympathetic nature which formed lasting attachments, and was quick to resent a fancied injury; took pleasure in athletic contests, delighted in society, and, above all, was passionately fond of dancing—in spite of the corporeal punishment which he invariably suffered when detected in a sin so peculiarly offensive to Quakers. When he attended a military parade in 1773 and prepared to organize the Kentish Guards, the "meeting" gave him three several warnings and asked him for an explanation, being reluctant to take extreme measures against the son of a father so highly respected; but these warnings had no effect upon him, and he continued his military investigations. No alternative remained but to dismiss him from their communion, which they promptly did. All of his differences with the Quakers were, however, of small consequence, except in the matter of education. This was of lasting importance. His father was one of the most prosperous men in the colony, and abundantly able, had he so chosen, to give his son a thorough education and send him either to Harvard, Yale, or King's College. (Rhode Island College, afterward Brown University, was not fully established till he was thirty years old.) But his father did not so choose; such a course would have seemed to him most sinful. He employed an itinerant teacher in the long winter evenings to teach his eight boys to read, write, and cipher. Having mastered these, the Holy Scriptures and the writings of George Fox and Robert Barclay were considered as affording all knowledge that was needful or useful. Against this programme Nathanael

ANTECEDENTS AND EDUCATION.

the younger instinctively rebelled. At the age of fourteen he made the acquaintance of a young man named Giles, who was passing his college vacation in the village of East Greenwich, a short distance from his father's home. The result of his conversations with Giles about college and books led him to ask of his father better means of study; and after much hesitation his father so far yielded as to allow him to study geometry and a little Latin under a teacher named Maxwell, in East Greenwich. This taste of knowledge suggested to the lad that he devise means within his own control for procuring books, and accordingly he made toy anchors and other toys of iron. The next time the sloop took her load of wares from the forge and the mill to Newport he went in it, and promptly sold his toys for cash. With this he proceeded to the bookstore and remarked that he wanted to "buy a book." The bookseller sharply asked, "What book?" And the boy, abashed, was unable to reply. But it happened that in the bookstore at the same time was the Rev. Ezra Stiles, then pastor of the Second Church in Newport, and afterward for many years President of Yale College. He was much interested in a lad who showed such positive but ill-defined desire for knowledge, and at once began to give him welcome advice about the choice of books. Through this kindly assistance young Nathanael became acquainted with Locke on the Understanding and Watt's Elements of Logic, which, in connection with Euclid, formed strong, wholesome food for an acquiring and eager mind of fifteen. In his trips to Newport he also formed the acquaintance of Lindley Murray, the future grammarian, who, although younger than himself, was being well educated and anxious to talk about books and studies. In his nineteenth year the death of his two stepbrothers led to a law-suit concerning the disposition of their property, of so complicated a nature that it was sent to England on appeal. His father instructed him to collect evidence and confer with the lawyers, and this induced him to purchase Jacob's Law Dictionary and diligently study it. A little later he purchased an Oxford edition of Blackstone, in four quarto volumes; then the Dictionary of Arts and Sciences, in four volumes. Further additions to his stock were made from time to time, but it was not until he moved to Coventry and built his own house that he could fully gratify his taste for books. Then he had a library of two hundred and fifty volumes, well chosen and solid books, which had cost him no little hard-earned money, and which he thoroughly studied, reading many of them over and over again—English and Roman History, Vattel and Hume, translations of Homer, Cæsar, and Horace, Butler's Analogy, Plutarch's Lives, Turenne's Memoirs, Ferguson's History of Civil Society, the Spectator, Pope, Swift, and Sterne, and others equally good.

In these days of circulating libraries and countless novels, magazines, and newspapers, we are apt to forget that a good education can be obtained from a library of one hundred well-selected volumes, especially if they be obtained only by persistent effort and the sacrifice of time and money. Then they are appreciated, are pored over and thought out, read and re-read, stored away in the memory with an enduring lodgment that no easily-gained and lightly-read book can secure. Such a library did Nathanael Greene slowly accumulate and ardently devour, although to the close of his life he felt conscious of the defects of his early education. Doubtless he lacked the benefits of mental training and discipline, yet he overcame this deficiency, by his own unguided and persistent efforts, to such an extent that he was never considered by his associates an uneducated man; he acquired a good style, barring certain errors of grammar and spelling which were then almost universal; he wrote lucidly and concisely, and was agreeable in conversation. Above all, he had a clear mental vision and sound judgment. His mind saw realities, and not pictures.

CHAPTER II.

EARLY LIFE IN RHODE ISLAND.

In the year 1770, when Nathanael Greene was twenty-seven years old, his father gave him charge of the forge and mill at Coventry. This establishment had grown to such an extent that over one hundred families were dependent on it for their livelihood, and a local manager was necessary. Nathanael Greene moved there, built himself a comfortable house, of which the best room was reserved for his books, and established himself. Ten years before, one of his half-brothers had left him in his will an estate in West Greenwich; with this he had qualified under the property test and had been admitted as a freeman in Warwick in 1765. Immediately after his removal to Coventry he was elected to the General Assembly, and he was re-elected in 1771, 1772, and 1775. His father died a few months after his removal to Coventry in 1770.

At the time he took his seat in the Assembly the population of the thirteen colonies was about 2,300,000, and of these, about 55,000, or one fortieth part, lived in "The English Colony of Rhode Island and Providence Plantations." Newport was the principal town, having a population of about 11,000, which was reduced to less than half that number during the Revolutionary War, and which was not regained

EARLY LIFE IN RHODE ISLAND.   11

until nearly a century later. It was then exceeded only by New York, Philadelphia, and Boston. It had an extensive commerce, about two hundred ships being engaged in the foreign trade with Europe, Africa, and the West Indies, and about four hundred in the coasting trade. It imported large amounts of sugar and molasses from the West Indies, and exported New England rum to Africa. Its surplus stock of West India goods was shipped to Boston and New York, and there exchanged for British manufactures, of which its consumption was valued at £120,000 a year. Providence had a population of less than 4,000, and there were no other towns of any importance. But there were several villages scattered along its water front, which was singularly long in proportion to the area of the colony, and the inhabitants of these were for the most part engaged in maritime commerce in a small way. The rest of the population was employed in agriculture, though the soil was largely rock and sand, which yielded poor returns. The mother country looked askance at any attempt to introduce manufactures into the colonies, and called sharply for explanation of any efforts in that direction. In 1766 the Lords Commissioners for Trade and Plantations called for "a particular and exact account of the several manufactures which have been set up and carried on within the colony since the year 1734, and of the public encouragement which has been given thereto." No answer having been returned, in 1768 the Earl of Hillsborough, Colonial Secretary, warned the Governor "to pay exact obedience" to the request; and the Governor (Lyndon) humbly replied: " Ten forges for making iron out of ore; two furnaces—

one for making iron into pigs and the other for making hollow ware out of ore; six spermaceti works; twelve potash works; three rope walks; and one paper mill, at which is manufactured wrapping, package, and other coarse paper. These, my Lord, are the only manufactures which have been set up in the colony since the year 1734; and neither for these nor for any other manufactures is any bounty or other public encouragement given by the colony." Rhode Island is now the most densely populated State (319 per square mile) on the American continent, and three-fourths of its inhabitants are engaged in or dependent upon manufactures; but at the beginning of the Revolution none of these had come into existence, except a few iron forges and furnaces, of which those owned by Nathanael Greene and his brothers were the most important.

In means of education Rhode Island was behind its adjoining colonies. Land had been given for the support of a school in Newport in 1640, and in Providence in 1663, and subsequently in the other towns; but the free public schools had not been established until 1768, and then only in the face of active opposition on the part of those who would be most benefited by them. Harvard had been established in 1636, Yale in 1701, Princeton in 1746, and King's College (Columbia) in 1754. Rhode Island College (Brown University) was founded in 1764, with the primary object of affording education for Baptist clergymen. It was first situated in the town of Warren, but in 1770 a change was determined upon, and the various towns offered subscriptions as an inducement to cause its removal. Nathanael Greene labored actively to secure it for East Greenwich, but

EARLY LIFE IN RHODE ISLAND.

the subscription of Providence exceeded that of any other place, and it was removed there. Failing to secure the university for his section of the colony, he set to work to establish a public school in Coventry, and in this humbler but still useful task he was entirely successful.

The local politics of the colony when he took his seat in the Assembly had for many years turned on the contentions of the rival factions of Hopkins and Ward, the standing candidates for Governor. The origin of the contest was trivial, but the struggle was none the less active and bitter. Greene's family was connected by marriage with that of Governor Ward, and his sympathies were naturally with that faction; but he does not seem to have taken, any very active part in the controversy. In fact, just before he entered public life the struggle was brought to a close in face of the vital issues then coming forward in reference to the right of the British Parliament to tax the colonies without their consent. Governor Ward was in office when the Stamp Act was passed, in 1765, and was the only one of the colonial governors who refused to take the oath to enforce it. He was re-elected in 1766, but was defeated by Hopkins in 1767. At the close of Hopkins's term both parties agreed to withdraw from the contest; they joined hands in opposing the pretensions of Parliament, and henceforth worked together in the interests of the colony, which, as it was now evident, were tending toward independence from Great Britain. They jointly represented the colony in the first Continental Congress, and Ward died in Philadelphia in the spring of 1776.

It does not appear that Nathanael Greene took a

prominent place in the Assembly during the four years in which he was a member of it. One or more of his brothers were deputies from Warwick at the same time, but no record has been preserved of any speeches or acts by any of them which attracted special attention. It is probable that he gained influence among his fellow-members, for otherwise it is impossible to explain the confidence they showed in him on the outbreak of the war, but of the details there is no record. During this period he formed intimate friendships with two men—Samuel Ward, Jr., and James Mitchell Varnum—which lasted through life. Ward's father and grandfather had been governors of the colony, and the family had long been prominent. Varnum had come from Massachusetts, where his father owned property on the Merrimac; after a year at Harvard he had been sent to Rhode Island College, and graduated at its first commencement in 1769. The graduating exercises consisted of a "Forensic Dispute" on the question whether it was good policy for the colonies "to affect to become an independent State." It fell to Varnum's lot to argue in the negative, although for the rest of his life he fought and argued in the affirmative. The debate has escaped the usual oblivion of baccalaureate efforts, and has been preserved in full. At the time it attracted wide attention. In 1771 Varnum began the practice of law in East Greenwich. He afterward rose to distinction in the army, at the bar, on the bench, and in Congress, being particularly famous as an orator. Ward had also graduated at Rhode Island College, two years later than Varnum, and settled at his father's home in Westerly. But Governor William Greene and Governor Samuel

EARLY LIFE IN RHODE ISLAND.

Ward had married sisters, and young Ward was a frequent visitor at his aunt's house in East Greenwich. Like Varnum, he served with distinction during the Revolution, but he did not enter political life. At the close of the war he removed to New York and established himself in mercantile pursuits.

To both of these young men Nathanael Greene was strongly attracted. They were younger than himself—Varnum by six years and Ward by fourteen years—and from all accounts they were as manly, handsome, and fine young fellows as were to be found anywhere. But to Nathanael Greene, who was so sensitive and almost morbid on the subject of his education, their chief attraction was in the fact of their being college graduates. This leveled the difference of age, and he wrote to them, on terms of equality, long letters on morals and manners and the theory of the universe—such letters as are common among thoughtful men at the collegiate age. "The pursuit of virtue where there is no opposition is the merit of a common man; but to practice it in spite of all opposition is the character of a truly great and noble soul. . . . What I call false modesty is not to have resolution to deny an unreasonable request or power to oppose a corrupt custom. . . . Have you not felt, on seeing or reading of noble deeds or generous actions, pleasant emotions mixed with the desire of imitation? These are the advantages that spring from choice books and the best of company. They inspire the mind to action and direct the passions." Evidently he utilized his college friends to improve his own education and gain practice in the composition of letters. But he was no snob or sycophant. "It is very fortunate for you to be able to enumerate a long train of noble ancestors, but to equal the best and excel the most is to have no occasion for any."

At this time he fell deeply in love with young Ward's sister; but she did not return his affection. He took it much to heart, and his letters for several months were of the most gloomy and melancholy character. But in the following year his spirits revived; he made the acquaintance of Miss Catharine Littlefield, of Block Island, who was an orphan adopted by her aunt, the wife of Governor William Greene, at East Greenwich. The acquaintance rapidly passed into friendship, love, and marriage. They were married on July 20, 1774, at East Greenwich, and he took his bride to his own home at Coventry. She was only twenty, while he was nearly thirty-two years old at the time of his marriage, but it was a happy union, blessed with two sons and three daughters, though for eight of the twelve years between his marriage and death he was absent in the army. But his wife, following the example of Mrs. Washington, joined him several times at the winter quarters during the long struggle.

During the year of his marriage the strained relations between the mother country and the colonies were rapidly approaching a crisis. The Boston Port Bill had passed in the spring, and as soon as news of it reached Providence the freemen met and proposed the idea of a general congress of the colonies, to decide on the best means of maintaining their rights. The idea was formally approved by the Assembly at its meeting in June, and Hopkins and Ward were elected the delegates. In order to be able to maintain their views, by force if necessary, military companies were organized in different parts of the colony. At the October session of the Assembly, Varnum, Nathanael Greene, his kinsman Christopher Greene, and Archibald Crary applied for and received a charter for an independent company to be formed in the towns of East Greenwich, Warwick, and Coventry, and to be known as the "Kentish Guards." Varnum was made captain, and Nathanael Greene was one of the privates. This little company enjoyed the distinction, as the war progressed, of supplying thirty-two officers to the regular or Continental army.

But Greene had no musket, and could not buy one in the colony. He therefore determined to go to Boston, ostensibly on business connected with his forges; his time, however, was employed on other matters. He watched the morning and evening parades of the British troops on the Common; he made several visits to Henry Knox's bookstore, and bought copies of Cæsar's campaigns, Turenne's memoirs, and other books; he purchased his musket, and he engaged a British deserter to go back with him as drill master for the Kentish Guards. He and the drill sergeant had to return by different routes, and the musket by still another, concealed in the straw of a farmer's cart; but they all arrived in safety, and the drilling began. At the December session of the Assembly Nathanael Greene, although not a member of the Assembly and only a private in the Kentish Guards, was appointed one of a committee of five—the other four being field officers of militia—to revise the militia laws. They reported in time for the new law to be passed at the same session.

Four months later the first blood of the Revolution was shed at Lexington. News of it reached Providence on the afternoon of April 19, 1775, and passing from mouth to mouth and house to house with extraordinary rapidity, the report came to Nathanael Greene at his home at Coventry after nightfall. He immediately mounted his horse and rode to the training grounds of the Kentish Guards at East Greenwich. The whole company was aroused and collected during the night, and at daybreak marched for Providence, Captain Varnum at the head, and Nathanael Greene with his brothers in the ranks with their muskets on their shoulders. They passed through Providence early in the morning, and on arriving at the colonial boundary line, a few miles farther on, they were overtaken by a messenger from the Governor with orders to return. The company obeyed the order, but Greene, with two of his brothers and a third companion, obtained permission to go on to Boston, and they started forward on horseback. Later in the day they learned that the British troops had returned to Boston, and they therefore retraced their steps to Providence, where, on the 22d, the Assembly, of which Nathanael Greene had this year again been elected a member, met in special session. It resolved that an army of fifteen hundred men should be raised for the defense of the colony, and to march out to the aid of other colonies if necessary. In order to co-operate with the adjoining colony of Connecticut, a committee of two—Nathanael Greene and William Bradford—was appointed to confer with the Connecticut Assembly concerning details. The Assembly met again on May 2d and passed an act in detail for raising the

EARLY LIFE IN RHODE ISLAND.

"army of observation" of fifteen hundred men, organizing it into a brigade of three regiments, and prescribing rules and regulations for its government. A loan of £20,000 was authorized to be raised by the issue of colonial bills. A Committee of Safety was appointed, whose duty it was to "provide arms, tents, provisions, and every accouterment necessary for the army"; they were also to pay the troops, and, in accordance with the usual practice, they were to "be allowed one and a half per cent for transacting the business." The committee consisted of six members, and among them was Jacob Greene, brother of Nathanael. Finally, the Assembly proceeded to the election of officers, and Nathanael Greene was elected brigadier-general in command of the army of observation. Varnum was elected colonel of the Third Regiment, which was to be raised in and about Warwick; Christopher Greene, the future hero of Red Bank, was elected major of this same regiment, and Samuel Ward, Jr., captain of one of its companies. The Governor (Wanton) had recently been re-elected, but he protested against the act for raising the army of observation; whereupon the Assembly promptly suspended him from his functions, and directed the secretary of the colony to issue the commissions to the officers. They were so issued under date of May 8, 1775, and before the end of the month the greater part of the little "army" was organized and on its march for Boston.

In the foregoing pages has been recorded practically everything that is known of the life of Nathanael Greene down to the time when he took command of the Rhode Island troops. It can hardly be called an extraordinary or remarkable career. He had gained his education by his own efforts, against his father's wishes and almost in spite of his father's opposition. He was the managing partner of an iron factory which, although it would now seem small, was then in fact of the same relative importance to the population and wealth of the colony as the largest cotton mills are to the State of to-day. He had served three terms in the Assembly, and had been a member of a few important committees. His travels were limited by Boston on one side and New York on the other. He had had no military experience beyond service for six months as a private in a militia company. Suddenly he was elected to command all the troops of the colony, at the outbreak of a struggle which had been long preparing, and the importance of which no one underestimated. His office was, next to that of the delegates to the Continental Congress, the most responsible which the colony had at its disposal. What led the Assembly to select Nathanael Greene for that office? From the records which have been preserved no satisfactory answer can be made to the question. His ancestor had been one of the founders of the colony, but this was one hundred and thirty-seven years before, and there were hundreds of his kinsmen who enjoyed this slight distinction; and while members of other branches of the family had held high office with credit, his immediate progenitors and his near relatives had not been in public life. His only acquaintance or connection of much influence in public affairs was Governor Samuel Ward, who was in Providence at the session of the Assembly in May, 1775, just before leaving for Philadelphia, where he took his seat in Congress on

EARLY LIFE IN RHODE ISLAND. 21

May 15th. Probably he advocated the choice of Nathanael Greene, who was well known to him through his intimacy with his son Samuel and otherwise; but of this there is no authentic record. If he did so, he not only showed his knowledge of character, but performed a signal service to Rhode Island and to the future United States. Whether he did so or not, the Assembly made the selection by unanimous vote, and this would not have been done on any one's recommendation unless Greene had already impressed his associates in the Assembly as a man who, though still young, was possessed of unusual intelligence, character, and determination. That the result was a most fortunate one, never regretted by the colony or the United States, the result abundantly proved. That he has now for more than a century been regarded as the most illustrious man that Rhode Island has produced, no one will deny. When it was a question, in 1866, of selecting the two foremost men of Rhode Island to be represented by statues in the Capitol at Washington, Roger Williams and Nathanael Greene were quickly chosen; but the latter solely by reason of what he had done after May, 1775. There is no distinct clew to what caused his selection for her most important station at that time. We can only conjecture that there must have been something in his manner and action which impressed his associates in the Assembly with a sense of his ability and integrity, and enabled them instinctively to discern the qualities for leadership which he undoubtedly possessed, and which only needed an opportunity for their proper development.

Whatever the cause, the choice was wisely made;

and at the age of not quite thirty-three he left his home, his young wife, his little manufacturing establishment, and his colonial surroundings, to take his place among the military leaders in a war of transcendent importance.

CHAPTER III.

BOSTON AND LONG ISLAND.

ON the 3d of June, 1775, Greene arrived at Boston. He had been detained at Providence during the month of May, collecting and forwarding his troops, and had not been able to visit his home and wife, to whom he wrote his farewell, commending her to the care of his brothers, from Providence on June 2d. He found two of his regiments encamped at Jamaica Plain, the third, under command of Varnum, not arriving until a few days later. The troops were without discipline or military training, and, although their fine tents and the artillery they had brought with them from old Fort George at Newport attracted much attention, yet they seemed to Greene sadly deficient in all the essential features of military proficiency. He set to work with all his energy to remedy these defects, instituted daily drills, instructed his men in the use of their arms, instilled in their minds the rudimentary principles of discipline—in a word, labored early and late to convert his enthusiastic, patriotic farmer lads into a body of soldiers; and with such success, that by the time Washington reached camp, while fully appreciating what they lacked, he was not ashamed of them. "Though raw, irregular, and undisciplined," he thought they were "under much better government than any round about Boston."

Colonel Reed, Washington's military secretary, wrote not long after that Greene's "command consisted of three regiments, then the best disciplined and appointed in the whole American army." He did not have an opportunity to test their quality at Bunker Hill on June 17th, for he was stationed at the opposite end of the line, and his troops were not brought into that engagement.

In addition to organizing his little force, he kept up a constant correspondence with Governor Ward at Philadelphia, who was habitually chairman of the Committee on the War. To him Greene wrote fully of the condition and requirements of the troops gathered around Boston and Ward acted on this information in the deliberations of Congress. Greene also carried on a daily correspondence with Governor Cooke, of Rhode Island, concerning the supplies and equipment of his troops; and he wrote frequently and fully to his brother Jacob Greene, who was a member of the Rhode Island Committee of Safety. From this very full correspondence it is possible to follow quite closely his life during the nine months of the siege of Boston. It contained no striking episode. The period was one of preparation and organization, and Greene was incessantly hard at work, drilling, studying, writing, and thinking; but the fruits of this work were visible not at Boston, but in the Jerseys and the Carolinas in the years that followed.

Washington arrived at Cambridge on July 2d, and Greene sent a detachment of two hundred men, under command of a colonel, with a letter of address to welcome him to camp. Washington "returned a very polite answer, and invitation to visit him at his quarters." Thus was formed an acquaintance which soon grew into a friendship destined to remain unbroken, and year by year to grow stronger throughout the rest of Greene's life. On the one side it was based upon profound respect and admiration, unquestioning loyalty, willing obedience, and unbounded faith; on the other, upon the fullest confidence, affection, and esteem. Greene's temper was quick, and in his voluminous correspondence he was not slow to criticise others, and particularly members of Congress—sometimes unwisely. But no word of his has ever been found in which he expressed a thought of jealousy, or lack of faith or confidence in Washington. He had already studied with care Washington's career in the French wars and the Virginia House of Burgesses, and it was a career which peculiarly appealed to a man of his temperament and tastes. Personal acquaintance only confirmed the high opinion he had formed in advance, and this opinion was never changed, or even for a moment clouded with a doubt.

The arrival of Washington effected a complete transformation in the troops about Boston. They ceased to be colonial militia and became the Continental army. Four major-generals were appointed by Congress—Artemas Ward, Charles Lee, Philip Schuyler, and Israel Putnam; and eight brigadiers—Pomeroy, Montgomery, Wooster, Heath, Spencer, Thomas, Sullivan, and Greene. Gates was appointed adjutant-general. Before the end of the war all of these, except Putnam, Gates, Heath, and Greene, had disappeared from the army list, and all but Greene had ceased to hold active command. The return which Washington called for immediately on his arrival showed the strength of the army to be as follows:

	Regiments.	Officers.	Noncommissioned Officers.	PRIVATES.	
				Present for duty.	Total present and absent.
Massachusetts	26	789	1,326	9,396	11,688
Connecticut	3	125	174	2,105	2,353
New Hampshire	3	98	160	1,201	1,644
Rhode Island	3	107	108	1,041	1,085
Total	35	1,119	1,768	13,743	16,770

These were organized into three divisions and six brigades. Ward commanded the right at Roxbury facing Boston Neck, Lee commanded the left at Prospect Hill facing Charlestown Neck, and Putnam commanded the center or reserve under Washington's own eye at Cambridge. Greene was assigned to the second brigade in Lee's division, consisting of the three Rhode Island regiments and four from Massachusetts; the total strength of his brigade was twenty-seven hundred and ninety-eight men. Lines of defense were laid out from the Mystic on the north to Dorchester on the south, and, in addition to constant drills, the men were now engaged in building field fortifications. When these were completed there were occasional small skirmishes with the enemy, but no serious engagement. Washington was keenly sensitive to the general desire that he should attack Boston, and to the criticisms which he anticipated would be made upon him for not doing so; but his judgment was against it, and he declined to entertain the idea of sacrificing his men in what he felt confident would be an unsuccessful assault. He called several councils of war to discuss the question, and they uniformly sustained his judgment. Greene, being the junior, next to Gates, was obliged to express his opinion first, and it is evident that with his ardent temperament he was seeking to convince his own mind of the advisability of an assault; but still his judgment was always finally against i . At the council of October 18th he voted "that it is not practicable under all circumstances, but if ten thousand men could be landed at Boston, thinks it is." Writing to his brother in the following February, he expressed the views he had always held— viz., that "an attack upon a town garrisoned with eight thousand regular troops is a serious object, and ought to be well considered before attempted. I always thought an attack with twenty thousand men might succeed. I still think so; and were the bay to be frozen over, I should be glad to see the attempt made." But it was neither possible to get an army of twenty thousand men nor to land ten thousand in Boston. Moreover, there was not enough powder for a bombardment preliminary to an assault. What little they had must be carefully husbanded for use in their muskets in case the enemy made an attack. There was nothing to do but to keep at work drilling and organizing.

The tedium of this was, however, somewhat relieved by pleasant social relations. Many of the general officers had served in the French wars, and were men of distinction in their colonies. They received Greene with much consideration, and he was flattered by it, though, in his letter to his brother, he is careful to say that he considers these "flattering attentions" due to his office and not to himself. "I shall study to deserve well, but can not but lament the great defects I find in myself to discharge with honor and justice the important trust committed to my care. . . . I hope God will preserve me in the bounds of moderation, and enable me to support myself with proper dignity, neither rash nor timorous,* pursuing a conduct marked by manly firmness, but never bordering on phrenzy." In the late autumn Mrs. Washington came to camp, and Greene immediately sent for his wife. She came, bringing with her their infant son, born since he had left home, who was christened in camp and named George Washington. A warm friendship sprang up between Mrs. Washington and Mrs. Greene, which was renewed in subsequent winters at Morristown and Valley Forge, and lasted through life.

In September his friend Ward volunteered to join Arnold in his expedition to Quebec. Greene felt it incumbent on him to advise him against going, but to such a spirited young fellow his formal advice counted for nothing in face of his remark that it would be "a very pretty tour." Doubtless Ward felt that if his rank had been less, Greene himself would have been among the volunteers. Ward was taken prisoner at the assault of Quebec, and was not exchanged until the following summer. Then he was assigned to another part of the army, and Greene saw no more of him until they went into camp at Valley Forge in December, 1777.

As the year 1775 drew to its close, so did the term of enlistment of the men around Boston. On December 10th Greene writes to Governor Ward that

---

* The motto on the family arms of his English ancestors, "Nec timeo nec sperno," was singularly applicable to his character.

"the Connecticut troops are going home in shoals to-day." New Hampshire, on the other hand, "behaves nobly; their troops engage cheerfully." The Massachusetts troops are also beginning to enlist very fast, but he is very solicitous about his own colony. "I sent home some recruiting officers, but they got scarcely a man. . . . I feel for the honor of the colony, which I think is in a fair way . . . . to receive a wound. It mortifies me to death that our colony and troops should be a whit behind the neighboring governments in private virtue or public spirit." In truth, Rhode Island had undertaken almost more than it could carry out. The commerce of Newport had been ruined by the British cruisers; and whereas this town formerly paid one sixth of the taxes, it was now so reduced that the poor had to be supported out of the colonial Treasury. Bristol had been bombarded, and Wallace's ships went up and down the bay plundering on both shores and on the islands. Over seventeen hundred officers and men had been sent to Boston and Canada, and now two regiments had to be raised for the defense of the colony itself. Instead of re-enlisting for the defense of Boston, it was a question of protecting their own homes. Greene, however, looked at the matter with different and perhaps broader views. From the first he saw that the contest involved the united colonies, and that their independence was at stake; he felt that success could only be gained by united action, even if his own colony was the greatest sufferer. He wrote to his brother: "We must expect to make partial sacrifices for the public good. I love the colony of Rhode Island, and have ever had a very great affection for the town of Newport; but I am not so attached to either as to be willing to injure the common cause for their particular benefit." And to Governor Ward: "The interests of our colony are no ways incompatible with the interests of another. We have all one common interest and one common wish—to be free from parliamentary jurisdiction and taxation." And as to the expense, "what signifies our being frightened at the expense? If we succeed, we gain all; but if we are conquered, we lose all."

Fortunately, the year passed away without his fears being realized. The British did not know how weak Washington's army was at the end of December, 1775, or, if they did, they took no advantage of it. The new army was enlisted for the year 1776, and took the place of the old; and, so far as Greene was concerned, on January 4th he felt strong enough at Prospect Hill to defend himself "against all the force in Boston." Finally the siege came to an end in March. Washington collected eighty large boats, and stationed Sullivan and Greene with four thousand men on the shore near Cambridge, ready to cross the Back Bay and attack Beacon Hill if the British interfered with his movements. He then seized Dorchester Heights, which commanded the bay as well as the British lines at Boston Neck. Howe had either to storm this position or leave. The memory of Bunker Hill was still fresh, and he sailed away for Halifax. Washington entered Boston, and assigned Greene to the command of the city.

The most memorable feature of Greene's service at Boston was his correspondence with Governor Ward at Philadelphia, and especially two letters dated October 23, 1775, and January 4, 1776. In the first, he argued in favor of a declaration of independence, not only because there was no alternative except subjugation, but also because without it no help could be expected from France. He shrewdly and correctly reasoned that " France, as a real enemy to Great Britain, acts upon a true plan of policy in refusing to intermeddle until she is satisfied that there is no hope of accommodation. Should France undertake to furnish us with powder and other articles, and the breach between Great Britain and the colonies be afterward made up, she would incur the hostility of her rival without reaping any solid advantage." In the second letter he argues still more forcibly for independence, and expresses his views about the military measures necessary to achieve it. He says—speaking of George III's speech on the opening of Parliament, news of which had just reached camp—" Heaven has decreed that tottering empire to irretrievable ruin; and, thanks to God, since Providence has so determined it, America must raise an empire of permanent duration, supported upon the grand pillars of truth, freedom, and religion, based upon justice, and defended by her own patriotic sons. . . . Permit me, then, to recommend from the sincerity of my heart, ready at all times to bleed in my country's cause, a declaration of independence ; and call upon the world, and the great God who governs it, to witness the necessity, propriety, and rectitude thereof. My worthy friend, the interests of mankind hang upon that truly worthy body of which you are a member. You stand the representative not of America only, but of the whole world, the friends of liberty, and the supporters of the rights of human nature. How will posterity, millions yet unborn, bless the memory of those brave patriots who are now hastening the consummation of freedom, truth, and religion!" In regard to military measures he says: "No doubt a large army must be raised in addition to the forces upon the present establishment. . . . How they must be divided, and where stationed, is a matter at present problematical. However, one thing is certain: the grand body must be superior in number to any force that the enemy can send. All the forces in America should be under one commander, raised and appointed by the same authority, subjected to the same regulations, and ready to be detached wherever occasion may require. . . . An army unequipped will ever feel the want of spirit and courage; but properly furnished, fighting in the best of causes, will bid defiance to the united force of men and devils. When a finishing period will be put to the present dispute God only knows. We have just experienced the inconveniences of disbanding an army within cannon shot of the enemy and forming a new one in its stead—an instance never before known. Had the enemy been fully acquainted with our situation, I can not pretend to say what might have been the consequence. A large body of troops will probably be wanted for a considerable time. It will be infinitely safer, and not more expensive in the end, for the continent to give a large bounty to any number of troops, in addition to what may be ordered on the present establishment, that will engage during the war, than to enlist them from year to year without a bounty."

These letters were written at a time when a large party in Congress was still trying to devise measures for a reconciliation; when Pennsylvania required the members of its Assembly to take the oath of allegiance to King George, and instructed its delegates in Congress to reject any proposition looking toward independence; when Washington was hampered in his command by the constant instructions of a committee of Congress, and New England delegates were proclaiming that "enlistment for a long period is a state of slavery; a rotation of service in arms is favorable to liberty." In the face of this confusion of ideas Greene saw clearly that the political object of the war was not a mere redress of grievances by parliament or king, but the independence of the united colonies; and that the military means for accomplishing it were troops enlisted for the war, well armed and equipped, ready to serve wherever ordered, and all directed by the single mind of one commander-in-chief. The Declaration of Independence came six months later—sooner than almost any one anticipated; annual enlistments continued for several years longer and were never fully abandoned; the course of events in another year gave Washington full military control as commander-in-chief; the measures for raising money to equip the army properly were never taken, no central government being formed with power to tax. But Greene at least had no illusions; he saw plainly what was before him, and pleaded for what ought to be done. No one will now dispute the soundness of his views. He could not secure their adoption in full, but he could at least devote his life to the cause; he had started to get his musket and join his company before midnight on the date of the battle of Lexington, and he was still fighting after Yorktown had surrendered, nearly seven years later.

These letters afford the clew to his selection to command the Rhode Island troops. They were written less than a year after his appointment, and the man who could write them was easily among the foremost men in his colony, and must have so impressed his fellow-members in the Assembly, even though he was only a private in the Kentish Guards.

Boston was evacuated on March 17th, and on the 18th Washington sent Heath, with his brigade of six regiments, a battalion of riflemen, and two companies of artillery, to New York *via* Norwich and the Sound. With the rest of the army he waited to make sure of Howe's departure. On the 27th the fleet sailed away —for New York, Washington naturally supposed, although in fact it was for Halifax. Leaving five regiments in Boston under Ward, the American army started for New York as rapidly as transportation could be collected. Washington himself left Boston April 4th, and arrived in New York on the 13th. His army was all there before the 1st of May.

Greene received his marching orders on March 29th, and left Boston on Monday, April 1st, at sunrise. His brigade consisted of two of his Rhode Island regiments and three from Massachusetts, with a detachment of Knox's artillery. Their route lay through Providence and past his old home to New London, where they took vessels for New York, arriving on April 17th. Just as they started, word was received from Governor Cooke that the English fleet had appeared at Newport, and Greene hurried on, expecting to fight in defense of his own colony. But it proved to be a false alarm. On arriving at New York two changes were made in succession in the organization of his brigade, but at the end of April, with five regiments containing seventeen hundred and sixty-one men, of whom thirteen hundred and seven were fit for duty, he was ordered to take post on Long Island. Other troops were ordered to the same position, and Greene, as senior brigadier, commanded them all. On August 9th he was promoted to the rank of major-general, and the troops on Long Island were formed into a division under his command.

Washington had about twelve thousand men, subsequently increased by militia to twenty thousand, of whom not more than two-thirds were fit for duty. He rightly anticipated that Howe would soon appear at New York, and endeavor to secure control of the line of the Hudson and thus cut the colonies in two. He therefore set to work to dispose his little force to the best advantage in order to make as much resistance as possible. Fortifications were laid out and built on both shores of the lower end of Manhattan Island, south of Canal Street, on Governor's Island, and on Long Island. To the latter Greene was assigned. Brooklyn was then a small village of less than one thousand inhabitants, situated in the vicinity of the present City Hall. Gowanus Bay on one side and Wallabout Bay on the other, with the creeks and marshes which drained into them, stretched up into the land behind it so as almost to create an island about three miles long and one to one and a half miles wide. Fortifications were laid out to defend this peninsula on both sides. On the water front a battery of seven guns was built on the commanding position of Brooklyn Heights, which completely dominated New York as well as the entrance to the East River; this entrance was further protected by a battery of five guns on Red Hook, just north of the present Erie Basin, which, in connection with a similar battery on Governor's Island, would prevent ships from passing through Buttermilk Channel. On the land side Greene traced and built his line of works substantially on the ground selected by Charles Lee when he was in New York three months before. It consisted of four small redoubts, mounting in all twenty guns, and a line of connecting intrenchments protected by abatis. The line was judiciously selected, and the works were well built; for, after his victory of August 27th Howe did not dare to assault them, but sat down to a regular siege, and thus gave Washington an opportunity to withdraw the remnants of the Long Island force to New York.

While the works were in progress Greene kept constantly drilling his men, trying to bring his new regiments up to the standard of those he had commanded at Boston; and he also reconnoitered the whole country from Hell Gate to Gravesend Bay, and out as far as Jamaica, making himself thoroughly familiar with every road and hill and piece of woods, so as to be prepared for the British attack which it was expected would be made from the south and east of Brooklyn; for the British could not sail up the Hudson River and leave this strong post on their flank and rear. He also accompanied Knox and other officers in reconnoissances over Manhattan Island, and he was frequently summoned to Washington's headquarters to attend a council of war or receive instructions. On one of these occasions he walked from the ferry up through what was then an open field used for parades and is now the City Hall Park. A company of artillery was being drilled, and Greene

BOSTON AND LONG ISLAND.   37

was attracted by the earnestness and vivacity of the young captain in command, as well as by the proficiency of the company. He stopped for some time to watch them, and finally, at an interval in the drill, he sent one of his aids to compliment the captain on his excellent drill and to learn his name. It was Alexander Hamilton. Greene invited him to dinner, and at once formed a very high opinion of his abilities. At the earliest opportunity he introduced him to Washington, who soon after observed his fine conduct at the battle of White Plains and in the Jerseys, and in the following spring invited him to a place on his staff. The intimacy between Greene and Hamilton dated from this parade-ground episode, and it was never broken. Hamilton was fifteen years younger than Greene, but his marvelously precocious mind took no account of difference in age. Throughout Greene's life, and after his death, Hamilton was at all times his stanch adherent and admirer. The warmth of his eulogies was possibly due in some measure to his gratitude to Greene, who was the first among military men to recognize his merit.

While at Long Island, Greene also, as at Boston, found time to carry on a voluminous correspondence. His friend and mentor, Governor Ward, had died of the smallpox at Philadelphia just as Greene was leaving Boston. His loss was greatly mourned, but his place as correspondent was taken by John Adams, whose acquaintance Greene had probably formed or possibly revived at Cambridge. Adams was now chairman of the Board of War in the Continental Congress, and to him Greene wrote at length on the political and military situation. In three of these letters he used the expression "the desperate game which you are playing"; and this led Mr. Bancroft, in the earlier editions of his history, to speak of Greene at this time as "despondent," and to say that "Greene had once before warned John Adams of the hopelessness of the contest; and again on the 14th [July, 1776] he wrote: 'I still think you are playing a desperate game.'" In the last edition this is altered so as to read: "Greene, on the 14th, while facing the whole danger without dismay, wrote to John Adams: "I still think you are playing a desperate game." The latter comment is the exact opposite of the one first made, but it is the correct one. Greene was not hopeless or despondent, but he saw the danger of relying upon a militia, which came and went almost at pleasure, as the military means of securing independence; and the desperate game he referred to was the attempt of Congress to carry on a revolution without an adequate military force. On this subject he had written to Governor Ward in January. He now wrote to John Adams; and in the following autumn, when the approaching close of the year brought with it another dissolution of the annual army, he wrote to Governor Cooke in Rhode Island; and always what he pleaded for with all his strength was an army enlisted for the war, a system of bounties to encourage enlistments, pensions to provide for the families of those who should fall, thorough discipline and equipment of the men, and sufficient pay for the officers to enable them to maintain themselves with dignity. In his letter to Governor Cooke (October 11, 1776) he states the philosophical basis on which discipline is justified, with uncommon force and clearness, as follows: "The Americans possess as much natural bravery as any people on earth, but habit must form the soldier. He who expects [that] men brought from the tender scenes of domestic life can meet danger and death with a becoming fortitude, is a stranger to the human heart. There is nothing that can get the better of that active principle of self-preservation, but a proper sentiment of pride, or being often accustomed to danger. As the principle of pride is not predominant in the minds of the common soldiery, the force of habit must be called in to its aid to get the better of our natural fears, ever alarmed at the approach of danger."

In all this Greene was simply in advance of his time. Washington advocated the same views in favor of a permanent army with even more force; but it does not appear that the other officers of the army laid stress upon them, and in Congress they fell upon deaf ears. Nor is this to be wondered at. The militia was one of the colonial institutions—as much a part of the machinery of government as the governor, assembly, or courts of justice. It had been instituted in the earliest days of each colony, and been used with success in the Indian and French wars, which were the only contests which the colonies had had to sustain. Its essential principle was that every able-bodied man should bear arms, should have his musket always ready, and when danger appeared should promptly rally to suppress it—and then as promptly return home.

It was not to be expected that these habits and traditions of five generations would be laid aside in a moment. On the other hand, there was an almost rabid prejudice against standing armies, which were regarded as the instruments of autocratic power, and their name as synonymous with tyranny and oppression. Not a few members of Congress thought that a standing army was a greater evil than any which had been inflicted by Parliament, and if independence could not be secured without a standing army it were better not to attempt it. Finally, there was not only a contempt for the pomp and pride of war, but a jealousy of the honors which war would confer on the successful military leaders. This is well illustrated by John Adams, who, after seeing Washington escorted out of Philadelphia, after his election as commander in chief, with bands of music and companies of militia, went to his lodgings and wrote to his wife: " I, poor creature, worn out with scribbling for my bread and my liberty, low in spirits and weak in health, must leave others to wear the laurels which I have sown, others to eat the bread which I have earned."

In view of the feelings which all the public men of the day had imbibed from their childhood concerning the dangers of a standing army and military heroes, and the advantages of a militia in a free state, it is not surprising that Washington and Greene never succeeded in persuading Congress fully to adopt their views in regard to the proper organization of a military force. It is none the less to Greene's credit that he, although brought up in the same atmosphere and surroundings, saw so clearly the inherent defects of the militia, and advocated so earnestly the correct military policy.

While Greene was completing his fortifications, drilling his men, and writing to John Adams, Howe's army arrived at New York and landed on Staten Island. Greene writes, on July 14th: " I wrote you some time past I thought you were playing a desperate game. I still think so. Here is Howe's army arrived, and the re-enforcements hourly expected. The whole force we have to oppose them don't amount to much above nine thousand, if any. I could wish the troops had been drawn together a little earlier, that we might have had some opportunity of disciplining them. However, what falls to my lot I shall endeavor to execute to the best of my ability." Two weeks later, Clinton and Cornwallis arrived from the South, and on the 12th of August came twenty-five hundred fresh troops from England and eighty-six hundred Hessians. With the keenest interest Greene had watched them all sail into the bay and land on Staten Island, and he made his preparations to receive them as warmly as possible in case their attack should be against the Long Island fortifications, as seemed probable. But just at this time he was taken ill with a raging fever contracted in the swamps of Gowanus Bay. He was for several days at death's door, and was then removed to the Sailors' Snug Harbor, at what is now Broadway and Ninth Street. It was a cruel misfortune. He had been for fifteen months in the army, and had as yet seen no actual fighting except a few slight skirmishes around Boston. The first large battle of the war was now to be fought—against his own men and on his own ground —and he lying in bed with his mind wandering in a fever. "Gracious God! to be confined at such a time!" he writes to his brother as soon as he recovers. But there was no help for it. The battle was fought without him, and was a crushing defeat. To what extent he could have prevented this defeat had he remained in command is mere matter of conjecture, but all historians concur in attributing the disaster largely to his sickness and absence. Bancroft speaks of this as "an irreparable loss." While success with nine thousand militia against twenty-four thousand of the best troops of Europe would seem to have been impossible, yet, when we see what Greene accomplished in the South four years later, in the face of odds almost equally great, there is room to believe that he would at least have retarded the British advance with small loss, and brought his men within their lines in good condition. At all events, with Putnam and Sullivan in command, a terrible defeat was suffered, and but for Washington's extraordinary skill and quickness of action the whole army would have been captured. After the battle of the 27th of August, Howe pressed up to Fort Greene, but the abatis and fallen timber were thick, the lines looked strong, and Bunker Hill was still not forgotten. He decided to besiege, and not to try an assault. In forty-eight hours, from under his very eyes, Washington had taken the army over to New York. It is doubtful if a more brilliant military operation of this kind was ever performed. The whole army rang with Washington's praises, and Greene among the first. He tells his brother that, "considering the difficulties, the retreat from Long Island was the best effected retreat I ever read or heard of."

CHAPTER IV.

FORT WASHINGTON.

AFTER the retreat from Long Island Washington reorganized his army into three divisions. The first, consisting of five brigades under Putnam, was stationed in the city at the lower end of the island; the second, consisting of seven brigades under Spencer (to whom Greene's brigades were temporarily assigned), was ordered to march to Harlem to prevent a landing in that vicinity; the third, of two brigades, was posted at Kingsbridge. The paper strength of these twelve brigades was about twenty thousand men, but one third of them were sick, and the militia were deserting in swarms—going off, in Washington's words, " in some instances almost by whole regiments, in many by half ones and by companies at a time." His effective force probably did not much exceed ten thousand men.

Howe, having seen with chagrin Washington escape from him on Long Island, gradually extended his right flank along the shore of the East River as far as Flushing, and leisurely prepared to land on the upper part of Manhattan Island, hoping by the aid of his fleet in the North River to coop up Washington's entire force and capture it. Washington, on the other hand, " never sparing the spade and pickaxe," put every man at work throwing up fortifications along the East River, at Kingsbridge, and across the narrow neck from Fort Washington to the Harlem River.

On September 5th, after being three weeks in bed, Greene had so far recovered as to be able to write, and on that day he wrote a long letter to Washington advising " a general and speedy retreat " from Manhattan Island, and the posting of the army at Kingsbridge and along the Westchester shore. He further advised the burning of the city, reasoning that if once lost it could not be recovered for lack of a naval force, and that the enemy should not be allowed to use it. In this view he was supported by John Jay and others. But Congress, on September 3d, had passed a resolution instructing Washington, " in case he should find it necessary to quit New York, that no damage be done to the said city by his troops on their leaving it, the Congress having no doubt of being able to recover the same, though the enemy should for a time have possession of it." Whether the burning of New York would have been justifiable is a matter of doubt, but as to regaining it Congress was wrong and Greene was right; the British held it without interruption until after the close of the war.

On receipt of Greene's letter Washington called a council of war for September 7th. An exact record of its proceedings was not kept, but on the following day Washington reported to Congress the substance of its deliberations. " There were some general officers, in whose judgment and opinion much confidence is to be reposed, that were for a total and immediate removal from the city, . . . but they were overruled by a majority, who thought for the present a part of our force might be kept here and attempt to maintain the city a while longer." It was therefore concluded to post five thousand men in the city, nine thousand at Kingsbridge, and the balance at intermediate points. In this report Washington stated, "Nor were some a little influenced in their opinion, to whom the determination of Congress was known, against an evacuation totally, as they were led to suspect that Congress wished it to be retained at all hazards." Congress did not relish this remark, and tartly informed him, by resolution of the 10th, that they did not mean that the army should remain in New York "a moment longer" than he thought proper. Just as Washington received this resolution he also received a petition signed by Greene and six brigadiers asking for a second council. Washington promptly called one for September 12th, and at this council the previous vote was reconsidered, Heath, Spencer, and Clinton alone voting against it. It was decided to evacuate the city and all of the island except Fort Washington and its vicinity, for the defense of which eight thousand men were to be left. Washington immediately began the removal of stores and prepared for a retreat, which was somewhat hastened by Howe's movements. On Sunday, September 15th, Howe sent five frigates, mounting between seventy and eighty guns, up the East River, and, under cover of their fire, he transported a part of his force across the East River from Newtown Creek to a point (foot of Thirty-fourth Street) between Turtle and Kip's Bays. Washington hurried down from his headquarters near Harlem, and with two brigades endeavored to oppose Howe's landing. But the troops, although some of them had been engaged before, ran at the first fire, leaving Washington but a short distance from the enemy, by whom he narrowly escaped capture. A hasty retreat was made to Bloomingdale, and Washington sent word to Putnam to evacuate the city immediately. Had Howe marched over to the North River he would have completely cut off Putnam and captured his force of five thousand men; but instead of doing so, he stopped to lunch at Mr. Murray's house (Park Avenue and Thirty-sixth Street), and Putnam, by following the roads along the North River shore, was enabled to escape with the loss of fifteen men wounded, about one hundred stragglers missing, and his cannon and stores. At night the troops were hurriedly assembled and posted along the heights on the north of Manhattanville. The men slept without tents, were wet through by a heavy rain, and were greatly dispirited. Howe had completed his landing during the afternoon and advanced his troops to a line extending from Bloomingdale, through the heights in what is now the northern part of Central Park, to Hell Gate at Eighty-ninth Street. The armies were about two and a half miles apart, separated by the flat Harlem plains.

Before daylight on the following morning (September 16th) detachments of both armies were in motion. General Leslie left the British lines and moved along the high broken ground west of what is now Morningside Park; Colonel Knowlton, with his battalion of "rangers" or scouts, was sent forward over this same ground to ascertain the position of the British. The two detachments came together, apparently, in the vicinity of 110th Street, and a skirmish ensued, Knowlton gradually retreating toward Manhattanville. Washington was at his headquarters at the Morris House (161st Street) engaged in writing to Congress a report of the preceding day's retreat. Word was brought to him that the enemy had appeared in force on the Harlem plains, and, leaving his dispatch to be finished and forwarded by his secretary, he rode rapidly to the hill where the Convent of the Sacred Heart now stands (133d Street), and where Greene was posted with his division, of which he seems to have then just resumed the command. On arriving there he heard the firing and saw the skirmish in progress on the hills across the Manhattanville valley. He then went forward to the advanced pickets on the "Point of Rocks" (Ninth Avenue and 126th Street), where Knowlton met him and reported that the force opposed to him did not exceed three hundred men. Washington at once planned to effect their capture by making a demonstration against their front with a detachment of volunteers from Greene's division, while Knowlton with his rangers, re-enforced by a part of a Virginia regiment under Major Leitch, was to steal around their right flank and gain their rear. The plan partially succeeded, the British rushing down into the Manhattanville valley to attack the small force which was making a feint against their front. But Knowlton, instead of gaining their rear, attacked on their flank, and a sharp engagement took place, in which Knowlton was killed and Leitch was wounded. In spite of this loss, the men stood their ground, although it was evident that the British force was larger than anticipated. Washington therefore sent two Maryland regiments to their aid. The British, after a vigorous defense, were forced back about half a mile, when the Forty-second Highlanders came up as re-enforcements and they made a stand about noon. Howe now ordered additional re-enforcements, and two regiments of Hessians arrived, but they were unable to hold their ground and were finally driven back in considerable confusion nearly to 110th Street. Washington, not deeming it prudent to hazard his advantage any further, then stopped the pursuit and recalled his troops to their positions between the Point of Rocks and the Morris House. A large body of British re-enforcements arrived just after the Americans withdrew, but they made no effort at pursuit. In the evening, however, their pickets advanced to the heights just south of Manhattanville valley, only a short distance from those of the Americans at the Point of Rocks on the north of it.

The losses in this engagement were not very heavy, being about eighteen killed and ninety wounded on the British side, and considerably less on the American, but it was an engagement of great importance, because it showed that, in spite of their disgraceful conduct of the previous day, the men could be relied upon to fight. It had a wonderful effect in reanimating the spirits of the army. It brought Howe to a standstill for four weeks, and caused him to write home to the ministry that " the enemy is too strongly posted to be attacked in front, and innumerable difficulties are in the way of our turning him on either side." He plainly said that the war was not to be finished in one campaign, and asked that large re-enforcements be sent in the spring.

In this action Greene first came under fire. His troops were not engaged (except a small party of volunteers), but he, as well as Putnam, and Tilghman

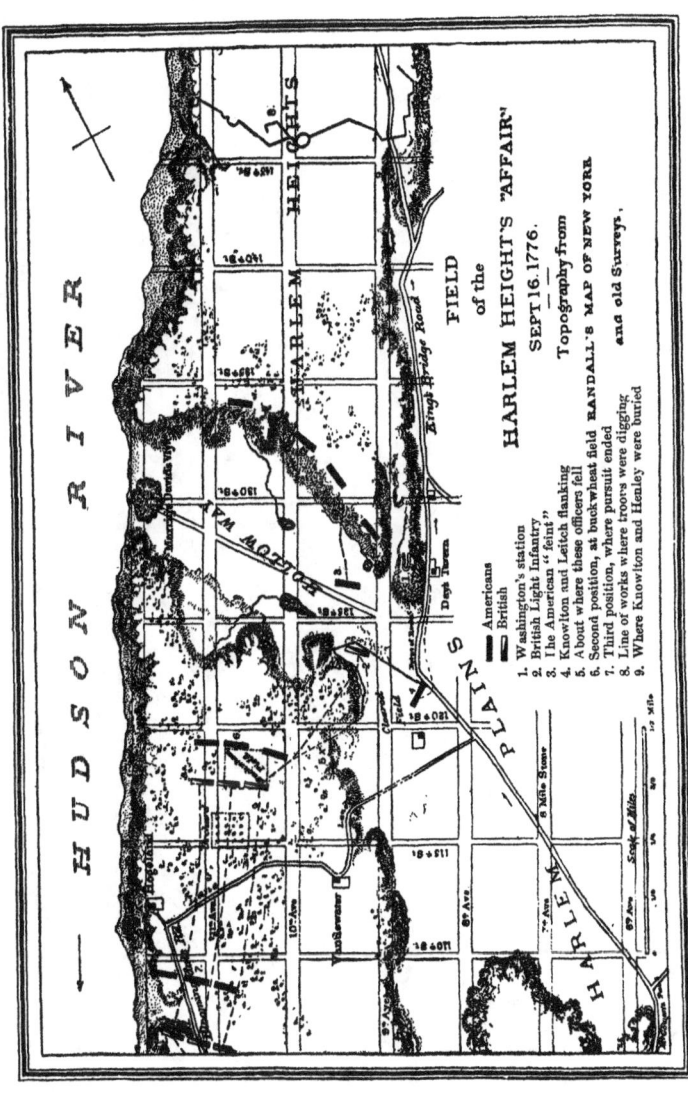

of Washington's staff, volunteered to take part in order to encourage the men, and they were in the thickest of the fight. Reed, the adjutant-general, also performed similar service, and, on account of his knowledge of the ground, acted as guide to Knowlton's turning column. As Reed wrote to his wife, it was rash for officers of their rank to expose themselves in this way, but they felt it was necessary to do so in order to encourage the men. They evidently wished, at any cost, to prevent a repetition of the shameful business at Kip's Bay.

Greene had now regained his health, and, as at Long Island, Washington gave him a semi-independent command, while retaining the bulk of the army under his own eye. It was all-important to preserve control of the line of the Hudson River, and, if possible, prevent the British ships from ascending it; at the same time holding possession of both banks, so that the army could move in either direction as the course of events might require. With this view the high ground at Mount Washington, about 180th Street, had been selected as the site of a fort even before the battle of Long Island; and when it was determined at the council of war, on September 12th, to evacuate New York, it was unanimously decided to hold Fort Washington. After the battle of Harlem Heights, Putnam's division was stationed in the vicinity, and the fort was under Putnam's command. Greene, on the other hand, was detached with his division, numbering fifty-seven hundred and seven on paper, and thirty-five hundred and twenty-one fit for duty, and sent over into New Jersey, with headquarters at Fort Lee, at the southern end of the Palisades and immediately opposite Fort Washington.

Greene remained in this position for the next two months. In the middle of October Howe began his turning movement, intending to get in rear of Washington by way of Throgg's Neck and New Rochelle, and then march across to the Hudson. With Lord Percy's detachment at Bloomingdale Heights on the south, his main army on the north, and his ships on both rivers, Howe hoped to surround and capture the whole American force. But as Howe extended his right by way of Long Island Sound, Washington as steadily extended his left along the line of the Bronx. Finally Washington reached White Plains, and there assembled his entire force, except what was left at Forts Washington and Lee, twenty miles distant, from which his communication was entirely severed. An indecisive engagement was fought at White Plains on October 29th, and then Washington retreated northward a few miles and took up a strong position at North Castle. Howe had been completely baffled in his efforts to turn Washington's left flank, and he thought it unwise to risk an assault at North Castle; he therefore marched across to the Hudson River at Dobb's Ferry and down to Kingsbridge. Washington saw that this meant an attack on Fort Washington. He therefore left Lee with seven thousand men at North Castle in case Howe should return to that point, posted Heath with three thousand in the Highlands near West Point, and sent the rest of his little force—about four thousand men—across the Hudson and down behind the Palisades to Hackensack, about nine miles in rear of Fort Lee. He himself arrived at the latter point on the afternoon of the 13th.

In the meantime Greene had made a small raid

into Staten Island and captured a few prisoners, had begun the formation of depots at convenient points on the road to Philadelphia, to be provided with stores for twenty thousand men for three months, and had done everything possible to strengthen the defenses of Fort Lee. Putnam commanded Fort Washington until about October 25th, when he was summoned to White Plains, and Greene, whose command had originally been limited to the troops on the Jersey shore, took charge of Fort Washington. Before Washington started for White Plains he had given orders that Fort Washington should be defended to the last extremity.

Putnam had placed some obstructions in the river, but they were not effectual in barring the navigation, although they rendered it more difficult. Early in October three frigates sailed up the river in spite of the obstructions and the fire of the forts, whereupon Congress passed a resolution (October 11th) directing Washington, "by every art and at whatever expense, to obstruct effectually the navigation of the North River between Fort Washington and Mount Constitution" [Fort Lee]. Putnam then added to the obstructions in the river and hastened the work on his batteries, and Greene continued to do the same after Putnam was called away to White Plains. On the 27th another ship tried to pass up the Hudson, but it was so badly damaged by the forts that it had to retire. At the same time a demonstration was made on the land side by the troops which had been left at Harlem under Lord Percy, but it was not seriously pressed and was easily repelled. This encouraged Greene to hope that a successful defense could be made at Fort Washington, and as Washington was some distance away, he sent a report of the affair direct to Congress. On the 28th, Fort Independence, which was on the heights just north of Kingsbridge, was evacuated under orders received direct from Washington; and on the 29th the Hessians under Knyphausen appeared on the plain just south of Kingsbridge. On the 31st, Greene, who only a week before had become responsible for Fort Washington, wrote to Washington for instructions: "I should be glad to know your Excellency's mind about holding all the ground from Kingsbridge to the lower lines. If we attempt to hold the ground, the garrison must still be re-enforced; but if the garrison is only to draw into Mount Washington, and keep that, the number of troops is too large. . . . I shall re-enforce Colonel Magaw (at Fort Washington) with Colonel Ralling's regiments until I hear from your Excellency respecting the matter." It took several days for this letter to reach Washington, so that he did not reply till November 5th, and then he gave no positive instructions. His secretary wrote: "It depends upon so many circumstances that it is impossible for him to determine the point. He submits entirely to your discretion, and such judgment as you will be able to form from the enemy's movements and the whole complexion of things." On the 6th a frigate and two transports passed up the river. Greene promptly notified Washington of it on the following day, and his secretary wrote to Greene to watch the shores carefully and give the earliest information of any movement of the British to cross the river. On the following day, having fully considered the matter and being convinced that an attack on Fort Washington would be

FORT WASHINGTON.   53

the next move on Howe's part, Washington wrote to Greene in these words. It is this letter which leads Bancroft to accuse Greene of disobedience of orders, and hence its language should be carefully noted, for the accusation is devoid of any foundation in fact:

" The late passage of three vessels up the North River, of which we have just received advice, is so plain a proof of the inefficacy of all the obstructions we have thrown into it that I can not but think it will fully justify a change in the disposition which has been made. If we can not prevent vessels from passing up, and the enemy are possessed of the surrounding country, what valuable purpose can it answer to attempt to hold a post from which the expected benefit can not be had ? I am therefore inclined to think that it will not be prudent to hazard the men and stores at Mount Washington ; but, as you are on the spot, I leave it to you to give such orders as to evacuating Mount Washington as you may judge best, and so far revoking the order given to Colonel Magaw to defend it to the last.

" The best accounts obtained from the enemy assure us of a considerable movement among their boats last evening, and, so far as can be collected from the various sources of intelligence, they must design a penetration into Jersey, and to fall down upon your post. You will therefore immediately have all the stores removed which you do not deem necessary for your defense."

This letter contains four things : First, a positive order to remove the stores from Fort Lee. Second, a revocation of the former order to defend Fort Washington to the last. Third, authority to General Greene to evacuate Fort Washington whenever he thinks best. Fourth, Washington's opinion that probably it would be best to evacuate it. It contains no order to evacuate Fort Washington. When Washington wished to give an order he did so in very plain language, but in this case he merely threw out a suggestion ("I am inclined to think that it would not be prudent to hazard") which evidently implied a desire for the expression of Greene's views.

Greene promptly replied on November 9th, saying that he had already given orders for the removal of the stores at Dobb's Ferry, and stating fully his opinion in regard to Fort Washington.

"The passing of the ships up the river is, to be sure, a full proof of the insufficiency of the obstructions in the river to stop the ships from going up; but that garrison employs double the number of men to invest it that we have to occupy it. They must keep troops at Kingsbridge to prevent a communication with the country, and they dare not leave a very small number for fear our people should attack them. Upon the whole, I can not help thinking the garrison is of advantage, and I can not conceive the garrison to be in any great danger; the men can be brought off at any time, but the stores may not be so easily removed, yet I think they can be got off in spite of them if matters grow desperate.

"This post is of no importance only in conjunction with Mount Washington. I was over there last evening. The enemy seems to be disposing matters to besiege the place, but Colonel Magaw thinks it will take them till December expires before they can carry it. If the enemy don't find it an object of importance they won't trouble themselves about it. If they do, it is a full proof they feel an injury from

FORT WASHINGTON. 55

our possessing it. Our giving it up will open a free communication with the country by the way of Kingsbridge that must be a great advantage to them and injury to us."

On the 10th Greene wrote again to Washington stating what dispositions he had made for the removal of the stores on the west bank of the Hudson, but saying nothing further about Fort Washington. Washington had given him discretion to evacuate Fort Washington if he thought best; Greene had replied, stating at length why he thought the evacuation unnecessary and unadvisable. He then waited for further instructions.

Washington left White Plains on the 10th, was at Peekskill on the 11th, crossed the river at King's Ferry (Verplanck's Point) on the 12th, and arrived at Fort Lee on the afternoon of the 13th. At what point he received Greene's letters of the 9th and 10th is not known. Washington made no reply to them, as was evidently unnecessary, in view of his intention to see Greene in a few days, unless he wished to give a positive order to evacuate the Fort, and this he was not prepared to do, for his own mind was not fully made up. After Washington's arrival, of course, all responsibility on Greene's part ended. The commander in chief was on the spot, and it was for him to give orders. Washington's report to Congress of the 16th, his letter to his brother of the 19th, his letter to Reed, August 22, 1779, and his letter to Gordon, March 8, 1785—all tell the same story. He arrived at Fort Lee and found the fort had not been evacuated or the stores removed. His own opinion was that it should be abandoned, yet he recognized its importance, and if it could be held, undoubtedly it would be of the greatest advantage. On this point his mind was not clear; personally he thought it could not be defended with success; but Magaw, who was in command of the post, and Greene, in whose judgment he had great confidence, thought that it could. He therefore came to no decision; the opposing opinions caused, in his own words, "that warfare in my mind, and hesitation, which ended in the loss of the garrison."

Washington did not visit Fort Washington on the 14th, but went back to the Hackensack to examine the ground over which he felt sure he would soon have to retreat. Here, on the afternoon of the 15th, he received a brief note from Greene, inclosing one from Magaw, saying that Howe had demanded the surrender of the garrison. Washington returned at once to Fort Lee, reaching the river bank at dusk.

In the meantime Howe had closed in on Fort Washington from all sides; from Kingsbridge on the north, with Knyphausen's division of Hessians; from Harlem on the south, with Earl Percy's detachment; and on the east bank of the Harlem, with detachments from his main force at Yonkers under Cornwallis and Matthews. In all, the assailants numbered about nine thousand men. The garrison, including the re-enforcements sent over by Greene, numbered about twenty-eight hundred. It was not stationed in the fort proper, but in the outlying works, at the point of the hills near 195th Street on the north and the old lines at Morris House and beyond it as far as 147th Street on the south, the distance between the two extreme points being over two miles. Rawlings commanded at the point of the hill north of Fort Washington, Baxter at the hill just east of him, overlooking the Harlem River, and Cadwalader at the lower lines facing Manhattanville. Magaw commanded the whole force, with his headquarters at Fort Washington.

On the 15th Howe sent his adjutant-general under flag of truce from Kingsbridge to Magaw's headquarters, demanding a surrender. Magaw replied that he would defend his post to the last. He immediately sent a copy of his reply across the river to Greene, who told Magaw to defend his post until he received other orders, and sent the letter on to Washington, as already stated. Greene then went across to see Magaw, accompanied by Putnam, who had crossed the river at King's Ferry a few days before, marched down behind the Palisades, and taken post at Hackensack. They spent an hour or more with Magaw, who assured them of his ability to defend his post, and they were just returning to Fort Lee when Washington met them at the shore with the intention of crossing. He was so assured by their report that he decided not to cross, and all three returned to Greene's headquarters on top of the Palisades for the night.

On the morning of the 16th Howe's columns converged on the fort from the north, south, and east. The resistance was at first quite spirited, but, being overpowered in numbers and being taken in flank and rear by the column under Cornwallis from the east, they yielded and retreated to the fort in considerable confusion. Had a defense like that at Bunker Hill been made at the fort, the British would have been held at bay, and the garrison could probably have been brought off in safety. Washington, who was watching the affair from the heights of

Fort Lee, saw this, and sent word to this effect by a gallant officer who made his way to the fort, but just before he arrived Magaw had surrendered his entire command. The British loss was about four hundred and fifty in killed and wounded; the Americans had lost fifty-four killed and less than one hundred wounded; they surrendered two hundred and twenty-one officers and twenty-six hundred and thirty-seven men. All the cannon and a considerable amount of stores which were in the fort fell into the hands of the British.

It was a terrible disaster. Charles Lee, jealous of the growing reputation of Greene, who was already talked of as the probable successor of Washington in case accident should befall him, did his utmost to cast discredit on Greene; but Washington assumed the full responsibility, and neither then nor afterward censured Greene in any manner for his action. Had such a defense been made as was made at Bunker Hill, or had the Americans fought as they fought at Harlem Heights two months before, Howe would have suffered such losses as would again have brought his campaign to a standstill, and Greene's opinion would have been vindicated and Washington's hesitation justified. But no such defense was made, an almost irreparable loss was sustained, and such blame as, judging after the event, attaches to it, must be shared equally by Washington and Greene. Since the place was lost, Greene's advice in favor of trying to hold it was perhaps an error of judgment; had his opinion been the other way, he would have withdrawn the garrison under his discretionary orders, and it would have been saved. But no one can divide the responsibility of the commander in

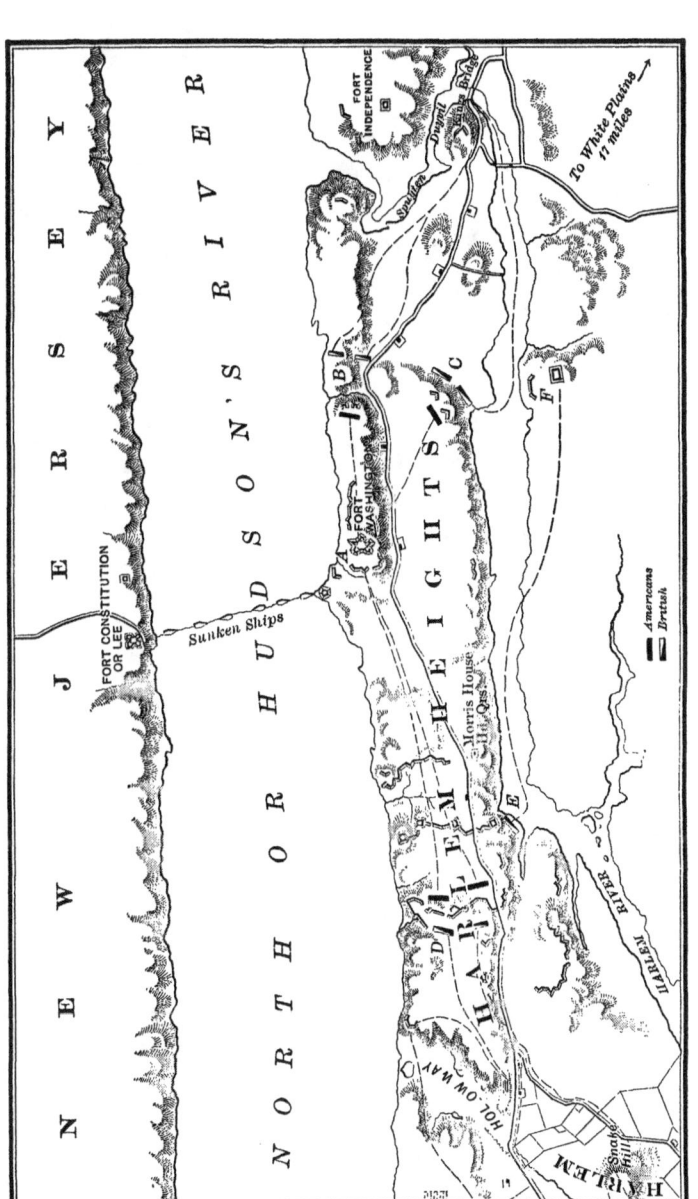

CAPTURE OF FORT WASHINGTON.

A. Col. Magaw commanding the fort. *C.* Cornwallis attacking Col. Baxter. *E.* Lieut.-Col. Stirling intercepting Cadwallader.
B. Knyphausen and Rall attacking Col. Rawling. *D.* Percy attacking Col. Cadwallader. *F.* British redoubts covering Cornwallis.

chief. Washington was on the ground for nearly three days before the assault was made. The skill which withdrew a much larger force from Long Island in actual contact with the enemy, was quite equal to withdrawing this garrison had its possessor so decided. But he made no such decision, not being sufficiently sure of his own opinion to overrule the strong opposite opinion of Greene, supported by that of all the officers of the garrison.

Washington fully realized his error and was deeply mortified. He saw that he should have supported his own judgment with a positive order, and he substantially says so in his letter to Reed three years later. Had he done so, none would have rendered more prompt and cheerful obedience than Greene. On the other hand, Greene felt at once that he would be blamed for the loss, and on the following day he wrote to Knox: "I feel mad, vexed, sick, and sorry. . . . This is a most terrible event; its consequences are justly to be dreaded. Pray, what is said on the occasion?"

This misfortune was the basis on which Lee and Gates founded their opposition to Washington; but as between Washington and Greene it only cemented their confidence in each other. Washington never attempted to shirk his own responsibility by pleading the advice of his subordinate; and Greene never answered the criticisms on his advice by calling attention to the indecision of his chief. He sought ever more and more to merit Washington's confidence by unflagging devotion to duty; and he pondered much on the mistake he had made, so as to avoid a similar one in the future.

CHAPTER V.

THE JERSEYS.

HAVING gained possession of Fort Washington, the British promptly turned their attention to the corresponding fort on the west bank of the river, Fort Lee. Washington anticipated this, and under his direction Greene began at once to remove the stores. But before this could be accomplished Cornwallis caused boats to be transported through Harlem River into the Hudson and up to Yonkers. On the night of November 19th, which was dark and rainy, he crossed at this point with a force of fourteen battalions, numbering about six thousand men, and marched toward the rear of Fort Lee. Greene heard of this on the morning of the 20th, and immediately marched out of Fort Lee with its garrison of about two thousand men, to join Washington at the Hackensack bridge, five miles in rear of the fort. Greene had the longest distance to march, but he reached the bridge in advance of Cornwallis, and held it. Cornwallis then moved over and took possession of the fort, where large quantities of stores had necessarily been abandoned. His force greatly outnumbered Washington's, and had he made a vigorous attack at once he might possibly have routed and dispersed Washington's army. But he did not make the attempt.

Washington withdrew behind the Passaic and remained in the vicinity of Newark for a week, then retreated by successive stages to New Brunswick, Princeton, and Trenton, where he arrived on December 7th, Cornwallis following him very closely during the latter part of the retreat. It was impossible for him to give battle, as his little force was wasting away by expiration of the year's enlistment and by desertion, so that he had not more than three thousand men in hand; and all efforts to bring out the Jersey militia were fruitless. On reaching the Delaware he collected all the boats within a distance of seventy miles, and, as Cornwallis was close behind him, he crossed the river on the 8th, after breaking the bridges, and stationed his force along the bank opposite Trenton. Cornwallis made no effort to cross, but disposed his force in winter quarters, partly along the opposite bank of the Delaware and partly in detachments as far back as Amboy. He himself returned to New York and prepared to sail for England on leave of absence, confident that no military operations would take place before spring.

Washington, however, had no such intentions. The American cause was at its lowest ebb, and he wrote to his brother: " If every nerve is not strained to recruit the new army with all possible expedition, I think the game is pretty nearly up." Everything depended upon the handful of men along the Delaware, and still more on Washington's iron nerve. In this desperate strait he resolved on striking a blow, which captured a force one third as large as his own and drove the British back to New York! We hear so much of Washington as the modern Fabius, that we are apt to forget that no general ever lived who was quicker to seize a favorable opportunity, and by prompt and vigorous action turn it to advantage. He had shown this the preceding summer in the retreat from Long Island, and was to show it again in his march to Virginia in 1781. But never did he show it so clearly as in this midwinter stroke at Trenton, which brought the sunshine of victory out of the gloom and darkness of a long series of disasters.

During the two weeks following his arrival on the Delaware he had managed to augment his little force. A part of Lee's army had at last reached him under Sullivan's command after Lee had been captured; Schuyler had sent a detachment from the Northern Department, and some militia had been raised in Philadelphia. These, with what remained of the force he had brought from Fort Lee, carried his strength up to about seven thousand men. He determined to cross the river at three points, attack the British and Hessian posts, and, if successful, push on to New Brunswick and capture the large depot of British stores. A part of the militia was to cross near Burlington and strike the British left; another part was to cross at Trenton and hold the roads at that point; while the Continental troops, about twenty-four hundred strong, in two divisions, under Sullivan and Greene, were to cross nine miles above Trenton and take it in flank. The time chosen was the night after Christmas, when the Hessians would be heavy with carousing and their guards slack. The night was intensely cold and stormy, with alternations of snow and hail, and the river was filled with floating ice. Both detachments of militia failed to get across, and accomplished nothing; but the Continentals were all across by about four o'clock in the morning and marching toward Trenton, Sullivan on the right along the river road, and Greene on a road a few miles to his left. Washington in person accompanied Greene's column. At daylight they reached the town, entering by converging streets. Greene's division entered first, seized their artillery, and cut off the retreat to Princeton; Sullivan arrived a few minutes later. The Hessians were surprised, but turned out briskly; there was a short, sharp fight in the streets, in which their commander, Colonel Rall, and thirty others were killed and wounded; then about five hundred escaped by the road which the militia detachment was to have held if it had crossed at Trenton, and the rest, to the number of about one thousand, surrendered. The American loss had been two privates killed, two frozen to death, and three wounded.

It was a success almost equally startling to friend and foe. Gordon states that a council of war was immediately held, and that Greene and Knox were in favor of pushing on at once toward Princeton, but the other officers—Sullivan, Stirling, Mercer, St. Clair, and Stephen—opposed it, and Washington did not feel justified in acting against the opinions of the majority. He therefore retired during the afternoon to his old positions on the south bank of the river.

On hearing the news of this affair, Cornwallis abandoned the idea of going on leave, and started at once for Trenton, picking up the detachments at Elizabeth and New Brunswick as he came. At the same time the British and Hessian detachments on their left flank near Burlington and Mount Holly retreated hastily toward Princeton. On the 28th, Washington sent Greene across the river again into Jersey with a force of about three hundred men, and on the next day he followed in person with the Continentals, numbering about eighteen hundred. He was then joined by the Pennsylvania militia, which had succeeded in crossing at Burlington and had been increased by fresh arrivals from Philadelphia. His force varied from day to day, according to the accessions of militia on one hand and the desertions and expiration of service on the other. On January 1st it was about five thousand men in all. On the morning of January 2d Cornwallis moved out from Princeton with his army of about eight thousand men. It was only ten miles to Trenton, and midway of the distance he met Colonel Hand's regiment of riflemen, who annoyed him with their fire and delayed his march. Early in the afternoon Greene was sent out with six hundred men and two guns to re-enforce Hand, and he disposed this little force to such advantage that Cornwallis spent the whole afternoon before he could force Greene back into Trenton. It was four o'clock of a short winter day before he reached the town, so that he was obliged to postpone his attack until the following day. In the meantime Washington had formed his main body behind a little stream which runs through Trenton, and was prepared to make as good a defense as his small numbers would permit. But Cornwallis prudently decided to put his men into bivouac for the night, his pickets in contact with those of Washington. During the night Washington executed a movement of extraordinary boldness and skill. Sending his baggage down to Burlington, and leaving his camp fires burning, he withdrew from Cornwallis's front, marched around his left and rear, and at daylight was at Princeton. Here he met and overwhelmed with heavy loss three British regiments on their way to join Cornwallis at

Trenton. He had intended to push on to New Brunswick and seize the British stores, but his men were too exhausted to justify the attempt, and he moved off toward the north, and by easy stages reached Morristown on the 6th of December. Cornwallis, dumbfounded at the absence of Washington's army on the morning of the 3d, started quickly for Princeton as soon as he heard the firing in that direction. He arrived just as Washington had left, but, instead of following Washington, he marched straight to New Brunswick to secure his stores.

From Fort Lee to Morristown Washington had thus described a figure ∞, with Cornwallis always in pursuit, until the latter gave up the chase at Princeton. At one time he was in a corner at Trenton, and it seemed as if the end must speedily come, either in an attack by overwhelming force, or in the disintegration of the army by expiration of enlistment and general discouragement and apathy. The English felt so confident of the latter result that they deemed it unnecessary to waste blood in an attack. But at the darkest hour Washington's bold strokes at Trenton and Princeton sent Cornwallis back to the line of the Raritan, and secured for himself a strong position on the British flank, where he could safely provide for the reorganization of his army and at the same time could paralyze his adversary's advance. Howe's Jersey campaign was at an end. For the next six months his force was neutralized, and he attempted nothing but a few feints. Finally he gave it up, and sent his troops around by sea to attack Philadelphia from the south.

To what extent Greene participated in planning these movements it is impossible to say. In the funeral oration pronounced by Hamilton before the Cincinnati in July, 1789, he says: " As long as the enterprises of Trenton and Princeton shall be regarded as the dawning of that bright day which afterward broke forth with such resplendent luster, . . . so long ought the name of Greene to be revered by a grateful country." Hamilton served through the campaign, and at its close became Washington's secretary, so that he was well qualified to speak. But something must be allowed to the warmth of eulogy in a funeral oration upon a most intimate friend. To the Committee of Congress that congratulated him upon the victory, Washington with his usual generosity replied : " I assure you, the other general officers, who assisted me in the plan and execution, have full as good a right to your encomiums as myself." To which Bancroft, never partial to Greene, adds : " The most useful of them all was Greene." That Greene's relations to Washington were of the most cordial and confidential nature there is no doubt, but, being associated in daily intercourse with him, there is but little record of it extant in writing. Greene was fully cognizant of the plans against Trenton, for on December 21st he wrote to Governor Cooke, of Rhode Island : " I hope to give the enemy a stroke in a few days." At the same time the Eastern delegates applied to have him sent to Rhode Island, which had just been invaded by a detachment from New York, but Washington would not consent to his leaving the army in Jersey, and Spencer was sent in his stead. The outlook for the coming year was so gloomy, that Washington felt compelled to write to Congress in the most earnest terms urging it to make provision for an army, and asking for enlarged

THE JERSEYS. 67

powers for himself. This he did on December 20th, and on the following day Greene wrote a similar letter advocating the same measures, and arguing that while the principle might be dangerous yet the situation was critical, and that there was no danger that Washington would exceed his powers. " There never was a man that might be more safely trusted, nor a time when there was a louder call." No one but his closest friend would have assumed to write such a letter. The joint appeal was not without effect, and at Baltimore, where it had retired from Philadelphia, Congress passed, on December 27th, a resolution conferring upon Washington almost dictatorial powers for the period of six months. A few months later Washington selected Greene to proceed to Philadelphia and appear before Congress in person, in order to explain fully the requirements of the army and his plans for the future.

The next six months were passed in and about Morristown in comparative inaction. Greene went to Philadelphia in March, as already stated, and in May he was sent with Knox to examine the defences about West Point and give such instructions as he might deem necessary for the greater security of the passes in the Highlands. Upon the surrender of Ticonderoga, in July, it was proposed to send him to the Northern army under Schuyler, but Washington again declined to part with him, and Lincoln and Arnold were sent in his place.

The winter quarters at Morristown were brightened, as in the preceding year at Cambridge, by the presence of ladies. Mrs. Washington joined her husband, and several other ladies came to camp. But Mrs. Greene was unable to come. Her second child

—Martha Washington Greene—was born in March, and she was subsequently very ill for several weeks; so that she did not arrive in Morristown until the middle of July, a few days before the army marched to Delaware.

In the comparative leisure of this winter Greene resumed his voluminous correspondence with John Adams in Congress, Governor Cooke in Rhode Island, Generals Spencer and Arnold, who commanded in Rhode Island, and others. With Spencer and Arnold he discussed plans for driving the British out of Newport, but with the others his principal topic was always the raising of a permanent army to take the place of the annual levies and the ever-vanishing militia. During the preceding September Congress had acknowledged the principle of a regular army, and had voted eighty-eight battalions, or sixty-six thousand men, to be raised by the various States and armed and equipped by them; the men to serve during the war, and receive a bounty of $20 and a grant of land. Two months later it was resolved to give the men the option of enlisting for the war or for three years; but in the latter case there was to be no grant of land. On December 27th the same resolution which conferred dictatorial powers on Washington for six months authorized him to raise from any part of the United States, in addition to the army voted in September, sixteen battalions of infantry, three thousand light horse, three regiments of artillery, and a corps of engineers; and he had authority to appoint the officers, equip the men, and establish their pay. But, as Washington had written to Congress in October, "there is a material difference between voting battalions and raising men." Enlist-

THE JERSEYS.

ments were slow, and the New England States, in order to encourage them, offered a large bounty in addition to that promised by Congress. This put a stop to recruiting in other States until they should offer the same inducements; and it did not help matters in New England, for the recruits held off in the hope that the bounty would be still further increased. Finally, Rhode Island, after ordering the two battalions allotted by Congress, entered into competition with them by ordering two regiments specially intended for defense against the British troops in Newport. Washington highly disapproved of this course, and Greene was specially mortified that, after all his arguments in favor of a strong Continental army, his own State should take a course so opposite to his views. He erroneously supposed that the two regiments were to be enlisted for service in the State only, and he wrote a vigorous letter to Governor Cooke protesting against the measure, and pointing out that if each State was simply to provide independently for its own defense the general cause must surely fail. The Governor was offended at the letter, laid it before the Assembly, and replied that the two regiments were to be enlisted for the defense of the United States in general and their own State in particular, but that they were liable to service in any State, and differed from the Continental battalions only in the fact that their term was for fifteen months instead of three years. Greene replied, apologizing for his error, and saying that love for his native place and zeal for the cause had led him to write so strongly, because he could " not help feeling himself wounded when anything transpired to the prejudice of the State." He was glad to know that the proposed regiments differed from the Continentals only in length of service; but still he thought the measure unwise, because it would delay the formation of the Continental battalions.

In fact, the Assembly was hardly to blame. It simply followed the system, or lack of system, which characterized all the military measures of the day. When the State was invaded, a convention of representatives from all the New England States had met at Providence to devise means of repelling it, independent of Congress. Then Charles Lee, without consulting Washington, had sent to the Governor a fussy Frenchman named Malmédy, on the ground that there was no one in the State competent to command the troops; this gentleman contributed little to its defense, but occupied his time in writing letters in all directions, complaining that he had not been given sufficient rank, until finally Washington lost patience and notified him, on May 16th, that his " scruples were exceedingly perplexing, and he wished them to cease." Washington sent Spencer to take command in Rhode Island, and, after being there four months, this officer wrote to the Governor, without consulting Washington, requesting him to raise troops specially for the defense of the State—the very thing that Washington and Greene complained of. Finally, in April, Congress passed a resolution specifically calling on the State and the other New England States to collect their " entire force " and drive the British out of Rhode Island. Everywhere the militia ideas prevailed of calling out troops for a special emergency and then disbanding them, instead of conducting a well-considered campaign with a regular army under one head for the benefit of the whole country. Washington and Greene were almost the only officers who appreciated the necessity of unity of command and a permanent force in order to secure ultimate success. In July, Greene came into sharp collision with Congress on a question of promotion. French officers were beginning to arrive in considerable numbers, under contracts made with Silas Deane, in Paris, by which they were to have very high rank. At their head was M. du Coudray, and it was rumored that he was to be appointed chief of artillery in place of Knox, with the rank of major-general, to date from August 1, 1776, which would antedate the commissions of Sullivan and Greene. Du Coudray had been a colonel of artillery in France, and, while a man of undoubted talent, had seen but little service. Greene did not relish the idea of being overslaughed, and though he afterward conceived great admiration and friendship for Lafayette, Steuben, and Kosciusko, at this time he looked with distrust upon the advent of foreign adventurers. Moreover, Knox, who was to be directly supplanted, was his particular friend, for whom he had the highest regard.

During the months of May and June Washington had several times written to Congress, and twice personally to Richard Henry Lee, expressing his anxiety concerning these appointments, which might lead to the army being overrun with foreigners, and stating in particular that the appointment of Du Coudray to the command of the artillery would "involve the most injurious consequences." In the intimacy which Greene enjoyed with Washington he must have been cognizant of these letters, and doubtless the matter was fully discussed at headquarters. No heed being paid to Washington's warnings, Greene determined to act on his own responsibility, and on the 1st of July, therefore, he wrote to the President of the Congress a brief letter, stating the rumors he had heard, and added: "If the report be true, it will lay me under the necessity of resigning my commission, as his appointment supersedes me in command. I beg you'll acquaint me with respect to the truth of the report, and, if true, inclose me a permit to retire." Sullivan and Knox * wrote similar letters by the same mail.

Congress was highly incensed, and, after deliberating on the matter two days, unanimously passed a resolution that the letters be sent to Washington, " with directions to him to let those officers know that Congress considers the said letters as an attempt to influence their decisions, an invasion of the liberties of the people, and indicating a lack of confidence in the justice of Congress; that it is expected by Congress the said officers will make proper acknowledgments for an interference of so dangerous a tendency; but if any of those officers are unwilling

---

* Mrs. Knox showed quite as much spirit in the matter as her husband. A few weeks before, she had written to him from Boston: "A French general (Du Coudray), who styles himself commander in chief of the Continental artillery, is now in town. He says his appointment is from Mr. Deane; that he is going immediately to headquarters to take command; that he is a major-general, and a deal of it. Who knows but I may have my Harry again? This I am sure of: he will never suffer any one to command him in that department. If he does, he has not the soul which I now think him possessed of." It is easy to believe that the views of John Adams and the Continental Congress would weigh but little in Knox's mind against an opinion of this sort from his "dear Lucy."

to serve their country, under the authority of Congress, they shall be at liberty to resign their commissions and retire."

Washington simply forwarded the resolution without remark to the officers in question, and on July 12th notified Congress that he had done so.

The resolution had been drawn by John Adams, chairman of the Board of War. He also wrote a short private note to Greene, calling on him to apologize or resign. Greene did neither. He made no reply to Adams, but broke off his correspondence with him, and did not resume it until five years later. To Congress he wrote a dignified reply, and doubtless his knowledge of Adams's character enabled him to draft it so skillfully. He had already had considerable correspondence with Adams on the subject of foreign officers, and also of rank in the army. Adams could form no conception of the sentiments of pride and honor which actuate a soldier. In March he had written to Greene: "This delicate point of honor, which is really one of the most putrid corruptions of absolute monarchy . . . must be bridled. It is incompatible with republican principles. I hope, for my own part, that Congress will elect annually all the general officers. If, in consequence of this, some great men should be obliged at the year's end to go home and serve their country in some other capacity, not less necessary and better adapted to their genius, I do not think that the country would be ruined."

The same hasty temper that wrote these words had evidently drafted the resolution of Congress. Greene had no trouble in writing a calm and convincing reply, which caused Congress to drop all further reference to resignation or apology, and, after much deliberation, to appoint Du Coudray Inspector-General of Ordnance and Military Manufactories, with the rank of Major-General, to date from August 11th of the year 1777. Thus Knox was not displaced, and Sullivan and Greene were not superseded in rank.

Sullivan and Knox made no reply to Congress, Greene's answer being apparently considered sufficient for all three. It was somewhat lengthy, but its tone was admirable and its logic was unanswerable. He begins by saying: "I confess that it was a matter of infinite surprise to me that an interpretation of so deep a complexion should have been put upon a meaning so innocent and inoffensive as that contained in those letters. Nor can I be persuaded but that Congress, upon a dispassionate review of the matter, will readily perceive that they have embraced ideas by no means deducible from anything we have done, and will in justice recall a censure equally severe, unmerited, and injurious." He then explains fully the rumor which had reached camp concerning Du Coudray's appointment and his reasons for believing it to be true, and continues : " My feelings as a soldier forbid my holding a command that was linked with evident signs of personal degradation. . . . Whatever influence I could have must be in proportion to the importance of my military character ; take this away, and I stand upon the footing of a common citizen; and it seems to me somewhat extraordinary that an offer to lay aside should be deemed to import such dangerous consequences as are imputed to it. . . . With respect to that part of the resolution which declares 'that if any of those

THE JERSEYS.

officers are unwilling to serve their country, under the authority of Congress, he shall have liberty to retire,' I answer that I have all the respect for Congress a free citizen ought to have for the representatives of himself and the collective body of the people, and that it is my glory and happiness to serve my country under the authority of those delegated by her to direct her councils and support her interests. I have not a single thought or wish inconsistent with this; but at the same time I as freely answer that I esteem it my duty to do it in a manner compatible with the dignity of the man, the citizen, and that of a soldier, while I sustain the character; and will immediately renounce any station in which I can not act with honor, and have recourse to that in which I can flatter myself I shall always be ambitious of, the character of a useful and good member of society. In my military capacity I have served and will serve my country to the utmost of my ability, while I hold it, but I am determined to hold it not a moment longer than I can do it unsullied and unviolated." This letter was read in Congress July 23d, and ordered "to lie on the table"; from which it was never taken up. The position and rank finally accorded to Du Coudray were such as to do no injury to Sullivan, Greene, or Knox; and the unfortunate Du Coudray himself—the unwitting author of this tempestuous little incident which, in the mind of John Adams, threatened such danger to American liberty—was accidentally drowned while crossing the Schuylkill River, a month after his appointment.

CHAPTER VI.

THE BRANDYWINE AND GERMANTOWN.

By the middle of May, 1777, Washington had succeeded in assembling in New Jersey a force of forty-three battalions of the new Continental levies authorized in September and December of the previous year. These came from New Jersey and the States to the south as far as Virginia, the New York and New England troops being ordered to the Northern army or the passes of the Hudson. Washington organized his force into five divisions of two brigades each. The division commanders were Sullivan and Greene, whose commissions dated from August 9, 1776, and Stirling, Stephen, and Lincoln, who had been promoted to be major-generals on the 21st of February, 1777. Knox was chief of artillery, and Pickering adjutant-general. The battalions were all small, the aggregate force amounting to eighty-three hundred and seventy-eight officers and men, and of these over two thousand were sick. The effective rank and file numbered fifty-seven hundred and thirty-eight.

On the 23d of May, Greene was sent to select a site for an intrenched camp in the high hills just north of the Raritan at Bound Brook, and the army was posted in this position during the next few days, Washington's headquarters being moved there on

THE BRANDYWINE AND GERMANTOWN. 77

May 29th. Sullivan's division was at Princeton in advance of the right wing, in order to keep up communications with Philadelphia. Arnold, who commanded temporarily at the latter point, was collecting militia behind the Delaware at Trenton. In this central position Washington waited to see what Howe would do. If he moved up the river to join Burgoyne, he would meet him at Peekskill; if he marched to Philadelphia, he would hang on his flanks; if he attacked him, he would make a good defense in a strong position of his own choosing. Howe did not feel strong enough to attack Washington, and he deemed it unsafe to march across to Philadelphia with Washington in his rear. In the month of April he had already decided to send his army by sea to attack Philadelphia from the south, but before embarking he determined to make a final effort to entice Washington out from his position in the hills, being confident that if he could meet him in the open country his superiority in numbers and discipline would gain him the victory. On the 13th of June, therefore, he moved out with a strong force from Brunswick to Princeton, thus cutting Washington's communications with Philadelphia, and took up a good defensive position on the south of the Raritan, in which to receive an attack. But Washington stood fast; he let go his communications with Philadelphia, Sullivan simply retreating from Princeton to the hills on the west. He rightly judged that Howe did not intend to march to Philadelphia. This manœuvre having failed, Howe retreated on the 19th to New Brunswick. Washington promptly sent Greene with his division, re-enforced by Wayne's brigade and Morgan's riflemen, in pursuit, at the same time ordering Sullivan to advance against his left flank, and Maxwell to intercept his retreat between Brunswick and Amboy. These latter did not receive their orders in time to take part in the movement, but Greene came up with the rear of the British at Brunswick on June 22d and pursued them through the town and across the Raritan, where they took position in their redoubts. They abandoned these as Greene advanced, and retreated to Amboy. He pursued them about five miles, and then, not wishing to get separated too far from the main body, he returned to Brunswick.

Having failed in his feint against Washington's right, Howe now tried to turn his left and get possession of the passes in the hills, which would bring him in rear of Washington's left flank. On June 25th he sent Cornwallis in the direction of Westfield and Scotch Plains. He had a sharp skirmish with Stirling's division, but, finding the passes well guarded, he retreated to Amboy. Howe then definitely abandoned New Jersey, and began the embarkation of his troops.

For the next six weeks contradictory reports concerning the destination of Howe's fleet followed in quick succession. At one time they were reported moving up the Hudson, at another toward Delaware or Chesapeake Bay, and at still another toward Charleston. Washington made corresponding moves with his army, now toward Peekskill and again toward Philadelphia, always holding his force well in hand and using his interior lines to be first on the ground wherever Howe should land. Finally, on the 22d of August, while Washington was near Trenton and intending to march for the Hudson, he received

THE BRANDYWINE AND GERMANTOWN.

positive intelligence that the fleet was two hundred miles up the Chesapeake. He turned about forthwith, marched his army through Philadelphia on Sunday, August 24th, the force drawn out to its greatest length in order to give an appearance of strength, and on the evening of the 25th, with Greene's division in the advance, reached Wilmington. Howe had landed in the northeast corner of Maryland, at the head of Chesapeake Bay, on the same day. The Continental battalions had been filling up, two brigades had been brought from the Hudson, and the militia of New Jersey, Pennsylvania, and Delaware had turned out in considerable numbers. All told, Washington's force numbered over fifteen thousand men, of whom eleven thousand were present for duty. Howe's muster rolls called for eighteen thousand, of whom fifteen thousand were available.

On the 26th, Washington and Greene rode forward to two hills—Iron Hill and Gray's Hill—about twenty miles south of Wilmington and six or seven miles from Howe's camp. Lafayette had been commissioned a major-general a few weeks before, and had joined Washington's headquarters as a volunteer when the army passed through Philadelphia. Washington invited him to take part in this reconnoissance, and here, or about this time, Greene first made Lafayette's acquaintance, and began that warm friendship which continued unbroken throughout the remaining years of Greene's life, and after his death was extended by Lafayette to Greene's son and grandson. But little was learned on this reconnoissance, which was, in fact, a foolhardy proceeding, and might easily have resulted in the capture of the entire party, as Lee had been captured near Morristown in the previous year. But, fortunately, the British did not suspect what large game was in their neighborhood, and the little party returned safely to Wilmington the following day.

Two days later Greene was directed to examine the ground still further, and select a position on which the army could be advantageously posted; for Washington had decided to accept battle. Greene selected the ground near Iron Hill, his idea being that it would be best to fight as close as possible to the landing place, so as to give Howe no room for developing his army; but before Greene's report reached Washington a council of war had been called, at which it was decided to post the army behind Red Clay Creek, a small stream about eight miles in front of Wilmington and twelve miles in rear of Iron Hill. When Greene saw this position he was of opinion that it could not be held. However, he faithfully complied with his orders, posted his division behind this stream, and the rest of the army came into line with him on September 7th.

Howe moved forward slowly from his landing place, and it was the 8th of September before his advance began in earnest. He then deployed Knyphausen's division in front of the Red Clay Creek, but with his main body moved off to the west to turn Washington's right flank. Washington detected the movement at once, called a council of war during the night, saw that the Red Clay Creek position was untenable (as Greene had predicted), and at 2 A. M. put his troops in motion toward the rear and right, to take position behind the Brandywine at Chad's Ford, twelve miles west of Wilmington. They reached the Brandywine during the morning of the

10th, and were all posted before night. Greene, with his own division, composed of Muhlenberg's and Weedon's Virginia brigades, re-enforced by Wayne's brigade and Maxwell's light troops, commanded the center, in rear of Chad's Ford. Sullivan, with his own division and those of Stirling and Stephen, commanded the right wing, posted about two miles along the river above Greene. The Pennsylvania militia, under Armstrong, was to watch the fords on Greene's left.

On the 10th Howe moved toward the Brandywine and assembled his force at Kennett's Square, about seven miles south of Chad's Ford. On the 11th he divided his army into two detachments—one, of about five thousand men under Knyphausen, which moved toward Chad's Ford, and the other, of over ten thousand under Cornwallis, which marched off to the left. About 10 A.M. Knyphausen deployed in front of Chad's Ford and began a brisk skirmish with Maxwell's light troops which crossed the river to meet him, but he made no real attack. Meanwhile the larger force under Cornwallis made a wide turning movement, crossed the river several miles above Sullivan's right, and during the afternoon appeared in the rear of his right flank—having marched completely around Sullivan without being discovered. It was the same flanking manœuvre which had succeeded so well at Long Island a year before, and it only failed of complete success here in consequence of the prompt action taken by Washington, and the skill and determination with which Greene carried out his orders.

During the morning Washington had sent officers to reconnoiter on the south side of the Brandywine, and from one of them, about eleven o'clock, he received intelligence that a large body of Howe's army, estimated at more than five thousand men, had passed along a road parallel to the river and moving westward. Washington at once suspected Howe's intention to turn his right flank, and he sent orders to Sullivan to move across the river and attack the turning column while still on the march; and at the same time gave orders to Greene to cross at Chad's Ford and attack Knyphausen. Some of Greene's men were already across the river about noon, when word was received from Sullivan that the officers sent out by him to reconnoiter had reported no enemy on the south side of the river opposite his position. Supposing Washington's orders to be based on erroneous information, he waited for further instructions. Unfortunately, Sullivan's information was wrong and Washington's was right; nevertheless, in view of the uncertainty, Washington was not justified in sending Greene's division to attack what might be the entire British army; he therefore revoked the order to Greene, and his troops withdrew to their original position after a brisk skirmish. The next intelligence was a note from Sullivan, dated 2 P. M., saying that "the enemy are in rear of my right about two miles, coming down." Between four and five o'clock the sound of heavy firing was heard in the direction indicated in Sullivan's dispatch. Washington set off at a gallop to join Sullivan, telling Greene to leave Wayne to hold his own against Knyphausen as long as he could, and with his two brigades of Virginians to come to Sullivan's aid with the utmost possible speed. Greene lost no time, and marched his men toward the sound

THE BRANDYWINE AND GERMANTOWN. 83

of the firing, most of the way at double quick, and covering nearly four miles of road in forty-five minutes. When he arrived on the ground between Dilworth and Birmingham meeting-house Sullivan's division had just broken, and, in spite of the most gallant efforts of Sullivan, Stirling, and Lafayette to rally the men, they were in full retreat. Greene opened his ranks to let the fugitives pass through, and then retired slowly and in good order before Cornwallis, contesting every inch, and using his artillery to great advantage. After falling back in this manner about half a mile he came to a narrow pass in the road well secured on each side by woods. Here he made a determined stand, and held his own until twilight against a force fully three times more numerous than his own. During his defense some order was established in the broken fragments of Sullivan's regiments in his rear; and Wayne's brigade, which had been driven back in confusion from Chad's Ford by the superior force of Knyphausen, also made good its retreat behind Greene's division. Finally, as night came on, Greene withdrew in good order on the Chester road. Howe did not pursue him, but went into camp at Dilworth for the night. He reported his losses as ninety killed and four hundred and eighty-eight wounded. The American loss was estimated at three hundred killed and six hundred wounded; the dead were left on the field, and the greater part of the wounded were made prisoners.

In this action more men were engaged than in any other battle of the war, and although the losses were not quite as heavy as at Germantown, three weeks later, yet there were more killed and wounded than in any engagement which had taken place up to that time. Superiority in numbers, a still greater superiority in organization, discipline, and equipment, and, above all, the failure of Sullivan thoroughly to reconnoiter the ground in his front and obtain accurate information of the enemy's movements, gave the victory to the British. It was a disastrous defeat, and ultimately gave the enemy possession of Philadelphia. Nothing but the skill and steadfast courage of Greene and the gallant Virginia regiments under his command saved this defeat from being turned into a rout and the destruction of the entire army. In his report, Howe claimed that another hour of daylight would have completed the "total overthrow" of the American army. But Greene fully realized the necessity of holding his position until dark, and during the last hour of daylight Howe was unable to make any progress against him.

On the day after the battle Washington retreated to Germantown. Howe did not follow him, but remained for two days in the vicinity of the battlefield to bury his dead. After giving his men one day's rest, Washington boldly crossed the Schuylkill again, determined to attack Howe. The two armies came together on the 16th, near White Horse Tavern, about twenty-five miles southwest of Philadelphia. But here an accident occurred, to which in these days of fixed ammunition armies are no longer subject. A violent rain-storm arose, and the men were so drenched that their ammunition, of which they had just secured a full supply of forty rounds per man, was completely ruined. There was nothing to do but to move up the Schuylkill as far as Reading Furnace, where there were fresh supplies. Several days of feints and manœuvres followed, at the close of

THE BRANDYWINE AND GERMANTOWN. 85

which Howe, having threatened Washington's right flank and induced him to move up the Schuylkill, rapidly countermarched, crossed the Schuylkill at Parker's Ford, and marched down to Germantown. Washington's army was worn out, and so badly clothed and shod and so deficient in transportation, that it was impossible for him to race with Howe for the possession of Philadelphia. Howe therefore took possession on September 26th, the main body of his troops, however, remaining in camp at Germantown.

Washington sent immediately to Putnam and Gates for re-enforcements, and moved up to Skippack Creek, about twenty miles west of Philadelphia. Here he waited for a favorable opportunity to attack Howe, for, in spite of its reverses, the army was in high spirits and felt confident of success in another battle. The opportunity came on the 3d of October, when Washington learned through intercepted letters that Howe had detached a portion of his force across the Delaware River to attack the forts below Philadelphia. Washington called a council of war, which was unanimously in favor of making an attack without waiting for further re-enforcements.

Germantown was then a straggling village, extending for about two miles along the high road which follows the ridge just east of and parallel to the Wissahickon. Twenty-two battalions, numbering probably about nine thousand men, of Howe's army were posted there in a line at right angles to the main road ; their center was at the market house, in the middle of the village, their left rested on the Wissahickon near its mouth, and their right was on the old York road.

Washington, with eight thousand Continentals and three thousand militia, was in rear of the Metuchen Hills, sixteen miles from the Germantown market house. His plan of attack was as follows: Sullivan was to command the right wing, composed of his own and Wayne's divisions and Conway's brigade, and was to follow the main road and attack the British left. Greene was to command the left wing, composed of his own and Stephen's divisions and McDougall's brigade, and was to follow the Limekiln road, which, coming from the northeast, meets the main road at the market house; he was to attack the British right. Stirling with his division was to form the reserve, following the main road, in rear of Sullivan. The Pennsylvania militia under Armstrong were to move down between the Schuylkill and the Wissahickon, cross the latter near its mouth, and strike the British left flank and rear. The Maryland and Jersey militia, under Smallwood and Forman, were to follow the old York road on the extreme left and attack the British right and rear. The troops were to move at dusk on the 3d of October, march all night, and, moving along four different converging roads, covering a front of five miles, were to attack at daybreak. It was certainly a bold design to attack the best regular troops of Europe with untrained Continentals and militia, on so complicated a plan; yet it came within an ace of success.

The army began moving from Skippack Creek at 7 P.M., and passed the Metuchen Hills at nine. Washington was with Sullivan's wing. Greene had two miles farther to march than the rest of the army. Whether his wing was in advance so as to insure his arriving in time is not recorded, but

THE BRANDYWINE AND GERMANTOWN. 87

Pickering, who was then adjutant-general, states that Greene's guide lost the road in the night and caused a serious delay. Day broke with a dense fog, which hindered the march along a road with which the officers were not familiar. From these causes Greene did not come into action until Sullivan had been engaged for three quarters of an hour, and his plans were much deranged by Greene's non-arrival. The Pennsylvania militia moved down within sight of the mill at the mouth of the Wissahickon, had a skirmish in which they lost twenty men, and then retreated. The Maryland and Jersey militia do not appear to have come into action at all, and a few days later the Jersey militia went home. Stephen's division left the road just as it was coming into action, and fired into Wayne's division and then retreated.* In this way nearly half the army was eliminated; the battle was fought by the divisions of Sullivan, Greene, Stirling, and Wayne.

Sullivan's column, with Conway's brigade in the advance, came upon the British pickets at Mount Airy, about two miles in advance of the market house, soon after daybreak. The alarm was at once given, and the Fortieth British Regiment, under Colonel Musgrave, was sent forward to support the picket. A sharp skirmish resulted, the British gradually falling back. Nothing being heard of Greene on the left, Sullivan deployed Wayne's division on the left of the main road and his own on the right, and continued to drive back the British until they reached a stone house belonging to Chief-Justice

---

* Stephen was tried by court-martial a few days after the battle, found guilty of intoxication, and dismissed.

Chew. Musgrave threw his regiment into this house and opened fire from the windows. Sullivan and Wayne pushed on toward the market house, while Maxwell's brigade was brought up from the reserve to attack the Chew house, but was unable to capture it. Wayne was at first brought back to assist in this attack, but was then sent forward again to join Sullivan; and the remaining brigade of the reserve under Nash was also brought up on Sullivan's right. By this time Howe had brought forward his entire force, and a very hot fight took place in the village just north of the market. Washington, with his usual impetuosity when confronted with danger, was in the thick of this fight, in spite of the remonstrance of his officers. Just as it was growing warm, Greene came up the Limekiln road, with his own division on the left and Stephen's on the right. Stephen left the road and marched through the fog toward the firing on his right. This brought him into collision with Wayne, and both divisions were thrown into confusion and began to retreat. In spite of these checks, however, the battle was not lost. Sullivan and Nash continued to push the British along the main road, and Greene with his own division pushed their right along the Limekiln road until he reached the market house in the center of the village. It was a very spirited engagement, which lasted for about two hours after Greene came up, and two hours and forty minutes from the time Sullivan's advance guard opened fire on the British pickets at Mount Airy. It was afterward learned that the British feared the day was going against them and made all their preparations for a retreat to Chester. Just as victory seemed within its grasp a panic seized the American army, and it began a precipitate retreat. The exact cause of this panic has never been clearly ascertained or stated. Washington attributed it to the dense fog, which made it impossible to see more than thirty paces, and left the different divisions to fight independently without common command. Moreover, a part of the troops had exhausted their ammunition. Some one seems to have raised the cry that they were surrounded, and color was lent to this idea by the firing in the rear, which still continued around the Chew house. Whatever its cause, the panic could not be arrested even by the most gallant efforts of the commanding officers, and the troops retreated precipitately by the main road, Greene's division bringing up the rear. As the retreat began, Cornwallis, who had been summoned from Philadelphia, arrived on the field and was sent in pursuit. Greene's division, with Pulaski's cavalry, protected the rear, and kept up a running fight with Cornwallis for about five miles, when the latter gave up the pursuit. Not a gun was lost in the retreat. By night the troops were all back at their original positions on Skippack Creek. Their losses were one hundred and fifty-two killed and five hundred and twenty-one wounded, and four hundred prisoners, many of whom were among the wounded. Howe reported his own loss at five hundred and thirty-five killed and wounded, although, from some papers afterward found in Germantown, there is reason to believe it was nearer eight hundred.

Greene seems to have felt very keenly the loss of this battle, which came so near being a decisive victory; for it is probably in reference to this that he wrote to Washington, six weeks later: "In one instance I thought I felt the lower of your Excellency's countenance, when I am sure I had no reason to expect it." But Washington replied in most cordial terms, subscribing himself "With sincere regard and affection," and stating, "You seem to have imbibed a suspicion which I never entertained."

At this time there was considerable jealousy in the army at Greene's influence and intimacy with Washington, and this jealousy was shared not only by the members of the Conway cabal, but by some of Washington's most loyal supporters. Greene probably feared that the unavoidable delay in his arrival on the field would be seized by his enemies as a pretext to throw the responsibility for the defeat on his shoulders. No open criticism of this character, however, was made by his contemporaries. Some hints of censure were made, but, as Henry Lee described them, "they were too feeble to attract notice when leveled at a general whose uniform conduct had already placed him high in the confidence of his chief and of the army." It was reserved for Bancroft, ninety years later, with characteristic malice, to make the charge, but no other historian has supported him. In fact, the charge was without foundation. Greene had shown both skill and courage on this day, and was in no way responsible for the disaster. It was one of those accidents to which untrained troops are always liable, no matter how great their individual courage.

After the battle of Germantown Washington remained in camp facing Howe for over two months. He was very anxious to attack him again, but his men were short of ammunition and badly clothed, and their numbers were inferior to those of the British.

THE BRANDYWINE AND GERMANTOWN. 91

Washington therefore sent Hamilton to visit Gates at Albany and Putnam at Peekskill, and obtain re-enforcements. Howe turned his attention to reducing the forts on the banks of the Delaware River below Philadelphia. In the first effort he was not successful. Count Donop with twelve hundred Hessians, on the 22d of October, attacked Fort Mercer at Red Bank, commanded by Nathanael Greene's kinsman, Colonel Christopher Greene. He made a gallant defense, for which Congress presented him with a sword and a vote of thanks. Donop was killed, and his force defeated with a loss of one third of its strength. On the 15th of November a combined land and naval attack was made on Fort Mifflin, which resulted in its capture. A few days later Cornwallis was sent to Chester with about three thousand men, and, being joined by twenty-five hundred re-enforcements from New York, he crossed the Delaware and advanced against Fort Mercer from the south. The place was untenable in face of such a large force, and was evacuated on the night of the 20th of November. As soon as Washington heard of Cornwallis crossing the Delaware at Chester, he detached Greene with his own division (Muhlenberg's and Weedon's brigades), re-enforced by McDougall's brigade, with orders to cross the river at Burlington and move south to the relief of Fort Mercer, and, if possible, to engage Cornwallis. But the movement was ordered too late. On the very day that Greene started from camp, Fort Mercer was evacuated. Varnum, who had lately arrived from the north with his brigade to re-enforce Christopher Greene at Fort Mercer, fell back to Mount Holly. Greene crossed the river at Burlington and reached Mount Holly on the 23d. Here he was joined by Morgan's light infantry returning from Saratoga, and he was expecting daily the arrival of Glover's brigade. In all, his force numbered between three thousand and four thousand men. Greene's instructions from Washington intimated a wish that he should attack Cornwallis. He was therefore placed in the same position, on a smaller scale, as Washington himself. In each case public opinion demanded an attack and a victory, and expressed its condemnation of Fabian tactics. And in each case the judgment of the commanding general and his subordinates was against an attack, because it had no prospect of success, on account of inferiority in numbers, discipline, and position. It was under these circumstances that, on November 24th, Greene wrote to Washington the letter from which an extract has been given so far as it related to Germantown. In relation to the case in hand, it stated that his own judgment and that of his brigade commanders were against the propriety of an attack., " But if your Excellency wishes the attack to be made immediately, give me only your countenance, and, notwithstanding it is contrary to the opinion of the general officers here, I will take all the consequences upon myself. . . . I will run any risk or engage under any disadvantage, if I can only have your countenance if unfortunate." It is small wonder that toward a subordinate who united such loyal devotion with intelligence and energy Washington should have been accused of partiality. When Washington received this letter he had information that Cornwallis was about to recross the Delaware, and that Howe was meditating an attack. He therefore recalled Greene, and two days later he sent a second order telling him to hasten his march. He arrived in camp on the 30th, and while he had not engaged Cornwallis, yet his good judgment was fully approved. Marshall sums up this week's campaign by saying: "That judicious officer feared the reproach of avoiding an action less than the just censure of sacrificing the real interests of his country by engaging his enemy on disadvantageous terms."

Washington's surmise that Howe meditated an attack was correct. On December 4th he moved out to Chestnut Hill in face of Washington's army, and, after manœuvring in front of him for four days, "decamped very hastily and marched back to Philadelphia," where he went into winter quarters. It was necessary for Washington to do the same. Greene's opinion was in favor of quartering in the town of Wilmington, but Washington finally decided in favor of Valley Forge, on the Schuylkill, twenty-five miles from Philadelphia. Here the troops arrived on December 19th, and began cutting trees to build their huts for the winter.

CHAPTER VII.

APPOINTED QUARTERMASTER GENERAL — VALLEY FORGE, MONMOUTH, AND NEWPORT—1777-'78.

THE winter at Valley Forge was destined to be one of historic hardship, but its beginning was not more uncomfortable than the summer and autumn had been. The men were in good spirits and cheerfully set about building their huts. Washington prescribed the manner of construction, personally watched their progress, and offered a reward for the squad which should finish its hut in the quickest and most workmanlike manner, and another prize to whomsoever should invent some practical method of roofing, as boards were not to be had. There were but two or three houses in or near the camp ground, and these were taken by Washington, Lafayette, and Knox. The other officers, including Greene, were quartered in huts a little larger than those of the men, but built in the same manner. Early in the winter Mrs. Washington came to camp, and she was soon followed by Mrs. Greene, Mrs. Knox, Lady Stirling, and the wives of other officers. In addition to Lafayette, there were Fleury, Armand, Duplessis, and other well-bred and agreeable young Frenchmen; De Kalb had lately arrived, and Pulaski was in command of the light horse; in Washington's staff were Hamilton and Laurens; and Greene's particular

APPOINTED QUARTERMASTER GENERAL. 95

friends Varnum and Ward were both present with their commands. On the 23d of February Steuben arrived, bringing with him letters of recommendation from the highest military authorities in Europe; and with him came his light-hearted young secretary, Duponceau, who describes Mrs. Greene as " a handsome, elegant, and accomplished woman, whose dwelling was the resort of foreign officers, because she spoke the French language and was well versed in French literature." * It was a charming society, though they lived in huts, were surrounded with deep snow, and had so little to eat or wear that the subaltern officers gave bachelor dinners of tough beefsteak and potatoes, with hickory nuts for dessert, to which no one was eligible who owned a whole pair of breeches. The principal officers and the ladies who were in camp met two or three evenings in the week at their own quarters or those of Washington; cards were prohibited, and there was no place to dance, but every one who could sing was called upon for a song.

---

* This remark must be interpreted rather as an evidence of Mrs. Greene's pleasing manners than as a statement of positive fact. Only a short time before, Greene, in writing to his wife, telling her to make arrangements for coming to camp in company with Mrs. Knox, had cautioned her to be very particular about her spelling, in which she was sometimes careless. Mrs. Knox, being the wife of a bookseller and fond of books herself, was quite proficient in this respect, and Greene did not wish his wife to suffer by comparison. Mrs. Greene had been brought up on Block Island, and prior to the war had never traveled beyond the homes of her relatives in Rhode Island. She had a good mind and was fairly well educated for the times ; and she was undoubtedly a very agreeable woman. But her knowledge of the French language and French literature must certainly have been less than Duponceau so politely states.

In the midst of these mild diversions, however, Washington was most anxious about the state of his army. It was deficient in discipline and drill, it was ragged and barefooted, and it was on the verge of starvation, the supply of food being so precarious that sometimes the men had no meat for three or four days at a time. Unless the discipline of the army and its methods of obtaining supplies could be speedily improved, it was likely to dissolve during the winter. Washington addressed himself to these problems as soon as the huts were finished, and he called on each of the general officers to submit his views on the subject in writing. From these he drew up his own plan, which was just completed when a committee of Congress, consisting of Francis Dana, Charles Carroll, Joseph Reed, Gouverneur Morris, and Nathaniel Folsom, came to camp to consult with him. They approved his plan, and it was subsequently adopted by Congress. The arrival of Steuben soon after enabled Washington to solve the military part of the problem. Steuben studied the situation, and, with the aid of advice which he says he received from Greene, Laurens, and Hamilton, he formulated a plan of inspection and drill which received Washington's approval. Steuben was appointed inspector general to carry it out. Though he had been a lieutenant general in Europe, and had served under the great Frederick, the first soldier of the age, yet he soon made drilling fashionable by forming a model squad of one man from each regiment and drilling them himself, musket in hand, and swearing alternately in German and French as he trudged through the snow.

For the administrative part of the problem Washington turned to Greene. The quartermaster's department was in a state of chaos, and the quartermaster general (Mifflin), though he still held office, had not been seen or heard of—except as he intrigued with Gates and Conway against Washington —for months. Washington pressed Greene to take the office and introduce some order into the department. The Committee of Congress seconded this appeal. But the place was not at all to his taste. A year later he wrote to Washington : " There is a great difference between being raised to an office and descending to one, which is my case. There is also a great difference between serving where you have a fair prospect of honor and laurels and where you have no prospect of either, let you discharge your duties ever so well. Nobody ever heard of a quartermaster in history." And in a letter to Knox, asking his advice while the matter was still pending, he says : " His Excellency also presses it upon me exceedingly. I hate the place, but hardly know what to do; the general is afraid that the department will be so ill managed unless some [one] of his friends undertakes it that the operations of the next campaign will in a great measure be frustrated." His tastes were entirely in the line of strictly military service, and he shrank from entering upon a semi-civil employment where his means would be unequal to his task, and where he well knew the least mistake or failure would be seized upon by his enemies and those of Washington to undermine his reputation. But Washington told the committee that he "would stand quartermaster no longer," and finally Greene yielded to his solicitations, and those of Reed and Morris of the committee in whose friendship and judgment he had great confidence, so far as to agree that he would direct the department for a year, provided he had nothing to do with the accounts and received no other compensation than that of a major general. This plan the committee declared was inadmissible. He then agreed to take the office on the same terms as his deputies could be engaged for, but he stipulated two conditions which were agreed to : first, that he should retain his rank in the line, and second, that he should appoint his subordinates. He chose as assistant quartermasters general Colonel Cox, a prominent merchant in Philadelphia, and Mr. Pettit, Secretary of State in New Jersey. The committee wrote to Congress with much satisfaction of their success, saying that they had "had great difficulty in prevailing upon these gentlemen to undertake the business," and that "nothing but a thorough conviction of the absolute necessity of straining every nerve in the service could have brought the gentlemen into office upon any terms." Congress made the appointments on March 2d, and, following the custom of the time, fixed their compensation at a commission of one per cent upon the money issued to the department, to be divided among the three as they should agree. Greene proposed an equal division of the commission.

The details of the measures which Greene adopted in reorganizing the quartermaster's department have not been preserved. We only know the general results. What the army needed most of all was means of transportation, and for lack of these its movements had been hampered and its plans frustrated more than once. It also needed clothing and tents for the men and forage for the animals.

APPOINTED QUARTERMASTER GENERAL. 99

Greene therefore scoured the country for horses and teams, and visited the State Legislature at Lancaster to confer with it in regard to impressment in case other means failed. He dunned Congress incessantly for money to buy shoes and cloth and canvas; and he established a chain of magazines or depots of supplies stretching from the head of Elk through Delaware, Pennsylvania, and Jersey to the Hudson, and containing in all eight hundred and forty thousand bushels of grain. He was obliged to insist to Congress on his right to appoint his subordinate agents if he was to be held responsible for his department, and he protested successfully against the attempts of the new Board of War to interfere in the management of his business and issue instructions for the purchase of supplies without consulting him. The net result of his labors is best stated in an extract from a letter of Washington written about two years later: "When you were prevailed upon to take the office in March, 1778, it was in great disorder and confusion, and, by extraordinary exertions, you so arranged it as to enable the army to take the field the moment it was necessary, and to move with rapidity after the enemy when they left Philadelphia."

While Greene was organizing the quartermaster's department and Steuben was drilling the squads, the spring had passed. Howe had been relieved of his command and Sir Henry Clinton had succeeded him. The questions which Washington was debating with his officers were, What will Clinton do? and What action shall the army take? These questions were considered at several councils of war. Lee had recently been exchanged and come back into the army amid much rejoicing, his weak and treacherous character not yet being appreciated by Washington or any of his subordinate commanders. He was assigned to the command of a division consisting of Poor's, Varnum's, and Huntington's brigades. Washington's force consisted of about twelve thousand Continentals and three thousand militia, and Clinton had nineteen thousand five hundred men in Philadelphia.

At the first council of war (April 20th) Greene was in favor of leaving the main body of the army under Lee at Valley Forge, while Washington with a picked corps of four thousand men made an attack on New York. But this proposition was not supported by the other officers. At the second council (May 8th) the opinion was unanimous to remain on the defensive and wait events. At the third council (June 17th) the question was propounded whether in case the enemy marched toward New York, he should be attacked on the way. Lee was strongly opposed to any attack, and such was still his influence that all the other officers supported him except Greene, Lafayette, Wayne, and Cadwalader. These were in favor of a vigorous attack at the first favorable opportunity. Washington shared the same views. In fact, he had not been listlessly waiting; his army was in complete readiness to move on short notice, and he was simply watching his chance to fall on Clinton the moment he left Philadelphia. This happened on the day after the council, and on the same day he put Lee in motion with six thousand men for Coryell's Ferry, above Trenton; the next morning he followed in person with the rest of the army. The two armies were thus marching in parallel lines across Jersey. Washington moved more rapidly than Clinton, who was encumbered with a baggage train twelve miles long, and he reached Princeton in time to head off Clinton's march on Brunswick, where he had intended to embark his men. The latter was therefore compelled to deflect to the right and march for Sandy Hook. At Hopewell, near Princeton, another council was held on June 24th, at which the question to be considered was the advisability of making a general attack. Greene, Lafayette, and Wayne advocated this, while Lee again opposed it and carried the majority of the officers with him. After the council Greene and the other two submitted their views in writing, urging that a strong detachment be sent against Clinton's rear and that the main body of the army be put in position to support this detachment and bring on a general engagement. Washington had the same opinion, and he gave the necessary orders the following morning.

The result was the battle of Monmouth, fought on Sunday, June 28th. It was well planned, the army was in fine condition, in excellent spirits, and better drilled and disciplined than at any other period of the war. The advantage of position was on Washington's side, and there was every reason to expect a crushing defeat and the possible capture of the British army. But, owing to Charles Lee's combined treason and cowardice, the result was a drawn battle and the escape of the British during the following night. The only redeeming feature was that Lee's career here came to an end. He was court-martialed, suspended for a year, and at the end of that period dismissed by Congress.

In this march and in the battle Greene acted in the dual capacity of quartermaster general and commander of the right wing. As the former he laid out the route and order of each day's march and selected the camping grounds. Lee being in command of a large detachment, comprising two fifths of the entire force, Greene was assigned in his place to the command of the right wing of the main body under Washington, the left wing being commanded by Stirling. This body came on the field about noon, just after Lee had made his disgraceful retreat, and it was formed on high ground between the Freehold meeting-house and Wenrock brook. Clinton made two vigorous attacks against this position, first trying to turn Stirling's left and then to turn Greene's right; but in both he was repulsed. Some artillery which Greene had posted on his extreme right not only aided to defeat Clinton's attack in that direction, but enfiladed his entire line; and this, combined with an advance of Wayne's brigade, caused him to retire about half a mile to the east of Wenrock brook. Washington intended to renew the attack, but, owing to the extreme heat and the approach of darkness, this was postponed until morning, and then the British were gone.

The American loss was sixty-nine killed, one hundred and sixty-nine wounded, and one hundred and thirty-two missing, many of whom were merely overcome by the heat and turned up in a day or two. Clinton reported his losses as one hundred and twenty-four killed, one hundred and seventy wounded, and sixty-four missing; but there was a serious error in these figures, as two hundred and forty-nine were buried by the Americans alone.

APPOINTED QUARTERMASTER GENERAL. 103

Clinton's total losses from battle, heat, and desertion, during his march across Jersey, were about two thousand men. This was the last of the series of battles begun at Long Island nearly two years before; there was no further fighting in this part of the country, and none under Washington's immediate direction until the siege of Yorktown, three years later. Had Greene or Stirling or Wayne been in command of the advanced detachment in place of Lee, it is probable that these three years of straggling warfare might have been saved by the capture of Clinton's army. The proof of Lee's treason was not discovered until seventy years later, but it is now evident that it resulted in far greater injury to the American cause than that of Arnold.

From Monmouth to Sandy Hook is a distance of only twenty miles. Clinton had a day's start, and on arriving at his destination would be under the protection of the guns of his fleet. Washington saw that nothing could be accomplished by following him, and he therefore marched for the Hudson River, to prevent any possible attack on the passes in the Highlands. He arrived in his old manœuvring ground, between White Plains and Haverstraw Bay, on July 20th.

While Washington was moving from Monmouth to White Plains, Greene had been, at various points along the Hudson River, engaged in collecting transportation and stores, selecting sites for camps, and otherwise attending to the business of the quartermaster's department. While thus employed he was subjected to one of those outbursts of temper from which Washington, in spite of his marvelous self-control, was not free. Hamilton, who lived in daily contact with Washington, was always anticipating an outburst of this kind, and he wrote to his father-in-law, General Schuyler, that he was determined, if a breach occurred, never to consent to an accommodation. When, therefore, Washington reproved him, one day in the spring of 1781, with what he considered unnecessary severity for a slight delay in answering his summons, he promptly resigned from his staff, and no persuasion could induce him to reconsider his determination. Greene acted very differently; he had the most profound regard and affection for Washington, and, instead of resigning, he replied with great dignity and calmness, disclaiming any intentional fault and expressing very clearly his sense of the injustice done him. The letter was all the more remarkable because Greene was himself a man of quick temper, very prompt at various periods of his career to resent the slightest reflection cast upon him by Congress or any of its members, or by any one in the army except Washington. The nature of Washington's reproof, whether verbal or written, has not been preserved, but it doubtless referred to something connected with his duties as quartermaster general. Greene replied at length from White Plains, July 21st: "Your Excellency has made me very unhappy. I can submit very patiently to deserved censure; but it wounds my feelings exceedingly to meet with a rebuke for doing what I conceived to be a proper part of my duty, and in the order of things. . . . If I had neglected my duty in pursuit of pleasure, or if I had been wanting in respect to your Excellency, I would have put my hand upon my mouth and been silent upon the

APPOINTED QUARTERMASTER GENERAL.

occasion ; but as I am not conscious of being chargeable with either one or the other, I can not help thinking that I have been treated with a degree of severity that I am in no respect deserving. . . . Your Excellency well knows how I came into this department. It was by your special request, and you must be sensible that there is no other man would have brought me into the business but you. The distress the department was in, the disgrace that must accompany your operations without a change, and the difficulty of engaging a person capable of conducting the business, together with the hopes of meeting your approbation and having your full aid and assistance, reconciled me to the undertaking. . . . As I came into the quartermaster's department with reluctance, so I shall leave it with pleasure. Your influence brought me in, and the want of your approbation will induce me to go out."

There is no record of what Washington replied. Doubtless, either by word or letter, he removed the sense of injustice and reassured his loyal subordinate. Their relations continued on the same intimate and friendly footing as before.

While Washington had been marching from Monmouth to White Plains the French fleet had arrived. The treaty of alliance with France had been signed in Paris on February 6th, and on April 13th a fleet of twelve ships of the line and four frigates, containing four thousand troops, all under the command of Count d'Estaing, had sailed from Toulon. It arrived at the mouth of the Delaware on July 8th, and after landing the French minister it proceeded to Sandy Hook. Here Washington sent letters on board by his aids-de-camp Laurens and Hamilton.

It was at first proposed to sail into the harbor and give battle to Howe's fleet, while Washington made a land attack on New York. But the pilots declared that the ships could not be taken across the bar, and this project was abandoned. The fleet therefore sailed for Newport on July 22d.

In anticipation of this movement, Washington had already written on July 17th to Sullivan, who commanded in Rhode Island, to call upon the States of Massachusetts, Rhode Island, and Connecticut for five thousand militia. These States responded so fully and promptly that inside of three weeks about seven thousand militia were assembled in Rhode Island. As soon as Washington learned, by a note from Hamilton, that the fleet would go to Newport, he detached Glover's and Varnum's brigades, with two batteries under Jackson, and, placing them under command of Lafayette, directed him to march at once for Providence and place himself under Sullivan's orders.

Both public and private reasons strongly urged Greene at this time to go to Rhode Island. When the British first occupied Newport after the fall of Fort Washington in 1776 the eastern delegates asked Washington to send Greene to take command in Rhode Island; but Washington was then in a critical position on the Delaware and declined to part with him. Spencer was sent in his stead. Spencer resigned in the spring of 1778, and again it was proposed to send Greene to take this command; but Washington was then urging him to take the position of quartermaster general, and the other idea was abandoned. Now it was evident that the scene of active operations would be around Newport and not New

APPOINTED QUARTERMASTER GENERAL. 107

York; there would be fighting in his own State, and there would be much work for the quartermaster's department. Greene was anxious to go in person to take part in both. Moreover, in going he would necessarily pass his own home, where he had not been for over three years, except for one night on the march from Boston to Long Island. His wife was there with his two children, one of whom he had never seen, and a third child was soon expected. He therefore asked Washington to send him, and his request was promptly granted, as it was evident he would be very valuable in this movement on account of his local knowledge of men and ground. Lafayette had already started, but Washington wrote to him explaining the situation, and stating that the troops under Sullivan would be divided into two divisions—one to be commanded by Greene and the other by himself. The generous young Frenchman accepted the arrangement with perfect cordiality and good grace. Greene left White Plains on the morning of July 28th, and arrived at his home at Coventry on the evening of the 30th. He stopped to rest one day, then went on to Providence and immediately gave his whole time to organizing the expedition under Sullivan.

Newport, as has already been stated, was the fourth town in the colonies in size and importance. After the close of the campaign around New York and the retreat of Washington through the Jerseys in December, 1776, a fleet of seventy-six ships was sent from New York, with over eight thousand men under command of Clinton and Percy. They landed a few miles north of Newport and took possession of the place, which was guarded by only a few hundred militia. In the following spring Clinton and about half the force were recalled to New York to take part in the expedition to the Delaware, and Percy went home on leave. The command devolved on General Prescott, an unenterprising and brutal commander who undertook no military movements but did all the damage in his power to unarmed inhabitants. He was captured in his bed in the summer of 1777, and the following spring was exchanged for Charles Lee. A short time after his release he was superseded by Sir Robert Pigott. This officer was now in command with about six thousand men, half of whom had only arrived on July 15th, having been sent by Clinton from New York on his arrival there after the battle of Monmouth. The troops occupied two lines of works stretching across the island just north of Newport; a detachment of Hessians was stationed opposite to them on Conanicut Island. D'Estaing arrived at the mouth of Narragansett Bay on July 29th, and Sullivan held a conference with him on board his ship the next day. Could a prompt attack have been made by the combined American and French troops, supported by a vigorous bombardment by the French fleet, it is quite possible that Pigott's force might have been captured. But it was only ten days since Sullivan had received Washington's instructions to call out the militia, and only a portion of them had arrived. Lafayette's troops, having two hundred miles to march from White Plains, did not reach Providence until August 3d, although Lafayette in person arrived on July 29th and visited the fleet the following day. Sullivan therefore fixed August 10th as the earliest day when he could be ready; and in the mean time suggested that D'Estaing should attack the British ships. D'Estaing moved up the east and west passages for this purpose on August 5th, and all the British ships, seven in number, were immediately set on fire or sunk. Their crews were sent to man the land batteries at Brenton's Point, Goat Island, and North Battery (opposite Rose Island); the Hessians had already been withdrawn from Conanicut on the first appearance of the fleet, and a detachment at Butt's Hill, on the northern part of Rhode Island, opposite Bristol Ferry, was brought back to Newport on the evening of August 8th.

It had been agreed between D'Estaing and Sullivan that on August 10th the American troops were to cross over by Howland's Ferry, from Tiverton on the mainland, to the northern part of Rhode Island near Butt's Hill; the French troops were to land on the west side, opposite Dyer's Island. In this way it was hoped to capture the British detachment on Butt's Hill, and then the united forces, numbering about fourteen thousand men, were to move south and attack the lines at Newport. In accordance with this plan, Sullivan united all his force at Tiverton on the 7th, and on the 8th D'Estaing sailed up the main channel, exchanging fire with the batteries near Newport, and anchored off the northern end of Conanicut, intending on the following day to land his troops, which had been on shipboard for nearly four months, and to cross to Rhode Island the day after, as agreed upon.

But Sullivan noticed on the morning of the 9th that the British position on Butt's Hill had been evacuated. Fearing that it might be reoccupied, he crossed from Tiverton at once, instead of waiting till the 10th, as agreed upon. This somewhat disconcerted the French admiral; but he visited Sullivan in his camp, and, on hearing his explanation, approved his action. As he was returning to his ship on the afternoon of the 9th the fog lifted, and, to his utter astonishment, disclosed a British fleet sailing toward the harbor of Newport, ten miles to the south of him.

In fact, Pigott had not been idle, but had sent word to Clinton at New York the day (July 29th) that the French fleet arrived off Newport. By a curious chance, a portion of Byron's fleet, which had sailed from Plymouth on June 5th in pursuit of D'Estaing, arrived at New York a few days after D'Estaing had left. Joining these to his own squadron, Lord Howe sailed for Newport and arrived there on the morning of August 9th. Washington wrote D'Estaing on the 8th, informing him of this, but the letter had not arrived when D'Estaing saw the fleet. While the latter was ready to conform his movements to those of the Americans as far as possible, yet the idea of merely assisting in a land attack while there was a chance of fighting a British fleet was not to be thought of.* On the morning of the 10th there

---

* Captain Mahan, in his Influence of Sea Power on History, says: "With the prevailing summer southwest breezes blowing straight into the bay, he [D'Estaing] was exposed to any attempts his adversary might make"; and he gives no other reason for D'Estaing's sailing out the next morning, when the wind unexpectedly blew from the north. While there is no question of the soundness of Captain Mahan's reasoning, yet it does not appear that D'Estaing was moved by such considerations; for in a long letter to Congress, dated August 26th, he gives his reasons for sailing out of Narragansett Bay, and he makes no mention of the

was a strong breeze from the north, and D'Estaing, after sending word to Sullivan of his intended departure, set all sail and bore down toward the British. As he had the windward there was nothing for Howe to do but to weigh anchor and sail out to sea until a change in the wind should give him a chance to fight on more even terms. The two fleets manœuvred to get to windward of each other for two days, and then they met a hurricane the memory of which survived for two generations. Both fleets were scattered and seriously disabled. Howe returned to New York, and D'Estaing only reached Newport, in a badly crippled condition, on the 20th.

Sullivan was thus left in the lurch. D'Estaing had promised to put the French troops under Lafayette's command, but, instead of leaving them to aid Sullivan when he went out to fight the British fleet, he took them with him in his ships—where they could only be in the way and do no good to any one. Nevertheless, Sullivan started to carry out alone the original plan as far as he could. On the 11th he pushed out light parties to the vicinity of the British lines and followed with his main body—Greene commanding the right wing, Lafayette the left, and John Hancock, formerly President of Con-

---

prevailing breezes—which possibly were not known to him, as he had only been there twelve days. He justifies his action on the ground that the British would have landed on Conanicut Island and erected batteries there, which, in connection with the batteries which they already possessed on Rhode Island, would have destroyed his fleet. In other words, he feared the influence of the land power on his ships.

All contemporary writers speak of his sacrificing co-operation in the land attack on Newport to the desire of fighting the British fleet.

gress and now major general in command of the Massachusetts militia, the second line. But the same hurricane which dispersed the fleets passed over Rhode Island on the night of the 12th, blew away the tents, killed several of the animals, injured some of the men, soaked their clothing, and ruined a large part of their ammunition. It left the army in a sad plight, and it took two or three days to put it in order again.

As soon as D'Estaing's fleet reappeared, Greene and Lafayette were sent to consult with him and arrange plans for the further conduct of the expedition. To their surprise, D'Estaing announced his intention of sailing for Boston to repair damages. They urged him to land his troops, make a vigorous assault on the Newport lines, and then refit his fleet in Newport, where the facilities were almost, if not quite, as good as in Boston. They urged that, with their large superiority of force and the discouragement of the garrison on having received no further aid from New York, success was certain. They spent the night with him trying to convince him of the soundness of these views, but without success. They then returned to Sullivan, and a solemn protest was drawn up and signed by every general in camp except Lafayette. But all to no purpose. D'Estaing sailed away on the 22d, taking with him his four thousand soldiers—which certainly were not needed to repair his ships in Boston.

This departure wrecked the expedition and set everybody by the ears. Sullivan wrote to Washington, telling him of his troubles and truly saying: "To combat all these misfortunes and to surmount all these difficulties requires a degree of temper and persevering fortitude which I can never boast of, and which few possess in so ample a manner as your Excellency." On the day after D'Estaing sailed away Sullivan issued a general order in which he first laments the departure of the French fleet and then contradicts himself by the remark that "he can by no means suppose the army or any part of it endangered by the movement." He goes on to say that "he yet hopes the event will prove America able to procure with her own arms that which her allies refused to assist her in obtaining." This insult was more than Lafayette could stand, and he called upon Sullivan to make a public retraction, which Sullivan attempted to do in an order of the 26th, but his language was so awkward that it left the matter almost in worse shape than before. Hancock started at once for Boston, where there was talk of not allowing the fleet to enter; the militia, which had been called out for only three weeks, were so angry at the departure of the fleet that they concluded they would go home, and over five thousand of them left in five days. The only man who seems to have kept his head was Greene. Washington wrote to him: "I depend much upon your temper and influence to conciliate that animosity which I plainly perceive, by a letter from the marquis, subsists between the American officers and the French in our service." This reliance was not misplaced. Greene had felt it his duty to sign the formal protest of the 22d, but after that his whole efforts were given to keeping the peace. He saw clearly that giving vent to feelings of disappointment and resentment would have a fatal effect upon the French alliance, now being put to its first test. He therefore did everything in his power to suppress any expression of feeling against the French. He also used every effort to conciliate the French officers, and Lafayette in a letter to Washington took occasion to express his appreciation of Greene's efforts as a peacemaker.

D'Estaing reached Boston on the 27th, and Lafayette, who had been urged by Sullivan and Greene to go there and if possible persuade the admiral to send his troops to Newport, arrived on the following day. In company with Heath and Hancock they called on the council, and a better feeling was established. D'Estaing promised to send his troops to Sullivan, and Lafayette rode back with all speed to carry the news, but on his arrival he found the army just retreating from Rhode Island.

Its position, in fact, had become very precarious. By the desertion of the militia its strength was reduced to between four thousand and five thousand men. With these it was attempting to besiege a force of greater strength than its own within the lines just north of Newport. Sullivan, in his anger, was ready to order an assault, but wiser counsels prevailed. During the night of the 28th the army retreated in good order to the position originally fortified by the British on Butt's Hill, at the northern end of the island. Pigott followed at daybreak in two columns, the Hessians taking the west road and the British the east road. They came up with the American pickets at seven o'clock, and a council was held at which Greene advised making a sharp attack and defeating the columns in detail before they united. But he was overruled, and it was decided to remain strictly on the defensive. The two

APPOINTED QUARTERMASTER GENERAL. 115

columns were thus allowed to unite. A determined engagement began about nine o'clock and lasted for seven hours. Greene commanded the right, and had with him the regiments in Varnum's brigade which had originally marched with him to Boston, Glover's brigade of Marblehead fishermen, a brigade of militia under Cornell, and a regiment of negroes recently organized in Rhode Island, of which his kinsman Christopher Greene, the hero of Red Bank, was colonel, and his old friend Samuel Ward was major. The Americans were gradually pushed back into the works on Butt's Hill, but the British, although they brought two ships to use their guns against Greene's right flank, were unable to make any further progress. After several hours of severe fighting they retired during the afternoon to their own lines on Quaker Hill. On the following day the British did not renew the attack, and during the night of the 30th the army was withdrawn over Howland's Ferry to Tiverton on the mainland; the boats being rowed by a militia regiment of boatmen from Providence, and by that same brigade of Glover's which had ferried the army across the East River after the battle of Long Island, and again across the Delaware at Trenton. The retreat was made just in time, for Lord Howe had sailed out of New York on the 27th with a large fleet, bearing Clinton and five thousand re-enforcements. Washington had notified Sullivan of this in a letter dated the 28th, which Sullivan received on the morning of the 30th. As the army climbed up the heights of Tiverton on the morning of the 31st the topsails of this fleet could be seen in the distance sailing into Newport harbor.

The American loss in the battle of August 29th

was thirty killed, one hundred and thirty-two wounded, and forty-four missing. That of the British is stated by S. G. Arnold in his history of Rhode Island to have been ten hundred and twenty-three, including prisoners. The Americans brought off all their wounded and saved all their artillery and stores. The balance of the militia now went home, and Sullivan's force, which had been ten thousand one hundred and twenty-four on the 4th of August, was reduced to about twelve hundred Continentals. He left a detachment under Lafayette at Bristol, which was soon withdrawn to Warren, and with the balance he retired to Providence. Greene went to Boston on business relating to the quartermaster's department. The British retained possession of Rhode Island until October, 1779, when Clinton voluntarily evacuated it, taking all the troops to New York for use in the South.

The Rhode Island expedition was thus a complete failure. Nothing was ever undertaken with fairer chances of complete success, and if it had succeeded it would have been of the greatest possible importance. Washington, in writing of it to his brother a few weeks later, said: "If the garrison of that place, consisting of nearly six thousand men, had been captured, as there was, in appearance at least, a hundred to one in favor of it, it would have given the finishing blow to British pretensions of sovereignty over this country; and would, I am persuaded, have hastened the departure of the troops in New York as fast as their canvas wings could carry them away." D'Estaing's orders enjoined him to be careful of his ships, and, in case of disaster, to go to Boston for repairs; but nothing

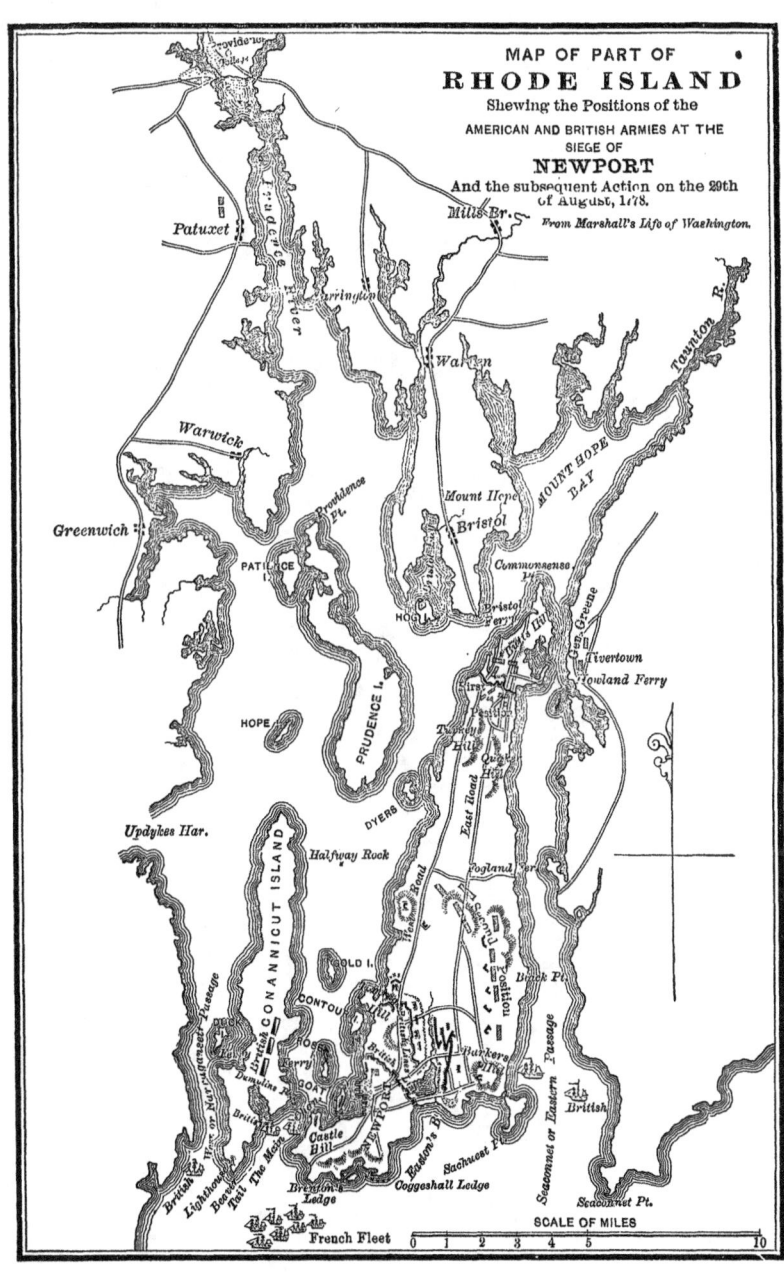

can justify his failure to put his land forces on shore at the earliest moment after his arrival. Had he done so, success would appear to have been certain. If Washington could have gone to Rhode Island, in all probability D'Estaing would have followed his advice, for Washington possessed an ascendency over the French as well as over his own countrymen which was not shared or even approached by any one else in the army. Washington, however, was not justified in leaving his central position at New York in face of the principal force of the enemy for any separate detachment, no matter how important. In view of Greene's subsequent success in an independent command in the South, and of the tact which he exercised in his intercourse with the French, it is probable that if he, in place of Sullivan, had been in command, the result would have been different. At the time, however, that Sullivan was sent to Rhode Island (March, 1778) the French fleet had not sailed from France, and the movement against Newport was not thought of. When it was undertaken, Sullivan was already in command, and there were no reasons sufficient to justify his removal. Nevertheless, his bad temper and lack of tact in dealing with the French were largely responsible for the failure.

CHAPTER VIII.

QUARTERMASTER GENERAL—SPRINGFIELD—
1778-1780.

THE two years following the expedition against Newport were years of inaction in the North. During the preceding year the Americans had been everywhere on the offensive, and while they had not gained the full measure of success which they had reason to expect, yet this was due to causes on their own side which could not have been anticipated, and not to any skill, energy, or courage on the part of the British. At Germantown the fog saved Howe, at Monmouth Charles Lee's treason saved Clinton, and at Newport dissensions between the allies saved Pigott. At the end of it all, the British found themselves just where they were in 1776—i. e., in possession of New York and Newport. All the other territory which they had gained had been lost again, and the prospect of bringing the Americans back to allegiance to the King and subjection to Parliament was as remote as ever. But the year of offensive operations had been very exhausting to the Americans. Congress was falling into contempt, its most distinguished members having returned to positions in the State governments, or gone abroad as diplomatic representatives. The finances were in a deplorable condition. Congress had no power (or, if it had, failed to exercise it) to levy taxation, and it attempted to meet the expenses of the war by issuing Continental bills. These had now reached the aggregate of over $120,000,000, and were more than doubled during the next year, with no definite prospect of redemption. The value of these bills decreased as their numbers increased. At this time they were worth about twenty cents on the dollar, and this value continued to grow less until they ceased to circulate at all, and the measure of complete worthlessness of anything was expressed in the phrase "Not worth a Continental." Congress still persisted in its opposition to a permanent army, and, while the act of 1776, calling for battalions to be enlisted for three years or the war, still remained on the statute books, yet it was not enforced; the States were afraid to undertake drafting with any determination, and laws were passed authorizing enlistments for one year or shorter periods accompanied by extravagant bounties, which of course nullified any efforts to get long-service men under the law of 1776.

Under these circumstances Washington was forced to remain on the defensive. He posted his army in the vicinity of New York, ready to move toward Philadelphia if Clinton repeated Howe's plan of 1777, or toward New England in case the force at Newport should take the offensive in the direction of Boston or elsewhere; and at all times covering the line of the Hudson and the posts in the Highlands, on the security of which depended his line of communications between the Eastern and Middle States, as well as the supply of food for his army, most of which came from west of the Hudson River.

On the other hand, the British, having campaigned

for two years in and around New York and from Philadelphia to Newport, and being at the end substantially where they were at the beginning, concluded to change the war to a new theatre. They therefore sent about thirty-five hundred men to Savannah, and thus began the Southern campaign, which was finally terminated at Yorktown and Eutaw Springs three years later. During all this period the British remained in New York without attempting any offensive operations beyond mere raids and forays.

As for the French, D'Estaing sailed away for the West Indies during the autumn of 1778 with his fleet and his soldiers. Lafayette went home during the winter to see if he could secure more tangible assistance in the way of money, supplies, and a force which would serve under Washington's orders. In this he was successful to an extent scarcely hoped for, but it was eighteen months before he was able to return with these substantial aids.

Everything being thus brought to a standstill, Washington was able in the following spring to detach five thousand men, under Sullivan, to inflict a well-deserved punishment upon the Indians and their Tory allies in central New York and northern Pennsylvania; and in the summer Wayne showed, in the brilliant capture of Stony Point with the bayonet alone, what his own daring and Steuben's discipline could accomplish. With these exceptions, the story of the two years—from September, 1778, to September, 1780—at the North is a story of military inaction.

The only busy man in the army (always excepting Washington, upon whose shoulders the whole burden of the contest now rested) was Greene. He was all the time engaged in the vexatious and impossible task of trying to keep the army supplied and equipped without cash. We left him at Tiverton just after the battle of Butt's Hill in Rhode Island. His home at Coventry was fifteen miles distant across Narragansett Bay. The sound of the battle was distinctly heard at his house, and its smoke could be seen. Two days later Greene rejoined his wife there, and on September 23d his third child was born. It was a daughter, and she was named Cornelia Lott, after the wife of a gentleman residing near Morristown, who had shown the warmest hospitality to Greene and his wife during the spring of 1777.

The business of the quartermaster's department kept him in New England for the next month, about half the time being passed in Boston and the other half at his home, whence he could ride into Providence every morning for consultation with Sullivan. Almost immediately after his arrival at home, John Brown—a leading merchant in Providence, and a member of the distinguished family to whose bequests Brown University owes its continued existence, who was then rapidly amassing a large fortune, and who had been a visitor to Sullivan's army—gave vent to very severe criticisms on the Rhode Island expedition, claiming that it had been badly planned and worse executed, and that Sullivan was incompetent. Sullivan and Greene had been division commanders together, and engaged in every campaign and battle from Boston in 1775 to Newport in 1778. Greene had the warmest affection for Sullivan, and an opinion of his abilities which was possibly higher than was justified. At all events, the idea of Sullivan, his brother officer, being abused by a merchant whose trade was being injured in consequence of the failure of the expedition, and this, too, at Greene's own home, seemed like an abuse of hospitality in addition to being grossly unjust. Greene thereupon took up the cudgels vigorously in Sullivan's defense, and wrote Brown a long letter—almost a pamphlet, in fact—reviewing the whole expedition, defending Sullivan and resenting the criticisms. Brown had attempted to censure Sullivan by quoting Greene's opinion and advice, but Greene repudiated any such argument. He insisted that "the expedition had been prudently and well conducted," and that there was "not a general officer, from the commander in chief to the youngest in the field, that would have gone to greater lengths to have given success to the expedition than General Sullivan." Finally he tells Mr. Brown, "I can not help feeling mortified that those that have been at home, making their fortune, and living in the lap of luxury and enjoying all the pleasures of domestic life, should be the first to sport with the feelings of officers who have stood as a barrier between them and ruin."

During his stay in New England Greene did everything in his power to restore the good feeling between the allies. At a meeting of the Assembly at Providence, at which he happened to be present, he contrived to prevent the reading of letters from Sullivan in which the latter gave full expression to his feelings toward D'Estaing, the publication of which could have done no good and might have done much harm. And a few days later, at Boston, he wrote the admiral a letter which D'Estaing describes as "of a nature to console me for the little irregularities which you perceived in General Sullivan's letter." D'Estaing adds: "It is from you and what you are, that it is doubtless suitable and flattering to judge of the respectable and amiable qualities of the American general officers."

On the 6th of October Greene returned to general headquarters, then at Fishkill on the Hudson. Sullivan had asked to have him stationed in Rhode Island for the winter, but Greene wrote to Washington that, however pleasant it might be to be near his family and among his friends, it would be "very unfriendly to the business of his department," and Washington therefore directed him to return. The headquarters were transferred for a time from Fishkill to Fredericksburg, on the Connecticut border, east of West Point; then to Middlebrook on the Raritan River, ten miles west of New Brunswick. Here they remained till the following summer, the men going into huts as at Valley Forge, but profiting by the experience of the previous winter to make them more comfortable. There was also a greater number of farmhouses available for the officers, and Greene as well as the other generals had each a house to himself. The ladies again came to camp; Mrs. Washington, Mrs. Greene, Mrs. Knox, Lady Stirling and her daughter Lady Kitty, and others. There were the same amusements as at Valley Forge with which to pass the long winter evenings, but here there were rooms large enough to dance in, and of one of these occasions, in March, Greene writes: "We had a little dance at my quarters a few evenings past. His Excellency and Mrs. Greene danced upward of three hours without once sitting down. Upon the whole, we had a pretty little frisk."

But the "little frisks" were mere oases in the desert of his troubles in the quartermaster's department, which increased steadily during the next eighteen months, until Greene finally threw up the office in disgust. The chief difficulty was the lack of hard money to pay for the necessary stores. Congress had little or no hard money, and when its paper promises were worth so little that it took four hundred dollars of them to buy a hat and sixteen hundred dollars to buy a suit of clothes, there were not enough printing presses in the country to supply what was needed to clothe the army and feed the animals. Impressment was occasionally resorted to, receipts being given for the property taken, but there was great objection to this method, and it was ineffectual. People concealed their property, and, in the general apathy in regard to the war which had now supervened, all the farmers and merchants assisted each other to evade the quartermaster's agents and defeat their intentions. The system of short enlistments was, moreover, most wasteful. The troops took but little care of public property, and at the close of their enlistments carried away large amounts of it; so that it required from two to three times the quantity of stores that would have sufficed for a permanent force—and still the men were never well supplied. Finally Congress and the Board of War attempted to interfere in the details of the management of the department in such a way as to destroy all system and discipline. This was not done from any malicious purpose, but simply from that lack of experience in executive management and organization which characterized the government of all the colonies at this time, and which continued until they were on the verge of anarchy, when the Federal Constitution was adopted in 1789. In dealing with this interference it must be said that Greene was not without fault. He had the most unlimited respect and admiration for Washington, and warm affection for his comrades in the army. But he did not entertain such feeling for the members of Congress, except for a few like Reed, of Pennsylvania, G. Morris, of New York, and Marchant, of Rhode Island. For the majority of the delegates he felt an indifference bordering on contempt, which was neither justified nor judicious; and this feeling was intensified when he saw the extravagant style of living in Philadelphia, the pursuit of pleasure to the postponement of business, and compared this with the sufferings of the officers and men in the huts at Valley Forge and Middlebrook. His temper was quick, and his affections strong. To a friend he was a stanch friend, and to an enemy a vigorous hater. Washington had these same good qualities, but to them he joined a discerning judgment, a patience, and a tact in dealing with men, which it is not too much to say has not been possessed by any other public man in our history, with the possible exception of Lincoln. Greene possessed these characteristics in a far smaller degree, and such measure of them as he did possess was often overbalanced by his feelings of indignation and resentment. Hence his tone in correspondence and intercourse with the committees of Congress was frequently harsh and unfriendly, and it resulted in bad feeling rather than good. Doubtless the provocation was great, but Washington had equal provocation, and it was his manner of meeting it which established his incomparable fame.

The bad feeling thus engendered was eagerly

seized by Greene's enemies and those of Washington to create all the trouble and embarrassment possible. The Conway cabal had failed, but some of its members were still in position to do mischief. Lee and Conway had, it is true, been dismissed, but Gates was in command at Boston, whence, as Washington was compelled to say to the President of Congress in April, 1779, he was practicing "little underhand intrigues" and "continually giving me fresh proofs of malevolence and opposition"; and Mifflin was in Philadelphia before a committee of inquiry into his administration of the quartermaster's department, and ready to join any intrigue which would injure his successor who had so enormously improved its efficiency. They and their adherents in Congress lost no opportunity of criticising such defects as still existed in the department and laying the blame on its chief, instead of on Congress which expected the war to be prosecuted without providing its sinews. They also accused the subordinates of peculation—a charge which, unfortunately, in some instances was probably true; and they hinted that Greene himself was making a fortune, and that he was filling the lucrative posts with his relatives and special friends. No direct charge was ever made against Greene's integrity, and his enemies well knew that there was not the slightest ground for any such accusation. But this did not prevent them from spreading innuendoes. As for his relatives, the matter was quickly disposed of. The only ones he had appointed to places in his department were his elder brother, Jacob Greene, who had been selected as chairman of the Committee of Safety of the Rhode Island Assembly in 1775, and was perhaps better qualified than any other man in that State to transact the quartermaster's business; and his cousin, Griffin Greene, who was connected with the Coventry forges and was a well-trained man of business. Both were men of the highest integrity, and well known as such to the public as well as to Greene, and their appointment to two out of the hundred places at his disposal was to be commended rather than criticised. In meeting the gossip that he was making a fortune, Greene was less fortunate, being embarrassed by the fact that he was being paid a commission. As already stated, he had first consented to direct the operations of the department without being connected with the accounts, and without other compensation than the pay of his grade in the army. The committee of Congress declined to accept this, and thereupon he agreed to serve on the same terms as his principal subordinates could be secured for. The committee fixed this at one per cent on the money disbursed by the department, and Greene divided this equally with Colonels Pettit and Cox. In these days this seems a bad arrangement, and such it undoubtedly was. But it was not so regarded at that time; it was the custom of the day, the arrangement was proposed by the committee and not by Greene, and it was considered by them, when made, a very economical method of compensation. Now it was used to cast discredit upon Greene; and in a letter written in April, 1779, to Mr. Duane, a delegate in Congress and President of the Treasury Board, he admits that "the emoluments expected from the office were flattering to his fortune, but not less humiliating to his military pride." The idea of its being flattering to his fortune, however, proved delusive, and a year later he wrote to a friend in Rhode Island that if certain private funds in his hands were not profitably invested he was poor indeed. "To be thought rich and at the same time to be poor, is the most disagreeable situation in the world." His one third of one per cent on the amount disbursed during the two years and six months that he held the office was probably about one hundred thousand dollars in Continental money. At the time he left the office this was worth one and two thirds cents on the dollar in the open market, and Congress was trying to redeem it at the rate of two and a half cents on the dollar, or forty for one. It is evident, therefore, that his compensation in actual value was small, and probably did not equal his expenses. It is certain that at the close of the war he was poorer than at the beginning. This was the case with all the general officers, but least of all with Washington. He had stipulated that he should receive no pay for his services, but have his expenses reimbursed; and on July 1, 1783, he submitted his accounts, kept with the most scrupulous care, of his expenditures during the preceding eight years, including depreciation, interest, and expenses of Mrs. Washington in coming to and returning from camp. The amount was $64,355.30 in specie, which would have been equivalent to more than one million dollars in Continental money at the average depreciation during the year 1779. Being reimbursed this amount, his only loss was for such expenditures as he had forgotten or neglected to enter in his accounts. This arrangement, while not so intended, proved more advantageous to Washington than any salary would have been. It is doubtful if any other general

QUARTERMASTER GENERAL—SPRINGFIELD. 129

received enough in pay and allowances to meet his actual expenses. Certainly Greene did not. In April, 1783, he wrote to Mr. John Collins, a delegate from Rhode Island in Congress, as follows: "Congress recommended to the several States to settle with their own officers. Will Rhode Island acknowledge me as one of hers? If she will, I should be glad to have a settlement, and if the State is not as poor as I am, I should be glad to get some advance. I have drawn no pay since '77, and you may well suppose my friends are tired of lending me money. The Southern States have voted me an interest, but it will be a long time before I can make it profitable either by sale or improvement."

The idea that Greene was making a fortune out of his commissions was therefore entirely false. Nevertheless, these rumors were industriously circulated by a clique in Congress, and they angered Greene very much. He felt that he was remaining in a very distasteful office solely from a sense of public duty and because Washington had asked it. Under these circumstances, to be accused of holding on to the office from mercenary motives seemed to him an evidence of the basest ingratitude. He could not keep his temper in dealing with men who so completely misjudged him.

His difficulties with Congress did not reach the acute period until the winter of 1779-'80. In the preceding April he had been in Philadelphia trying to get money to purchase stores and pay teamsters, so that Washington could make plans for a summer campaign. Congress seemed to him so indifferent and inattentive to his requests that he asked leave to resign; and he wrote at some length to Washington, explaining that it was impossible to carry on the business without financial resources; that there was a petty intrigue on foot to injure his reputation; that the office was in every way disagreeable to him, and that he desired to give it up and return to his place in the line. He stated that, as General Lincoln had just asked to be relieved from the Southern command on account of his wound, he would be glad to be ordered in his place. Washington replied, expressing sympathy for his troubles, but declining to give any advice; he added, that if Greene should resign from the quartermaster generalship and the appointment of a successor to Lincoln should be left to him, he should not hesitate in choosing Greene for the place. Congress, however, was not disposed to accept his resignation, and on the 7th of June, 1779, passed a resolution expressing "full confidence in the integrity and abilities of the quartermaster general." He therefore continued the business throughout the year, and did the best he could with the totally inadequate means at his disposal. When the year was over and the army went into winter quarters at Morristown, he determined to bring matters to a head, if possible. On December 12th he wrote a long letter to Congress: "It has been my wish for a long time to relinquish the office of quartermaster general. This is the close of the second campaign since I engaged in the duties of this office, and I feel a degree of happiness in having it in my power to say with confidence that every military operation, whether in the main army or in any detachment, has been promoted and supported, as far as it depends upon this department. The commander in chief has given me the most ample testimony of his approbation,* and the success in every other quarter sufficiently evinces the ample provision that has been made." But he goes on to say that he entered the department against his wishes; the office is "injurious to my health, harassing to my mind, and opposed to my military pursuits"; and "as interest was not the object which induced me first to accept the appointment, it would be my wish to resign, even if the emoluments could be made five times as large as they are, provided I could retire with the approbation of Congress and without injuring the public service." He then explains in detail the condition and needs of his department, and continues : "In this distressing situation, without money and without credit, necessity obliges me to give Congress information, and to ask their advice what are we to do. Here is an expensive army to support, and the difficulty hourly increasing; besides, the preparations necessary for another campaign is fast approaching, while we are without the means either to defray the current expenses or discharge our past contracts, which are now very great, owing to the poverty of the treasury for some months past. And so dissatisfied are the people at being kept out of their money, that they

---

* On September 3d Washington had written him as follows: "The services you have rendered the army have been important, and such as have gained my entire approbation, which I have not failed to express on more than one occasion to Congress in strong and explicit terms. The sense of the army on this head, I believe, concurs with mine. I think it is not more than justice to you to say that I am persuaded you have uniformly exerted yourself to second my measures, and our operations in general, in the most effectual manner which the public resources and the circumstances of the times would permit."

have begun to sue the public agents. . . . So strict are the laws of some States, and so attentive are the magistrates to guard the people's property, that the forage officers have been prosecuted and heavily fined for presuming to take forage on the march of the army (to save the public cattle from starving) by virtue of a press warrant granted by the commander in chief." He asks that Congress will take prompt steps to appoint his successor, and states that he will give every information and assistance in the matter that is within his power.

This letter was certainly courteous in tone, and related to matters of the highest importance. Congress made no reply, and, as far as could be learned, paid no attention to it. After a month had passed Greene wrote another letter, dated January 13, 1780, calling attention to his previous letter, and saying that, in view of "the alarming crisis to which things are drawing, and the necessity of applying a remedy before the evil becomes incurable," he "can not help pressing for an answer." He realizes that "there are many weighty matters before Congress," but he can not help thinking that the business of the quartermaster's department "claims their earliest attention." No reply was made to this, but on January 20th a resolution was passed appointing three commissioners to inquire into the condition of the staff, to introduce such changes as might be necessary, and generally to superintend its affairs. Schuyler, Pickering, and Mifflin were appointed on this commission. The first two were eminently qualified for any such duty, but Mifflin was still under investigation for his mismanagement and neglect of the business when he was himself quartermaster general, and he was known

QUARTERMASTER GENERAL—SPRINGFIELD. 133

to be personally hostile to Washington and Greene. His appointment was evidence that a faction in Congress had succeeded in using this commission to gratify private animosities instead of improving the public service. As Greene could get no reply from Congress, he wrote to his friend Reed, who was now Governor of Pennsylvania, for information, and Reed replied: "I will venture to tell you that you have nothing to expect from public gratitude or personal attention, and that you will do well to prepare yourself at all points for events. . . . Upon the whole, I still retain my opinion of the propriety of your being here as soon as possible, and in the meantime I can only inform you of two things with certainty: First, that the plan of the department will be altered as to commissions; second, that nothing but necessity will induce them to continue the present department, for, though it may have a great deal of the utile, it has little of the dulce on the palate of Congress. But you will be drilled on till the campaign opens, and, if they can not do better, they may keep you."

Greene hesitated to go to Philadelphia for fear that he would be accused of seeking to retain his place when in reality he desired to give it up. But Washington advised him to go, and he finally did so, arriving in Philadelphia on March 25th. He had a conference with a committee on the 27th, and learned that Mifflin and others had brought in a plan for the quartermaster's department, which Schuyler thought would "starve the army in ten days." Congress, having no money and having exhausted its credit, and being unable to devise any financial system, had adopted the idea of calling on the States to furnish supplies in kind. On this basis Mifflin had constructed a plan which added enormously to the duties of the commander in chief, which were already too heavy, and left the quartermaster general with almost nothing to do. On April 3d Greene wrote to Congress saying that on his arrival he had spoken to the committee of the injury he felt in having commissioners appointed to superintend his department, and had "requested to know whether there was the real want of confidence in my integrity or ability which those appointments but too strongly indicated, and urged this as a necessary step to a further explanation. I have been waiting a whole week for an answer, but as I find I am not likely to obtain one, and as I conceive my attendance is no longer necessary here, I propose to set out for camp the next day after to-morrow and there await the issue of the business."

The tone of this letter was not judicious, and its effect was heightened by the speech of a superserviceable friend in the debate which followed. A resolution was introduced on the 5th, expressing confidence in his ability and integrity, and requesting him to continue to act as quartermaster general, when this friend took occasion to say that Greene was " an officer in whom the commander in chief had the highest confidence; that he was the first of all the subordinate generals in point of military knowledge and ability; that in case of an accident happening to General Washington, he would be the properest person to command the army, *and that General Washington thought so too.*" All this was true enough, but it was put forward in an offensive manner, and it led another member to reply that he "had a very high opinion of General Greene's military abilities; that he believed the general had too; but that he believed no person on earth was authorized to say as much as the last words implied"; whereupon amendments were moved, the debate became very hot, and it was necessary to take an adjournment to allow the members to cool.

Greene returned to Morristown in a very uncomfortable frame of mind, and on April 25th wrote to Reed as follows: " If I force myself out of the department and any great misfortune happens, no matter from what cause, it will be chargeable to my account. If I stay in it, and things go wrong or any failure happens, I stand responsible. What to do or how to act I am at a loss. I think, upon the whole, your advice is prudent and on the safer side of the question; and therefore I determine to seek all opportunities to get out of the business. I feel myself so soured and hurt at the ungenerous as well as illiberal treatment of Congress and the different boards, that it will be impossible for me to do business with them with proper temper; and, besides, I have lost all confidence in the rectitude and justice of their intentions. The Board of Treasury have written me one of the most insulting letters I have ever received either from a public or private hand. I shall write them as tart an answer, and, as I expect it will bring on a quarrel, I shall have occasion to call on you and others to certify the manner of my engaging in this business, the circumstances it was under, and all other matters that may be necessary to give the public a proper idea of the part I have acted."

Just before Greene left Philadelphia [April 3d],

Washington had written to Congress pointing out
the utter impracticability of the system of getting
supplies in kind from the States, and urging the
adoption of some measures that would put the quartermaster's department in position to supply the
army so that a summer campaign could be undertaken. On receiving this, a committee, consisting of
Schuyler, Matthews, and Peabody, was appointed to
go to camp and consult with the commander in chief.
They arrived during the latter part of April, and remained at headquarters for several months. On the
2d of May they asked Greene to give his views concerning the system of State supplies, and other
matters pertaining to the quartermaster's department. Greene had never received any replies to the
various communications he had made to Congress
during the last four months, and he felt much ag-
grieved at its treatment of him. He replied to the
committee that he could not venture to give his
opinion on the matters in question until they had
made an inquiry into his past management of the
department. If they found it satisfactory in view of
the difficulties he had had to contend with, he would
cheerfully co-operate with them in any plans for the
future; but if they found it otherwise, it would be
improper for them to ask or him to give any opinion
on the matters in question. The committee made a
temperate reply, asking him to consider the public
welfare and waive his application, and give them the
benefit of his abilities and experience in their deliberations. But Greene felt that he had been badly
treated, and he was obstinate. He replied that he
must insist upon an examination of the general
policy of his department, so that the suspicions

which had been scattered broadcast might be removed. Until that was done he declined to act with the committee, and in any event he would refuse to serve under the orders of any superintending board, except the Board of War or a committee of Congress. The committee made no written reply. Doubtless Washington and Schuyler, for whom Greene had great regard, persuaded him in conversation that his position was untenable, for he soon after came into friendly relations with the committee, all of whom became warmly attached to him, and a few weeks later certified their full approval of his management of the department. He went to work with them in the heartiest manner, assisting them in their investigations, and honestly striving to work out some system for the improvement of the business.

Just as these pleasant relations were established, however, came another insulting letter from the Treasury Board about his accounts. He was ordered to send in his accounts before the end of the month, or be " published and prosecuted." Greene was doing everything in his power to get prompt returns, but his agents and subordinates were scattered from Massachusetts to Georgia, and it was manifestly impossible to get their returns in less than a month. The tone of the order was designedly offensive. Greene consulted Hamilton, who advised him to write a mild reply, but he rejected the advice and wrote them as sharply as possible. Another letter came from them in June, and then he laid the whole matter before Congress. His letter was dated June 19th, and with it he transmitted copies of all his correspondence with the Treasury Board. This board was attempting to hold him individually and personally responsible for any irregularities on the part of his subordinates in expending public money. He calls this a "strange, new, and unexpected doctrine," argues at length against the propriety or possibility of enforcing it, and flatly refuses to submit to it. "The duties of this office are very complex, extensive, and extremely disagreeable in the best state of things, from the great variety of tempers, characters, and applications attending it; but when these are multiplied by improper restriction, accompanied with orders from different boards, which in the nature of things can not be conformed to, the business becomes intolerable; nor do I choose to contend with such a complication of difficulties.

"I hold the office of quartermaster general not of choice, but with a view of obliging the public, and I can not think of exposing myself to so many unnecessary embarrassments and mortifications as beset me in my present standing.

"I beg Congress to give me their sense of the matter, without which I can not proceed further in the business."

Congress referred this letter to a committee composed of Ellsworth, Duane, and Madison. They considered it for a month, and then on July 24th reported a resolution, which was adopted, in which the doctrine of the Treasury Board in regard to responsibility is upheld as a general principle; but they say that as "abuses and frauds may possibly happen notwithstanding all the customary precautions, they will determine on the circumstances as they arise, and make such favorable allowances as justice may require." This was a decision directly against Greene in his controversy with the Treasury Board, and

QUARTERMASTER GENERAL—SPRINGFIELD. 139

would undoubtedly have caused his resignation. But several days before he received it he had already resigned in consequence of other action taken by Congress.

During the month of June Greene had a taste of purely military duty which offered a pleasant break in his long contest with Congress about the quartermaster's department. The sufferings of the troops for lack of food, clothing, and pay had caused a mutiny among some of the regiments, and when the British heard of this they sought to take advantage of it. Knyphausen was therefore ordered to cross from Staten Island to Elizabeth, about June 6th, and advance toward Morristown. The militia were called out, but there was no serious opposition to his progress until he reached the village of Springfield, about half way between Elizabeth and Morristown. Just back of this village is a broken country known as the Short Hills, and here Washington was posted with his army in compact formation, prepared to receive an attack. The stories about mutinies were evidently exaggerated, and Knyphausen retired to Elizabeth. Soon afterward Clinton sailed into New York Harbor, bringing with him about half of the force that he had used in the capture of Charleston. Washington anticipated that Clinton would make an attempt on the passes in the Highlands, which were thinly garrisoned, and therefore, on June 21st, he moved in the direction of the Hudson, leaving Greene in command at Springfield with Maxwell's and Stark's brigades, Lee's corps of light horse, and the militia. His directions to Greene were "to cover the country and the public stores." As soon as Clinton heard that Washington with the main body had moved toward the north, he instructed Knyphausen to make an attack on Greene's detachment at Springfield. Knyphausen did so on June 23d, with a force of about five thousand infantry, a considerable body of cavalry, and fifteen or twenty pieces of artillery.

This force moved in two columns on roads converging at Springfield, and when they arrived at this village a very considerable skirmish ensued in which Greene's loss was thirteen killed, forty-nine wounded, and nine missing. After about an hour's fighting, Knyphausen began to manœuvre with the evident intention of turning Greene's left flank; whereupon Greene moved backward about a mile and took a strong position in the Short Hills, covering the passes through which the roads led to Morristown. In this position he waited and hoped for an attack, but Knyphausen did not follow him. He contented himself with setting fire to the houses in Springfield, and then started in retreat to Elizabeth. Greene sent one of his brigades and the militia in pursuit, but the retreat was made so rapidly that it was impossible to overtake Knyphausen's force. He crossed over to Staten Island during the night, and his expedition thus came to an end. This was the last fighting on the soil of New Jersey during the war. About July 1st Greene joined Washington and the main body of the army, which was posted in New Jersey from Ramapo to Orange, waiting for developments on the part of Clinton and the arrival of the French fleet.

CHAPTER IX.

RESIGNS AS QUARTERMASTER GENERAL—WEST POINT—1780.

THIS pleasant little military episode at Springfield being over, Greene returned to his vexatious struggle about the quartermaster's business. He was waiting for a reply to his letter to Congress of June 19th, protesting against the attempt of the Treasury Board to hold him personally liable for any malfeasance on the part of his subordinates. Meantime he was in daily consultation with the committee, composed of Schuyler, Matthews, and Peabody, who had been sent to camp during the latter part of April to examine the quartermaster's department and had remained at headquarters ever since, moving from point to point as Washington moved. They had spent two months in studying the problem of supplies and gaining the information necessary to make an intelligent report on the subject of their investigations. Matthews, who had come to camp strongly prejudiced against Greene, had now conceived a great admiration for him, and the committee was about ready to adopt a plan for the quartermaster's department which had been proposed by Washington, Schuyler, and Greene, and as a part of which Greene had insisted that his compensation should be nothing but reimbursement of his actual expenses. Congress, however, after sending this committee to camp, did not in any way relax its own consideration of the subject, nor wait for reports from its committee. It was daily deliberating upon its own plan for the quartermaster's department, and it finally adopted this on July 15th. It was quite lengthy, and it had to be printed, so that it did not reach Washington in camp until July 26th. On the 10th of July, however, the French fleet arrived at Newport with the first division of the French army, amounting to more than five thousand men, under Rochambeau. Heath, who had succeeded Gates in the command of Providence, sent a messenger post-haste to Washington with the news, and he arrived at Washington's headquarters at Preakness, in Bergen County, New Jersey, on the 14th of July. Washington, with that promptness which characterized him in all emergencies of this kind, instantly made his plans for a prompt movement, in connection with the French forces, designed to capture New York. He sent Lafayette with letters to Rochambeau, and on the very day that Heath's messenger arrived he wrote to Greene, telling him to make arrangements for the supply of about forty thousand men, which it was expected would be used in an attack upon New York. He told Greene to apply to the States for the supplies in kind which they were required to furnish under the recent plan of Congress, and to make requisition on the Treasury Board for cash to purchase such supplies as the States were not bound to furnish, but which would still be necessary. He also says : " I have been in anxious expectation that some plan would be determined upon for your department; but as it has not hitherto taken place, and as it is impossible to delay

RESIGNS AS QUARTERMASTER GENERAL. 143

its operations a moment longer, I have to desire that you will yourself arrange it in some effectual manner to give dispatch and efficacy to your measures equal to the emergency. Your knowledge and experience in the business will be sufficient to direct your conduct without my going into more particular instructions." This order placed Greene in a very embarrassing position. He had himself written to Congress, stating substantially that, unless the pretensions of the Treasury Board were overruled, he should resign. He knew that Congress was deliberating upon a plan for the department, and he had reason to suspect that it would be impossible for him to act under it. There was a committee in camp which was also considering the subject. While all these matters were pending, Washington gave him a positive order to regulate the department himself in some manner, so that he could undertake an expedition against New York. He therefore thought it best to state his position clearly to Schuyler's committee, which he did in a long letter of the same date—July 14th—as Washington's order. At the same time he determined to do everything in his power to comply with Washington's order, and on the 15th he wrote to the governors of Rhode Island and Pennsylvania, making requisitions for the stores in kind. On the 16th the committee in camp replied, stating that they agreed with him in his views concerning his personal responsibility, and they took occasion to say that, after having examined his arrangement of the department, "we are convinced the measures you have taken and the principles on which these measures were founded were well calculated to promote the service, and they fully evince your attention to the public interest." They refrained, however, from expressing any opinion as to the conduct of his subordinates. For the next week, Washington, the committee, and Greene were all busy making plans for the attack on New York, but on July 26th Washington transmitted to Greene the copy which he had just received of the plan adopted in Congress on the 15th for the government of the quartermaster's department. It contained all the features which he had protested against as cumbersome and impracticable, and it moreover deprived him of the services of Colonel Pettit and Mr. Cox, the two deputies for whose appointment he had expressly stipulated on taking the office, two and a half years before. Greene decided instantly that he would not hold the office under this plan, and he sat down on the same day that it was communicated to him and wrote his resignation. Its language was peremptory, and was not altogether fitting. He felt so injured that he failed to keep his temper. He said: " I do not choose to attempt an experiment of so dangerous a nature where I see a physical impossibility of performing the duties that will be required of me. Wherefore I request that Congress will appoint another quartermaster general without loss of time, as I shall give no order in the business further than to acquaint the deputies with the new system, and direct them to close their accounts up to the first of August coming.

"It is unnecessary for me to go into the general objections I have to this plan. It is sufficient to say that my feelings are injured, and that the officers necessary to conduct the business are not allowed; nor is proper provision made for some of those that are. There is but one assistant quartermaster general, who is to reside near Congress, and one deputy for the main army allowed in the system. Whoever has the least knowledge of the business in this office, and the field duty which is to be done, must be fully convinced that it is impossible to perform it without much more assistance than is allowed in the present arrangement. . . . Systems without agents are useless things, and the probability of getting the one should be taken into consideration in framing the other. Administration seem to think it far less important to the public interest to have this department well filled and properly arranged than it really is, and as they will find it by future experience. . . . My rank is high in the line of the army, and the sacrifices I have made on this account, together with the fatigue and anxiety I have undergone, far overbalance all the emoluments I have received from the appointment. Nor would double the consideration induce me to tread the same path over again, unless I saw it necessary to preserve my country from entire ruin and a disgraceful servitude."

Greene sent a copy of this letter to the representatives of Congress in camp, and also to Washington. Washington made no written reply, but the committee consulted with him and wrote to Greene as follows: ". . . We are perfectly in sentiment with him 'that your declining to act at present will be productive of such a scene of confusion and distress that it will be impossible to remedy the evil or to reduce the business to a proper channel during the remainder of the campaign'; we have therefore most earnestly to entreat that you will continue to direct the department until the sense of Congress can be obtained on your letter of the 26th, and on ours of yesterday; but, as you positively decline acting under the plan established by Congress on the 15th inst., which has been officially handed to you by the commander in chief, and as the consequences which we have stated must inevitably follow, and probably be extended to eradicate every hope which the country entertains of an efficient operation against the enemy in conjunction with the force of our ally, we conceive it indispensably our duty, from these considerations, to require of you to continue the direction of the quartermaster general's department under the order of the commander in chief, as signified in his order to you of the 14th, and on the conditions stated in our letter of the 16th, until the further pleasure of Congress can be known; and we undertake to justify you for acting in consequence of this requisition, and will submit our conduct on this occasion to the judgment of Congress."

It was undoubtedly a most unfortunate time for such a change to take place. Clinton had started toward Newport with the view of attacking the French forces, and, as a counter move, Washington was just drawing up orders for a demonstration on his part against New York. The troops were to cross the Hudson River the following day and move down toward Kingsbridge. These considerations, and the support which the committee promised him in their letter, induced Greene to continue the business for ten days longer. Meantime his resignation was on its way toward Philadelphia, and it was followed by two letters—one from Washington and one from Schuyler's committee—in which it was stated that " unless effectual measures are immediately taken to induce General Greene and the other principal officers of that department to continue their services, there must of necessity be a total stagnation of military business. We not only must cease from the preparations for the campaign, but in all probability shall be obliged to disperse, if not disband, the army for want of subsistence."

Greene's letter of resignation reached Congress on Saturday, July 29th, and was referred to a committee to report on the following Monday. When Congress met on that day, the letters from Washington and their own committee were laid before them. Congress was in a rage, and its wrath was increased by the fact that its own committee in camp seemed to agree with Greene. There was a very hot discussion, and then Greene's letter was sent back to the committee, which brought in its report the following day, and recommended the passage of these resolutions:

"That General Greene's refusal be accepted.

"That General Washington be empowered and directed to appoint a quartermaster general.

"That General Greene be acquainted that Congress have no further service for him."

Greene stood too high, however, in public estimation to be turned out in this summary fashion. The report of the committee was taken up and debated every day for a week, but no action was had upon it. Finally, on August 5th, this resolution was passed: "That the absolute refusal of Major-General Greene at this important crisis to act under the new arrangement of the quartermaster general's department has made it necessary that the office of quartermaster general be immediately filled." They therefore proceeded to elect Pickering as quartermaster general, with the rank of colonel and the pay of a brigadier general, over and above his pay of one hundred and fifty-six dollars per month (in specie) as quartermaster general.

The feeling against the committee was almost as strong as against Greene. On August 2d a resolution was passed saying that the question of the quartermaster general's responsibility had been determined by Congress, "and, as the committee knew that the quartermaster general has requested the sense of Congress on so important a subject, they ought not to have interfered therein." A few days later Congress passed a resolution discharging the committee from any further attendance in camp and directing them to immediately report their proceedings to Congress.

Among the members of Congress who had been instrumental in forming the new system was Joseph Jones, of Virginia, who wrote to Washington on the 7th of August, giving a statement of the case, saying that Congress was greatly perplexed at Greene's refusal, and that "if General Greene thought the new system wanted amendment and had pointed out the defects, Congress would have considered the matter," and perhaps have made the necessary alterations; but, he went on to say, "the manner of these demands, made in such peremptory terms, at the moment of action, when the campaign was opened, the enemy in the field, and our ally waiting for co-operation, has lessened General Greene not only in the opinion of Congress, but, I think, of the public, and I question whether it will terminate with the acceptance of his refusal only."

This threat of summary measures against Greene

RESIGNS AS QUARTERMASTER GENERAL.

gave Washington an opportunity, which he quickly seized, to express his own views on the matter. Referring to the intimation contained in Jones's letter, he says: " Let me beseech you to consider well what you are about before you resolve. I shall neither condemn nor acquit General Greene's conduct for the act of resignation, because all the antecedent correspondence is necessary to form a right judgment of the matter, and possibly, if the account is ever brought before the public, you may find him treading on better ground that you seem to imagine; but this by the bye. My sole aim at present is to advertise you of what I think would be the consequences of suspending him from his command in the line (a matter distinct from the other) without a proper trial. A procedure of this kind must touch the feelings of every officer. It will show in a conspicuous point of view the uncertain tenure by which they hold their commissions. In a word, it will exhibit such a specimen of power, that I question much if there is an officer in the whole line that will hold a commission beyond the end of the campaign, if he does till then. Such an act in the most despotic Government would be attended at least with loud complaints. . . . Each will ask himself this question: If Congress, by its mere fiat, without inquiry and without trial, will suspend an officer to-day, and an officer of such high rank, may it not be my turn to-morrow ? and ought I to put it in the power of any man or body of men to sport with my commission and character, and lay me under the necessity of tamely acquiescing, or, by an appeal to the public, exposing matters which must be injurious to its interests ? . . . Suffer not, my friend, if it is within the powers of your ability to prevent it, so disagreeable an event to take place. I do not mean to justify, to countenance, or excuse in the most distant degree any expressions of disrespect which the gentleman in question, if he has used any, may have offered to Congress, no more than I do any unreasonable matters he may have required respecting the quartermaster general's department; but, as I have already observed, my letter is to prevent his suspension, because I fear, because I feel, that it must lead to very disagreeable and injurious consequences. General Greene has his numerous friends out of the army as well as in it; and, from his character and consideration in the world, he might not, when he felt himself wounded in so summary a way, withhold himself from a discussion that could not, at best, promote the public cause. As a military officer he stands very fair, and very deservedly so, in the opinion of all his acquaintance. These sentiments are the result of my own reflections, and I hasten to inform you of them. I do not know that General Greene has ever heard of the matter, and I hope he never may; nor am I acquainted with the opinion of a single officer in the whole army upon the subject, nor will any tone be given by me. It is my wish to prevent the proceeding; for sure I am that it can not be brought to a happy issue if it takes place."

Whether Greene's enemies in Congress could in any case have mustered enough votes to pass the proposed resolution dismissing him from the service is very doubtful; after the receipt of this letter from Washington it was not even attempted. The resolutions were never acted upon, and the resentment gradually simmered away to nothing.

The demonstration against New York made by

RESIGNS AS QUARTERMASTER GENERAL. 151

Washington on the 27th had been sufficient to recall Clinton with his troops to New York, but Howe's fleet went on to Newport and blockaded the French fleet there. Pending the arrival of the second division, the French fleet was inferior to the British, and De Ternay did not feel strong enough to risk an engagement. Rochambeau also did not consider his force sufficient to attempt any land operations. Washington certainly had not men enough to attack New York. The prospect of active operations held out in Washington's letter of July 14th to Greene was therefore postponed, pending the arrival of the second division of the French fleet. Washington moved the greater part of his army back to the west side of the Hudson, and established works on both sides at Dobb's Ferry. His headquarters were first at Orange, and then at Tappan, where he remained until September 18th, when he set out for Hartford to have a personal conference with Rochambeau.

Meanwhile Greene had to continue to act as quartermaster general, against his protests. He had agreed with the committee to serve for ten days from July 26th, the date of his resignation. He had issued circulars to all his subordinates to send in their accounts and close up their business. The ten days came to an end and nothing had been done. He asked Washington, on August 5th, to "take measures for relieving me as soon as possible from the disagreeable predicament I am in"; and he also asked Washington for his opinion on his conduct in the management of the quartermaster's department. Washington replied: "When you quit the department I shall be happy to give you my sense of your conduct, and I am persuaded it will be such as will be entirely satisfactory"; he said, however, that Greene must not leave the department until it was known what action Congress took on the letters from Washington and the committee, which were forwarded the day after Greene's resignation. On August 10th it was learned that these letters had angered Congress almost as much as Greene's resignation, and that Pickering had been appointed quartermaster general. Washington quietly comments on this as follows: "Whether he will be supplied with the means of procuring what is necessary in the department, or whether the new system is calculated to produce them, is yet to be known." The same messenger brought the letter of Joseph Jones, to which Washington replied on the 13th in the language already quoted. And on the 15th he gives Greene his opinion of his administration. The letter is a model for conciseness and temperate approbation, and it is given in full: "As you are retiring from the office of quartermaster general, and have requested my sense of your conduct and services while you acted in it, I shall give it to you with the greatest cheerfulness and pleasure. You have conducted the various duties of it with capacity and diligence, entirely to my satisfaction, and, as far as I have had an opportunity of knowing, with the strictest integrity. When you were prevailed upon to undertake the office, in March, 1778, it was in great disorder and confusion, and by extraordinary exertions you so arranged it as to enable the army to take the field the moment it was necessary, and to move with rapidity after the enemy when they left Philadelphia. From that period to the present time your exertions have been equally great. They have

RESIGNS AS QUARTERMASTER GENERAL. 153

appeared to me to be the result of system, and to have been well calculated to promote the interest and honor of your country. In fine, I can not but add that the States have had in you, in my opinion, an able, upright, and diligent servant."

Pickering was expected in a few days, and Greene therefore continued to act as quartermaster general without asking for further instructions. The few days, however, proved to be six weeks, and it was not until September 30th that he was finally relieved of this office. In the meantime the condition of the army grew worse instead of better. The plan of obtaining supplies in kind from the States was a total failure, and on August 20th Washington was obliged to write to Congress that he would have to dismiss the militia which were assembling, "or let them come forward to starve, which it will be extremely difficult for the troops already in the field to avoid." As there was almost nothing in camp to eat, for either men or animals, i became necessary to organize a raid and collect supplies from the Tory inhabitants along the west side of the Hudson opposite New York. As it was to be made in face of Clinton's army, a considerable force was necessary, and four brigades were detailed on August 24th, under Greene's orders. The raid was successful, and collected enough food to last about a month; but it led to unauthorized plundering, which Greene promptly suppressed. He asked Washington's authority to hang two of the culprits, and, on receiving it, he promptly did so.

On the 12th of September Washington received the news of Gates's total defeat at Camden, S. C., and he determined to go to Hartford to meet Rochambeau and decide upon a plan for future operations. He started on the 18th, leaving Greene in command of the army at Tappan. In his instructions to Greene he said: "I have such entire confidence in your prudence and abilities that I leave the conduct of it to your discretion, with only one observation: that with our present prospects it is not our business to seek an action, or accept one, but upon advantageous terms."

Nothing of consequence transpired at headquarters during the week that Washington was absent. Greene's principal occupation was in sending out foraging parties to collect food and save the army from starving. About midnight on September 25th he received a letter from Hamilton, dated at Verplanck's Point that afternoon, and reading as follows: "There has just been unfolded at this place a scene of the blackest treason. Arnold has fled to the enemy. André, the British adjutant general, is in our possession as a spy. His capture unraveled the mystery. West Point was to have been the sacrifice. All the dispositions have been made for the purpose, and 'tis possible, though not probable, to-night may see the execution. The wind is fair. I came here in pursuit of Arnold, but was too late. I advise you putting the army under marching orders, and detaching a brigade immediately this way."

It was a dark night, and the rain was falling fast; but if the Hudson, quietly flowing past Greene's tent, had suddenly burst into flames, it would have been less startling than this astounding piece of news. Greene instantly issued the orders which Hamilton had suggested, and then started a messenger to Congress with a copy of Hamilton's letter. At three o'clock in the night the army was paraded, and the

Pennsylvania brigade began its march up the river. A few minutes later came a letter from Washington, dated at Robinson's house at seven o'clock on the previous evening, directing him to march the left wing of the army to King's Ferry, and to hold the rest in readiness to march at a moment's notice. Greene replied that these dispositions had already been taken on the receipt of Hamilton's note. He waited for further orders, but none came until the next day, September 27th, when he received word from Washington that André and Smith had been sent to camp, and that André was to be kept in a decent room and " be treated with civility, but that he be so guarded as to preclude the possibility of his escaping." Washington had meanwhile taken other steps for the security of West Point, and on the 28th he arrived at headquarters at Tappan. Greene felt almost a personal shame at Arnold's treason. In a letter to his wife, on the 29th, describing the event, he says: " My pride and feelings are greatly hurt at the infamy of this man's conduct. Arnold being an American and a New Englander, and of the rank of major general, are all mortifying circumstances. The event will be a reproach to us to the latest posterity. Curse on his folly and perfidy." On the 29th Washington resumed command of the army, and appointed a court, of which Greene was president, for the consideration of André's case. It was composed of six major generals: Greene, Stirling, St. Clair, Lafayette, R. Howe, and Steuben ; and eight brigadiers: Parsons, J. Clinton, Knox, Glover, Paterson, Hand, Huntingdon, and Stark. Colonel John Lawrence was judge advocate.

Greene's careful study of Vattel now stood him

in good stead against the pretensions that André was protected by Arnold's flag of truce. This claim was not indeed raised by André, but by Clinton, in a letter to Washington which was laid before the court. André told his story briefly. No witnesses were examined. The court was cleared in the usual manner and the case considered. Beginning with the junior member, each in turn voted that André be considered as a spy and that he suffer death. The opinion of the court was written out, and Greene signed it as president and handed it to Washington. On the following day, September 30th, Washington approved it, and ordered that André be executed at 5 P. M. on October 1st. But on the 30th Washington had informed Clinton of the conclusions of the court, and Clinton instantly replied, saying that he had sent Lieutenant-General Robertson, Lieutenant-Governor Elliot, and Chief-Justice Smith to make a statement of the case, and he asked a hearing for them. Washington suspended the execution, and directed Greene to receive them at Dobb's Ferry. Greene met their barge at the water's edge on the afternoon of October 1st. He refused to allow any one but General Robertson to land, and he informed him that by Washington's order he met him as a private gentleman only, and not as an officer. Robertson endeavored to persuade Greene that André was acting under a flag of truce, but Greene replied that that question had been considered fully by the court and decided in the negative. Robertson then proposed that the question should be submitted to "disinterested gentlemen of knowledge of the law of war and nations," and suggested Knyphausen and Rochambeau as such arbitrators; but Greene declared that the deliberate decision of a competent tribunal could not be overruled in this fashion. Robertson then submitted a letter from Arnold justifying André's course—probably the most consummately impudent letter ever written. It is said that Greene read it and then threw it contemptuously on the ground. The interview lasted till nearly nightfall, and without any result. Then Robertson asked Greene to "represent my arguments to General Washington in the fairest light." Greene willingly promised to do so, and they parted, Greene riding back to Washington's headquarters at Tappan, and Robertson returning to his schooner anchored off Dobb's Ferry. On the following morning Greene wrote to Robertson: "Agreeably to your request, I communicated to General Washington the substance of your conversation in all the particulars so far as my memory served me. It made no alteration in his opinion and determination. I need say no more after what you have already been informed."

At noon on the same day, October 2d, a part of the American army was paraded under command of Greene, and in their presence André was taken out and hanged.

On the 30th of September, Pickering having arrived at camp, Washington issued an order announcing to the army his appointment as quartermaster general. In the same order he thanked Greene "for the able and satisfactory manner in which he had discharged the duties of that office." Greene was thus at last freed from this vexatious business, and with a light heart he returned to the congenial duties of the line. He was beyond question the most efficient quartermaster general of the war. With the slender resources placed at his command by a Congress which, whatever its virtues in other directions, was wholly lacking in administrative capacity, he accomplished far more than his predecessor Mifflin or his successor Pickering. Washington said deliberately that he had performed the duties "*entirely to my satisfaction,*" and nothing need be added to this. But, as Greene wrote Knox in the beginning, he hated the place; and he never overcame his repugnance to it. When, instead of gratitude for what he considered a great sacrifice on his part, he met criticism for defects beyond his control, and insinuations that he was holding the place from mercenary motives, he began the long contest with Congress which resulted in his peremptorily refusing to serve any longer. His manner of doing this was lacking in dignity. But for the fact that Washington so strongly urged him to take the place, and put the matter before him in the light of a public duty, it was a mistake for him ever to have taken it at all. Having taken it, and found it even more distasteful than he anticipated, he should have resigned at the end of the first campaign—in December, 1778—when he first learned from his friend Henry Marchant of the criticisms that were being made upon his administration by a faction in Congress. If he felt it his duty to continue in office for another campaign, he was fully absolved from this by the cavalier treatment which he received from Congress when it refused to answer his respectful, courteous, and most important letters of December, 1779, and January, 1780. A simple and positive letter of resignation would then have freed him from the office without giving the slightest cause for adverse comment. But he so often spoke of resigning, that he gave color to the belief that he was only making threats of resignation for the purpose of compelling the adoption of his own views in regard to the method of administration. After six months of wrangling, he finally had to resign just at a time when an important movement of the army was thought to be imminent. As to the manner of his resignation and the tone of his letters, Washington felt obliged to refrain from expressing any opinion. He could hardly fail to disapprove them, for they were very different from those which he himself adopted, though he had more than once as great, if not greater, cause for resentment.

But though his exit was not as dignified as might have been wished, he was at last out of the place, and he at once sought a regular command in the line. On the 5th of October he applied for the command at West Point, and Washington immediately granted it, only taking occasion to observe that it would not be an independent command, as he himself would probably make his headquarters in that vicinity. Greene accepted, and on October 7th began his march up the Hudson with two divisions. He set to work to complete the fortifications at West Point and place the garrisons in them. But he had been at West Point less than a week when Washington received from Congress a copy of their resolution of October 6th, directing him to order a court of inquiry on General Gates for his conduct at Camden, and also to appoint a successor to Gates. The same messenger brought a letter from Mr. Matthews (the same who had been on the committee of the previous spring to investigate the quartermaster's department), saying that he was authorized to communicate the wish of the delegates of the three Southern States that Greene should be selected for this command. Washington had wanted to send Greene there for more than a year, but the selection had never before been left to his discretion. Now that he had the authority, and especially since the choice of the Southern delegates was the same as his own, he lost no time in exercising it. On the 14th he offered the command to Greene in a letter full of good wishes, and Greene immediately accepted it. As he had been away from home (except for two weeks after the Rhode Island expedition of 1778) for more than five years, and was now going still farther away, he asked for a short leave in order to arrange his private affairs; but when Washington explained the necessity of his immediate presence in the South he withdrew his application. He, however, hoped that his wife, who was planning to make him a visit, would arrive before he started. But in this he was disappointed. She was already on the way, but her journey was delayed, and it was not the day of telegrams and limited expresses. He felt unable to wait longer than the 20th, and on that day, after writing a most affectionate farewell to her, he set out for Washington's headquarters at Preakness, in Bergen County, N. J. Here, on the 22d, he received his instructions from Washington, and went on to Philadelphia, where, on the 30th, Congress by special resolution ratified his appointment, and invested him with very extensive powers as commander in chief of the Southern army.

CHAPTER X.

TAKES COMMAND OF THE SOUTHERN ARMY—1780.

For more than five years Greene had been at Washington's right hand. He had been in every battle in which Washington had commanded, with the single exception of White Plains. Washington had detached him occasionally, as at Fort Washington, Mount Holly, Newport, and Springfield; but he had declined all requests to have him go far away or remain long. Greene had become the chief subordinate, in whom Washington placed his principal reliance. His first object had always been to strive to understand Washington's plans and wishes, and to support and execute them with all the devotion of a thoroughly loyal nature. Washington had grown to appreciate fully the merit of such a steadfast subordinate, and he had the most complete confidence in his judgment and ability. Now this intimate association was to come to an end. Greene was to be transferred to a distant theatre, where he was to act on his own responsibility. For the greater part of the next year Washington was to be inactive; the fighting and marching were to be done under Greene's sole command, and his responsibility was for the time to be scarcely if at all inferior to that of Washington himself.

In order to explain the condition of affairs at the

South when Greene took command, it is necessary to state as briefly as possible what had taken place there previous to his arrival. The war opened at the South with a skirmish between loyalists and State militia at Moore's Creek, near Wilmington, N. C., on February 26, 1776, which had the same relative importance in that region as the battle of Lexington at the North. The loyalists were defeated. At this time two bodies of British troops were on their way to invade the Carolinas: one was coming from Boston, and consisted of about two thousand regulars under command of Clinton, who had come out from England in the previous autumn as lieutenant general under Sir William Howe; the other was of about equal strength, and consisted of seven regiments under Earl Cornwallis. It left England under a convoy of ten ships, commanded by Commodore Parker. These two forces met at the mouth of the Cape Fear River early in May, 1776. But the militia had turned out in such large numbers, as a result of the victory at Moore's Creek, that Clinton deemed it imprudent to land in that vicinity, and he therefore sailed southward, with the intention of taking Charleston first and Savannah next. In attempting to reduce Fort Moultrie, in Charleston Harbor, on June 28th, Clinton met with defeat. His troops were unable to land, the fleet lost over two hundred in killed and wounded, and the ships were badly damaged. After making such temporary repairs as were possible, the whole expedition returned to the North, arriving at New York in time for the troops of Clinton and Cornwallis to take part in the battle of Long Island.

During the next two years, which were the most

TAKES COMMAND OF THE SOUTHERN ARMY. 163

active years of the war at the North, nothing was done at the South. Then Clinton determined to transfer the war again to the South in the hope of better success; and accordingly, in the autumn of 1778, a part of the garrison of Newport was withdrawn, and a force consisting of over three thousand troops, under Colonel Campbell, was sent to Savannah. General Robert Howe then commanded the American troops in the South, but he had only about twelve hundred men, more than half of whom were militia. Campbell made short work of him at Savannah, on December 29th — defeated him badly, captured all his stores and guns and about half of his men, and took possession of the town. He soon afterward took Augusta, and all resistance in Georgia was for the moment at an end.

General Benjamin Lincoln was then sent to the South to supersede Howe. He arrived at Charleston at the end of the year, and soon raised a force of about two thousand militia and six hundred Continentals. The greater part of these were sent under General Ashe to threaten Augusta, but in an engagement which took place at Brier Creek on March 3, 1779, Ashe was disastrously defeated and most of his force dispersed.

Lincoln, however, succeeded in calling out more militia, and began another movement against Augusta; whereupon the British marched toward Charleston, which caused Lincoln to retrace his steps, and after considerable marching and a slight skirmish each side returned to its former positions—the British along the line of the Savannah River, with an outpost at Beaufort, and the Americans at Charleston. In September, 1779, the French fleet under

D'Estaing which, during the year since the attack on Newport had been cruising in the West Indies, appeared off the Southern coast, and a plan was made for a combined attack by land and sea on Savannah. After a three weeks' siege an assault was made on October 9th, but without success. The British lost only fifty-five men, and the allies more than one thousand, Pulaski being among the killed. D'Estaing then sailed off to France with the greater part of his fleet, sending the rest to the West Indies.

As soon as Clinton at New York heard of this affair, he thought the time had come for a decisive blow at the South. He therefore withdrew the balance of the garrison from Newport, and adding to them a part of the troops in and around New York, he formed a force of eight thousand men, and with these he sailed in person for Savannah in December, 1779, taking Cornwallis with him. He immediately sent orders for Lord Rawdon to follow him with three thousand more men from New York, so that when all the troops brought from New York were joined to those already in the South, Clinton had between thirteen thousand and fourteen thousand men. At the same time Washington was hurrying forward reenforcements to Lincoln, but it was impossible to increase his force much beyond seven thousand men. Clinton started from Savannah in February to capture Charleston. After a siege of over two months, on May 12th, Lincoln surrendered with his entire army of over two thousand Continentals and three thousand five hundred militia. Clinton then left Cornwallis in command at the South with about five thousand men, and returned to New York with the rest of his force, arriving there, as we have seen,

TAKES COMMAND OF THE SOUTHERN ARMY. 165

just before the engagement at Springfield, in June, 1780.

While the siege of Charleston was in progress Washington had sent a re-enforcement of two thousand men under De Kalb to Lincoln's assistance, but they had gone no farther than North Carolina when Charleston fell. On receipt of this news, Congress, without consulting Washington, selected Gates, on June 13th, to take command in the South. He overtook De Kalb at Hillsborough, N. C., on July 19th. In the meantime Cornwallis had sent Rawdon to overrun the interior of South Carolina and raise a Tory militia. Rawdon was now at Camden, S. C., a meeting-point of several important roads, about one hundred and twenty miles north of Charleston and forty miles south of the North Carolina line. Gates began his march for this point on July 27th, and Cornwallis left Charleston for the same place about the same time. Gates arrived first, but he lost the favorable moment for attacking Rawdon before Cornwallis arrived. Gates had about three thousand men, of whom half were militia, and Cornwallis had about two thousand, including Rawdon's detachment, three fourths of whom were trained soldiers. On the 16th of August the battle was fought at Camden. Gates was ignominiously defeated, and fled back to Hillsborough, one hundred and sixty miles in rear; Baron De Kalb was killed, gallantly fighting to the last; the army was practically annihilated.

The British had thus in four months more than made up at the South what they had lost at the North during the two years between Long Island and Newport. Against the surrender of Burgoyne they had matched the capture of Lincoln, and they had offset the retreat from Pennsylvania and Jersey by the subjugation of the two Carolinas and Georgia, and the destruction of Gates's army.

Such was the situation when Greene was sent to the South, not so much to take command as to create an army. Within nine months from the time he arrived he had reconquered Georgia and the Carolinas with the exception of Charleston and Savannah, and, though defeated in several engagements, he had manœuvred Cornwallis into Virginia, where Washington with extraordinary rapidity fell upon him with the French army and what was left of the Continentals. Almost at the same instant Greene defeated the remnant of the British army in South Carolina at Eutaw Springs, and drove it into Charleston. These two events practically put an end to the war, although the treaty of peace was not finally signed until two years later.

Greene reached Washington's headquarters at Preakness, N. J., on October 22d, and there Washington gave him his instructions for the command of the Southern army. They were meager enough. "Uninformed as I am of the enemy's force in that quarter, of our own, or of the resources which it will be in our power to command for carrying on the war, I can give you no particular instructions, but must leave you to govern yourself entirely according to your own prudence and judgment and the circumstances in which you find yourself. I am aware that the nature of the command will offer you embarrassments of a singular and complicated nature, but I rely upon your abilities and exertions for everything your means will enable you to effect." More specific instructions were given him in regard to the inquiry he was to make into the conduct of Gates.

With these instructions and a letter to Congress, and flattering letters of introduction to the Governors of the Southern States, Greene rode on to Philadelphia. On the 27th of October he presented Washington's letter to Congress, adding one of his own, in which he says that it will be "my pride and ambition to merit the approbation of Congress, and I flatter myself that they will be charitably disposed to make just allowance for the peculiar difficulties I will have to contend with. . . . I am conscious of my deficiencies, but if I am clothed with proper powers and receive the necessary support, I am not altogether without hopes of prescribing some bounds to the ravages of the enemy. . . . At present I am wholly unacquainted with the intentions of Congress with respect to the plan and extent of the war they mean to prosecute in the Southern Department, as well as the number and condition of the troops they mean to employ, or the States in which they are to be levied. I am uninformed how they are to be paid, fed, and clothed, through what channels the quartermaster general's ordnance and hospital departments are to be supplied. I must request the orders and information of Congress upon all these points, and I will endeavor to make the most of the means put into my hands." This letter was referred to a committee of which his old friend Sullivan, now a member of Congress, was at the head; and two days later Greene wrote more specifically to this committee, giving estimates of articles required for the various departments of his army.

It was but little more than three months since Congress, in a rage, had discussed the idea of summarily dismissing Greene from the army; but now he was very kindly received. On the 30th of October they passed a series of resolutions, approving his appointment, directing Steuben to accompany him, specifying that his army was to consist of all the regular troops raised or to be raised in the six States from Delaware to Georgia inclusive, authorizing him to call on the Legislatures and executives of these States for "men, clothing, money, arms, intrenching tools, provisions, and other aids and supplies," and requesting these States to furnish them; and directing the heads of the staff departments to furnish him such articles as he could not obtain in the South. All the powers granted to Gates in June in reference to the appointment of officers and calling out the militia, were transferred to him, and to these was added the power to effect exchanges of prisoners. He was to "organize and employ the army under his command in the manner he shall judge most proper, subject to the control of the commander in chief." As his field of operations was over eight hundred miles from the latter's head quarters, and there were no means of communication except by horses, this control was almost nominal. In short, the entire military resources, such as they were, of six of the thirteen States were placed at his disposal; and with them he was to raise and equip an army and fight the enemy in whatever way he deemed best.

It is significant of the esteem in which Greene was held by his companions in arms that so many of the best men in the army sought the opportunity to

TAKES COMMAND OF THE SOUTHERN ARMY. 169

accompany him. Lafayette, Steuben, John Laurens, Henry Lee, and Dr. McHenry, afterward Secretary of War, all applied to be ordered with him. Lafayette in particular wrote him the most affectionate and flattering letters, asking "to have my fate united with yours." For various reasons these requests could not be granted, except in the cases of Steuben and Lee. Steuben was sent with him to organize and discipline the Southern army, as he had drilled the main army at Valley Forge three years before; and " Light Horse Harry," the famous father of his still more famous son, Robert E. Lee, was sent to a field where his talents as a cavalry leader would find full scope. On his arrival at the South Greene found the most distinguished lot of partisan chiefs which the war produced—Marion, Morgan, Sumter, Pickens, and William Washington. He gave them every opportunity to display their abilities, and never did they achieve as much as during the six months after his arrival; so that what the army lacked in men and resources it partially made up in the superb character of its chiefs.

Greene passed a short but busy week in Philadelphia, trying to get arms from President Reed, of Pennsylvania, clothing from Southern merchants, and wagons from the quartermaster general. Then leaving Colonel Feibiger with minute instructions for forwarding supplies, and writing a last word to Washington asking him to urge his wants unceasingly on Congress, so that they would not be forgotten the moment he was gone, he set out for his command on November 3d, in company with his two aids and Steuben and the latter's genial secretary, Duponceau. His first stop was at Annapolis, where he arrived on the 7th. The Legislature was in session, and he appeared before them in person, and also addressed them in writing, stating his wants and urging the formation of a regular army, by means of a draft if necessary. But he received little encouragement, the Legislature having "neither money nor credit, and, from the temper of the people, afraid to push matters to extremity." From Annapolis he also wrote to the Governor of Delaware, and appointed General Gist to present his requisitions in person, urge them upon the State, and forward all supplies that he could collect. From Annapolis he continued his journey southward, passing the afternoon and night of the 12th at Mount Vernon, whence Mrs. Washington was just starting to pass the winter, as usual, with her husband. Both Steuben and himself were delighted with the place and charmed with the reception they met. Greene wrote to Washington: "I don't wonder that you languish so often to return to the pleasures of domestic life. Nothing but the glory of being commander in chief, and the happiness of being universally admired, could compensate for such a sacrifice as you make." Thence he went on to Fredericksburg, stopping at the home of his former brigade commander, Weedon, who had fought so gallantly with him at the Brandywine three years before, and who was now absent in command of a detachment of militia. On the 16th he arrived at Richmond, and immediately entered into a long discussion of the situation with Thomas Jefferson, who was then Governor.

The ideas of Greene and Jefferson on military matters were naturally wide apart, and Greene therefore had once more to plead the same arguments in

TAKES COMMAND OF THE SOUTHERN ARMY. 171

favor of a regular force that he had used so often during the last five years. No one appreciated more fully than Greene the value of the militia in its proper place; but he well knew that it was not the proper instrument with which to carry on a long war against the best troops of Europe. But though Jefferson failed to see the deficiencies of the militia, he did everything in his power to provide supplies of clothing and wagons; he met with only indifferent success, however, because the State was without financial resources, and the people were growing tired of the war.

The arrival of General Leslie and his force from New York * had spread considerable alarm throughout the State, and the militia had been called out and placed under the orders of Muhlenberg and Weedon, who had commanded the brigades in Greene's division in the campaign of 1777. Greene decided to leave Steuben in Virginia, with instructions to organize and command this force, to send on such portion of it as could be spared, to collect and forward supplies, and to keep open his communications with the North. After remaining six days in Richmond to arrange these matters, Greene continued his journey on the 21st of November, and on December 2d arrived at Gates's headquarters, near Charlotte, N. C.

Gates had been his enemy throughout the war. As Fiske well says: "In every campaign since the beginning of the war Greene had been Washington's right arm; and for indefatigable industry, for strength and breadth of intelligence, and for un-

---

* See p. 182.

selfish devotion to the public service, he was scarcely inferior to the commander in chief." Greene being Washington's most trusted subordinate, Gates had intrigued against him on every possible occasion. Now Greene's hour of revenge had come; but he treated his rival with a magnanimity which made him his warm friend for the rest of his life. He came with orders not only to supersede Gates in command, but to put him on trial for his conduct at Camden. Yet his first act was to issue an order in which he "returns thanks to the honorable Major-General Gates for the polite manner in which he has introduced him to his command in the orders of yesterday, and for his good wishes for the success of the Southern army." The general officers necessary for Gates's trial could not be spared at this time, and Greene therefore postponed summoning the court; and as he studied the matter he came to the conclusion that Gates was the victim of misfortune rather than fault. He therefore reported to Washington that a council of war was of opinion that the court of inquiry could not be assembled without manifest injury to the service; he allowed Gates to proceed to Philadelphia and report to Congress and the commander in chief for orders; and he wrote to members of Congress expressing the opinion that no trial was necessary. None was ever held, and in August, 1782, Congress rescinded the resolution ordering an inquiry into Gates's conduct, and restored him to a command in the army under Washington at Newburg.

On assuming command of his army, Greene immediately called for returns, and from these he learned that its strength on paper was twenty-three

TAKES COMMAND OF THE SOUTHERN ARMY. 173

hundred and seven, of whom fourteen hundred and eighty-two were present, and the whole number "fit for duty, properly clothed and properly equipped, did not amount to eight hundred men!" The rest, as he wrote to Jefferson, and also to Washington, were "literally naked, . . . starving with cold and hunger, without tents and equipage."

As already stated, his army was to be made up of the Continental troops of the six States from Delaware to Georgia, and of such militia as he could raise in these States. By resolution of October 3, 1780, Congress had directed that the regular army, from and after January 1, 1781, should consist of four regiments of cavalry, four regiments of artillery, forty-nine regiments of infantry, and one regiment of artificers. Some slight changes in the proposed organization were made at Washington's suggestion, and, as finally agreed upon and ordered by resolution of October 21st, each infantry regiment was to consist of nine companies, and its strength was to be thirty-six officers, forty-seven noncommissioned officers, twenty-two musicians, and six hundred and twelve rank and file. The quota of the six Southern States was as follows:

Delaware.......	1 regiment of infantry.
Maryland.......	5 regiments of infantry.
Virginia........	8 regiments of infantry, 1 of artillery, and 2 of cavalry.
North Carolina..	4 regiments of infantry.
South Carolina..	2 regiments of infantry.
Georgia.........	1 regiment of infantry.
Total.........	21 regiments of infantry, 1 of artillery, and 2 of cavalry.

Or a total force of about fifteen thousand men.

But all this was on paper. It was even more true now than when Washington said it four years before, that "there is a material difference between voting battalions and raising men." Washington had about seven thousand men in the Northern army, and Greene had two thousand at the South; the rest of the forty thousand men called for by the resolutions of Congress did not exist. The regiments of South Carolina and Georgia had never been raised, and nearly all the regiments of Virginia and North Carolina had been made prisoners at the fall of Charleston. The regiments of Delaware and Maryland had marched from New Jersey to North Carolina, under De Kalb, in the spring of 1780. They had formed the Continental portion of Gates's army, and had been in the disaster at Camden. What was left of them constituted the eight hundred men fit for duty when Greene took command.

The so-called Southern army, as Greene wrote to Knox, was "rather a shadow than a substance, having only an imaginary existence." It was not only deficient in numbers, but lacking in organization, discipline, equipment, supplies, and everything that constitutes an efficient force. The men had little or no clothing, there were no wagons or other means of transportation, there was but little ammunition, there was no organized medical department, and there was no ready money to purchase supplies; the men were dispirited by defeat, and they were in the habit of going home when they felt so inclined and returning at their pleasure. The outlook was in the last degree discouraging.

Nevertheless Greene was hopeful, and he immediately set to work to introduce some degree of order.

His first step was to put a stop to men absenting themselves without leave. A deserter was tried, convicted, and hanged in the presence of the entire force. He next put Lieutenant-Colonel Carrington in charge of the quartermaster's department, and Lieutenant-Colonel Davie in charge of the commissariat—both excellent appointments. Though their resources were slender, yet they soon contrived to keep the army so far supplied that it was able to move. Greene kept up an incessant correspondence with his representatives in Virginia, Delaware, and Pennsylvania, urging them to forward men and supplies. He made arrangements for collecting a supply of boats to transport his stores up and down the rivers, and for another lot of boats to form an improvised pontoon train, which was of the greatest value a few months later in his rapid marches across the numerous rivers which run from the Alleghanies through the Carolinas to the sea. His army was so destitute of everything, that he was compelled in his correspondence to specify the urgent necessity of such minor articles as boards, nails, and horseshoes. Governor Rutledge, of South Carolina, came to Greene's camp and passed some time with him, consulting how his State could render assistance. He could do but little, as the State was completely occupied by British troops, and the Legislature could not convene. But the Legislature of North Carolina was in session, and Colonel Davie was sent to Governor Nash with letters explaining fully the needs of the patriot army.

The situation of the troops at Charlotte did not meet Greene's approval, as the surrounding country was destitute of supplies; he therefore sent his engineer, Kosciusko, to reconnoiter down the Pedee River and find a more eligible situation. He also opened correspondence with the partisan chiefs Marion, Pickens, and Sumter, with a view to bringing their operations under his control. As soon as Kosciusko made his report, and within two weeks of his arrival, Greene issued his orders for moving to his new camp at Cheraw, and, although the movement was delayed by rains, he arrived there before the end of the month. Meanwhile Steuben had been doing everything possible in Virginia to forward men to re-enforce Greene, but the first detachment he intended to send refused to leave Virginia, and they were discharged. Steuben succeeded, however, in getting together another detachment numbering four hundred and fifty-six men, enlisted for eighteen months, and they were started forward on December 14th. They arrived at the camp at Cheraw before the end of the month; and two weeks later Lee arrived with his legion, consisting of a little more than three hundred picked men, partly cavalry and partly infantry, in fine order. The arrival of these re-enforcements brought Greene's army up to about three thousand men, of whom perhaps two thirds were fit for service. In addition to these were the irregular, partisan troops of Marion, Pickens, and Sumter. It is impossible to give any accurate statement of their numbers, which varied from day to day. They were, in fact, what has been denominated in recent years under the more offensive term of guerrillas—farmers one day and soldiers the next. Their principal chiefs were commissioned as officers of militia and authorized to raise as many men as they could, but further than this they had no regular organization.

TAKES COMMAND OF THE SOUTHERN ARMY. 177

Marion operated in the eastern part of the State, in the swamps between the Pedee and Santee Rivers; Pickens in the western part, between Ninety-Six and Augusta; and Sumter in the northwestern part, along the Broad River and its branches. Having no regular cavalry except the small body in Lee's legion, Greene designed to use these partisan troops, so far as he could control their actions, to gain information of the enemy's movements and to threaten and harass their posts. The numbers of the three bodies aggregated between five hundred and one thousand men at different periods. In all, Greene had thus between thirty-five hundred and four thousand men at the opening of the campaign.

Opposed to Greene, in command of the British army in the South, was Lieutenant-General Earl Cornwallis, in many respects the best soldier that England sent to America. He came out in 1775, and served continuously for over six years, returning home a few months after his surrender at Yorktown. He subsequently attained great distinction during the seven years of his administration as Governor General of India, and three years as Lord Lieutenant of Ireland. He was four years older than Greene, and was now just forty-two years of age. He had been opposed to Greene in all the campaigns in New York, the Jerseys, and Pennsylvania, and had learned to respect him thoroughly. In the Jerseys Cornwallis had written: "Greene is as dangerous as Washington; he is vigilant, enterprising, and full of resources. With but little hope of gaining an advantage over him, I never feel secure when encamped in his neighborhood."

Next in command to Cornwallis was Lord Rawdon, who also in after-life, as Earl of Moira and Marquis of Hastings, was a famous governor general of India. He was now only twenty-six years of age, but he had had five years of unbroken service in America, beginning at Boston as a captain in the Sixty-third Foot. He had greatly distinguished himself at Monmouth, and in the following autumn had raised a regiment of provincials in New York, known as the "Volunteers of Ireland," and had been commissioned as colonel. With these and a considerable body of British and Hessian troops he had followed Clinton to Charleston, arriving there April 18th.

The third officer of importance on the British side was Lieutenant-Colonel Tarleton, who also was a youngster of twenty-six. He had come out as a major of dragoons under Cornwallis, in the spring of 1776, and had been continuously in active service ever since. He now commanded a force known as the "British Legion," numbering about four hundred and fifty men, and consisting, like Lee's Legion, of infantry and cavalry. His memoirs are full of vanity and egotism, but he possessed all the characteristics of a splendid partisan leader.

According to the returns in the British Record Office, the effective force under Cornwallis's command in December, 1780, numbered 7,384 in South Carolina, 968 in Georgia, and 2,274 on their way from Virginia to Charleston, under command of General Leslie, making a total of 10,622. This force consisted of two regiments of the Guards, the Seventh, Sixteenth, Twenty-third, Thirty-third, Sixty-third, Sixty-fourth, and Seventy-first (two battalions) Regiments of the line, the British Legion, the Hessian Yagers, and the regiment of Bose, a large detachment of royal artillery, the Volunteers of Ireland, De Lancey's and Cruger's battalions of New York Loyalists, and several battalions of Tory militia from North and South Carolina and Georgia.

On one side, therefore, was a force of regular troops, small in numbers, but composed of the best material in the British army, well trained, disciplined, and equipped, and supplied with everything that an ample military chest could purchase. Supporting these was a numerous body of Tory militia. On the other side was a force still smaller in numbers, composed principally of militia, deficient in every requisite of a well-equipped force, without money, and living on the country as best they could. On both sides were officers of the highest class—Greene, Morgan, and Lee on one side, and Cornwallis, Rawdon, and Tarleton on the other. The numbers were small, but the field of operations was immense, the marches prodigious, the manœuvring incessant. The game was played with the greatest skill on both sides, and no campaign in American history has illustrated the art of war in its highest branches more fully than the campaign of 1781.

When Clinton went North, in June, 1780, after the capture of Charleston, the instructions he gave Cornwallis were to march into the interior of South Carolina, capture the province, and then move north through North Carolina. He was to put down the Revolution and re-establish the King's authority in these two provinces; and when this was done he was to assist in a projected expedition up the Chesapeake against Baltimore.

In pursuance of this plan, Cornwallis overran the State soon after the fall of Charleston, and in the month of June established a circular line of posts on its western and northern borders, as follows: At Augusta, on the Savannah River, Lieutenant-Colonel Brown, with a detachment of militia; at a small settlement called Ninety-Six, Lieutenant-Colonel Balfour, with the Sixteenth Foot, three light companies and three battalions of provincials; at Rocky Mount, on the Catawba, Lieutenant-Colonel Turnbull, with a regiment of New York provincials and some South Carolina militia; at Camden, Lord Rawdon, with the Twenty-third and Thirty-third Regiments, the Volunteers of Ireland, Tarleton's Legion, a detachment of artillery, and two regiments of militia; at the Cheraws, on the Great Pedee River, south of the North Carolina line, Major McArthur, with the Seventy-first Regiment. There was a large garrison in Charleston, consisting of the Seventh, Sixty-third, and Sixty-fourth Regiments, two battalions of Hessians, and a detachment of artillery; and there were smaller garrisons on each flank at Georgetown and Savannah.

Having thus occupied the State with his troops, Cornwallis returned to Charleston to put the civil machinery in running order, and this occupied the entire summer. There were no military movements except the skirmishes with the partisan corps of Marion, Sumter, and Pickens, until the advance of Gates's army toward Camden, in August. Cornwallis came up from Charleston to meet him, and arrived just in time to take command in the battle which ensued, but after defeating Gates he did not pursue him; he returned to Charleston to complete the establishment of the civil government.

By the middle of September Cornwallis was ready

TAKES COMMAND OF THE SOUTHERN ARMY. 181

to begin the advance into North Carolina, and he again came up to Camden, bringing with him the Seventh Regiment, and drawing in the Seventy-first from the Cheraws; otherwise the "frontier" posts were not disturbed. Joining these two regiments to the force under Rawdon at Camden, Cornwallis marched across the State line and took possession of Charlotte. His reception was far from what he anticipated. Mecklenburg County was a hotbed of patriots; he found it difficult to collect supplies for his troops, and the raising of a Tory militia in this vicinity was out of the question.

Early in October a serious disaster overtook Cornwallis in the loss of one of his largest detachments. The communications between Ninety-Six, Rocky Mount, and Camden were kept up by a corps of light infantry and some militia, under command of Major Ferguson, of the Seventy-first Regiment. During the latter part of September seven American colonels, each with his band or corps of one hundred and fifty to two hundred men, mountaineers, backwoodsmen, and frontiersmen, well mounted on their own horses, and armed with hunting rifles and such swords as they could make out of domestic tools, assembled on the western border of South Carolina for the purpose of attacking Ferguson. They overtook him at King's Mountain on October 7th and annihilated his force. Ferguson and two hundred and twenty-five of his men were killed, one hundred and sixty-three were wounded, and the rest (about seven hundred and twenty) were made prisoners.

This was the first turn of the tide in favor of the Americans at the South. For two years the current had been strong against them, but now began a change. Cornwallis retreated from Charlotte as soon as he heard of the disaster, somewhat precipitately, abandoning part of his baggage. He established his camp at Winnsborough, in rear of the center of his line of posts. Gates advanced to and occupied Charlotte.

In the meantime the news of the British victory at Camden had reached Clinton at New York, and, supposing everything ready for Cornwallis's advance northward, he detached twenty-three hundred men under General Leslie and sent them to enter Virginia at the mouth of the James River, and then advance to meet Cornwallis on his way north, or make such other movements as Cornwallis might direct. Their arrival caused great excitement in Virginia. The militia were called out, and Steuben was left at Richmond when Greene passed through, in November, on his way South to take command of all the troops in the State and prevent Leslie from cutting Greene's communications with the North. But Cornwallis, as soon as he heard of Leslie's arrival in Virginia, sent orders to him to re-embark and come to Charleston. On arriving there, on December 13th, he found orders to join Cornwallis with a part of his force. Lack of wagons and horses prevented him from starting until December 30th. On that day he began his march with two battalions of Guards, the regiment of Bose, one hundred and twenty Yagers, and a detachment of light dragoons —in all, fifteen hundred and thirty men.

With the arrival of Leslie's force Cornwallis had more than ten thousand men under his command, and, without disturbing the large garrison in Charleston or the numerous posts on the "frontier," he intended to form a marching army of about four thousand men and resume his long-contemplated march into North Carolina, which had been postponed from various causes for more than six months, and had then been interrupted by the defeat at King's Mountain and the retreat from Charlotte to Winnsborough.

But his plans were disarranged by Greene, who boldly took the initiative. On arriving at Charlotte, Greene found that Gates had contemplated going into winter quarters. But Greene had no such plans. He intended to open a vigorous campaign just as quickly as he could get his troops in hand. But, in view of the disorganized condition of his army, he thought that at first he could do nothing more than organize a partisan warfare. Just before leaving Philadelphia he had written to Washington, October 31st: " My first object will be to equip a flying army, to consist of about eight hundred horse and one thousand infantry. This force, with the occasional aid of the militia, will serve to confine the enemy in their limits, and render it difficult for them to subsist in the interior county. I see but little prospect of getting a force to contend with the enemy upon equal grounds, and therefore must make the most of a kind of partisan war until we can levy and equip a larger force." With this idea in mind, immediately after taking command, he resolved to divide his army, small as it was, into two bodies, and on December 16th he issued the necessary orders. The first detachment, consisting of three hundred and twenty infantry of the Maryland line, two hundred Virginia militia, and Colonel William Washington's regiment of light horse, numbering less than one hundred men, was placed under Morgan's command. He was directed to cross the Catawba River, where he would be joined by the partisan corps of Davidson and Sumter. Morgan was instructed to use these forces, and any that might join him from Georgia, against the enemy on the west side of the Catawba, either offensively or defensively, as he might deem best. " The object of this detachment is to give protection to that part of the country and spirit up the people, to annoy the enemy in that quarter, to collect the provisions and forage out of their way." The second detachment, consisting of the rest of the army, was placed under command of General Huger, and directed to move down the Pedee River to the camp which Kosciusko had selected at the mouth of Hick's Creek, near the Cheraw hills. Greene accompanied the main body.

Greene was probably well aware, from his study of Turenne, of the military maxim against dividing a force and exposing it to the risk of being beaten in detail; but he seems to have felt that in the present instance there were imperative reasons which justified the risk. He knew that Cornwallis designed to march into North Carolina with his main body, leaving intact the garrisons in his numerous posts, and his only chance of delaying Cornwallis's advance while he was collecting his own army was in threatening these posts. By sending Morgan beyond the Broad River he threatened the important post of Ninety-Six, and by advancing down the Pedee with Huger he made a feint against Camden, and even against Charleston. He also placed Huger in support of Marion, who was raiding the country between the Pedee and Santee rivers. As he expressed it, in a letter written on January 24th to his old friend Varnum, now a member of Congress: "I am well satisfied with the movement. . . . It makes the most of my inferior force, for it compels my adversary to divide his, and holds him in doubt as to his own line of conduct. He can not leave Morgan behind him to come at me, or his posts at Ninety-Six and Augusta would be exposed; and he can not chase Morgan far or prosecute his views upon Virginia while I am here with the whole open country before me." While he threatened Charleston, however, he had no intention of really marching in that direction, for he fully explained how necessary it was for him to keep near the head waters of the streams where they could be easily crossed, and where the broken nature of the country would enable his inferior force to make a stand. Lower down, where the rivers were deep and the country open, he would have no chance against Cornwallis's superiority of force. But in order still further to disconcert Cornwallis, he made his feint against the posts on the seacoast as effective as possible, and as soon as Lee arrived with his legion he sent him to re-enforce Marion and try to capture Georgetown by a sudden dash. He even contemplated sending them, after making this attempt, entirely around the rear of Cornwallis to rejoin Morgan on the Broad River. The attempt against Georgetown failed, but the general result of the division of his force was just what Greene had desired. It arrested Cornwallis's march into North Carolina for nearly a month, and caused him to divide his own force. He could not go forward, leaving Morgan on his flank. He therefore detached Tarleton with the legion, the Seventh Regiment, one battalion of the Seventy-first, and two pieces of artillery—in all about eleven hundred men—and directed him to cross the Broad River and "push Morgan to the utmost." These instructions were sent to Tarleton on January 2d, and in the same letter Cornwallis asked Tarleton whether he thought that the moving of the whole or any part of the main body could be of use. At the same time he directed Leslie, instead of taking the direct route up the Congaree to Winnsborough, to follow the Wateree to Camden, so as to be prepared to meet any movements that Greene might make in that direction.

Greene's action in dividing his little force and threatening both of Cornwallis's flanks thus seemed to be fully justified, for it caused Cornwallis to divide his force into three bodies, and left him in great uncertainty how to act. Tarleton, however, promptly suggested a plan of campaign in response to Cornwallis's letter of the 2d. He proposed that he himself should move well to the west and then drive Morgan back on King's Mountain, while Cornwallis advanced with the main body to that point in order to strike Morgan in flank or rear on his anticipated retreat. Cornwallis adopted these suggestions, and on January 5th he wrote Tarleton in reply: "You have exactly done what I wished you to do, and understood my intentions perfectly." Cornwallis himself began his march on the 7th, but he moved very slowly, being still anxious as to what Greene might do against Camden, and waiting for Leslie to join him. In this way eleven days went by without finding Cornwallis farther advanced than Turkey Creek, only thirty miles from Winnsborough and about twenty-five miles south of King's Mountain. In the meantime the battle of the Cowpens had been

TAKES COMMAND OF THE SOUTHERN ARMY. 187

fought, with disastrous results to Tarleton. Cornwallis thus lost his only chance of complete success, which was to crush Morgan with his entire force before Greene could come to his assistance, and then throw himself quickly across the line of Greene's communications with Virginia.

Tarleton received his instructions on January 2d, promptly crossed the lower part of the Broad River, ascertained that Ninety-Six was in no immediate danger, and reported the facts to Cornwallis as we have seen. On receiving his reply approving his plans, he marched against Morgan, and after some manœuvring came up with him on the morning of January 17th. Morgan's force was now increased by the arrival of militia to about nine hundred and fifty men. His only trained troops were two weak battalions of the Maryland line, Washington's cavalry, and some Virginia militia, who had served their term of three years in the Continental line. Three fifths of his force was composed of militia from the two Carolinas and Georgia. He posted this force on the line between North and South Carolina, in the vicinity of one of the inclosures then common in that section of the country where cattle were driven in winter, known as Cowpens. He was in an open piece of woods, with the Broad River at his back, and without any protection on either flank. A better place for the British regulars to attack, and a worse place for ordinary troops to defend, could not be imagined. But Morgan had seen long service with the militia; he thoroughly understood their good and bad points, and he knew what he was about. He afterward justified his selection of the position, and said that he did not want any protection on his flanks, for he knew his adversary well and was satisfied he would have nothing but hard fighting. As for resting his flanks on a swamp : " I would not have had a swamp in the view of my militia on any consideration ; they would have made for it, and nothing could have detained them from it "; and as for a river at his back, it was what he wanted to keep the militia from going away, and make them fight. " Had I crossed the river," said Morgan, " one half of the militia would have abandoned me."

He disposed his force in three lines, about one hundred and forty yards apart: first, a line of skirmishers taken from the militia; next, the militia from the adjoining States ; and last, the Maryland line and the Virginia veterans. Washington's cavalry was posted as a reserve in rear, under cover of a slight eminence. Morgan had gone about among his men the evening before the battle, talking freely with them and telling them what they were expected to do. Then they had a quiet night's sleep, and a good breakfast in the morning. The formation was completed soon after sunrise, and the two lines of militia were instructed to fire two rounds carefully aimed and then retire, but not to run or take fright.

On the previous day Tarleton had learned by his scouts, and a prisoner whom they had taken, that he was in close proximity to Morgan. He therefore called up his troops at three o'clock in the morning and marched rapidly to attack Morgan before he should cross the river. At sunrise he came in sight of Morgan, who was posting his troops in their positions. Tarleton at once deployed his force: the Seventh Regiment, the Legion infantry, and the light infantry in a single line, with the two field pieces in the intervals; a company of dragoons was on each flank, and the rest of his cavalry, two hundred strong, and the battalion of the Seventy-first Regiment, formed the reserve, posted one hundred yards in rear of his left flank. As soon as the deployment was complete, Tarleton ordered his main line to advance on the militia skirmishers, two hundred yards away, and the advance was promptly and impetuously made. The militia waited until they were within fifty yards, fired their two rounds with the most careful and deliberate aim, and then retired around the left flank in accordance with their orders. The British were staggered by this reception, in which they lost heavily in officers; but as the militia retired they again pressed on until they came up with the Maryland line under Colonel Howard. Then a stubborn fight ensued for about thirty minutes, but they could make no progress. Tarleton thereupon brought up his reserve and threw it upon the right flank of the Continental line. But Morgan executed a change of front with the Virginia veterans, refusing his right flank, and this attack was brought to a standstill. Washington's cavalry was then brought up and charged Tarleton's right flank, causing it to retreat, and soon afterward Tarleton's cavalry, on the opposite flank, broke and ran. The panic was soon taken up by his infantry, which lay down its arms and surrendered, and nothing was left of the British but the detachment of Royal Artillery, who stood gallantly by their guns until every man was killed or wounded and the two guns captured.

Morgan's victory was as complete as it was brilliant. With a loss of only eleven killed and sixty-one wounded, he had practically removed Tarleton's force from the list of combatants. Cornwallis's returns of "rank and file, present and fit for duty," in the regiments which fought at the Cowpens, under the respective dates of January 15th and February 1st, are as follows:

	Jan. 15th.	Feb. 1st.
Seventh Regiment	167	....
Seventy-first Regiment, First Battalion	249	....
Sixteenth Regiment, three companies	41	....
Seventy-first Regiment, Light Company	69	....
British Legion	451	174
Total	977	174

The detachment of artillery and a company of militia which were also with Tarleton are not mentioned in the returns. They carried his strength to between ten hundred and fifty and eleven hundred, and of these, all that were "fit for duty" in the returns of the next three months were one hundred and seventy-four men of the Legion. Morgan turned over six hundred prisoners to the Commissary of Prisoners a week later; and this places the killed and wounded who were left on the field at about three hundred. Besides the prisoners, Morgan captured two field guns, eight hundred muskets, the colors of the Seventh and Seventy-first Regiments, thirty-five wagons, one hundred horses, and a large number of tents, which were very acceptable to the Americans, as they had none of their own.

CHAPTER XI.

THE RETREAT TO THE DAN AND THE BATTLE OF GUILFORD COURT HOUSE—1781.

MORGAN'S cool judgment was not disturbed by this victory. He had annihilated the force in front of him, and there was nothing more to be gained by remaining where he was. He knew that Cornwallis was either already on his way, or soon would be, with a greatly superior force, to cut off his retreat. Soon after noon of the day of the battle, therefore, he left the wounded under a flag of truce and began crossing the Broad River on his retreat eastward toward the main body under Greene. He was so much encumbered not only by the prisoners but by the valuable ammunition, muskets, and guns which he had captured, that he did not reach the north branch of the Catawba River until January 23d. He crossed the river on the 24th, and then halted in a secure place until he should ascertain what Cornwallis's intentions were. But Cornwallis was not heard from until the 25th, and then at Ramsour's Mill on the west fork of the Catawba, over twenty miles in his rear. Morgan therefore sent off his prisoners to Virginia by a route near the mountains where they could be easily guarded, and determined to wait until Cornwallis should come up; and in the meantime he hoped to be able to collect some militia.

Cornwallis on the day of the battle (January 17th) was at Turkey Creek, about twenty-five miles southeast of the battle ground. Leslie was moving from Camden to join him, and was a day's march in his rear. In the plan suggested by Tarleton in his letter of January 4th, and fully approved by Cornwallis in his reply of the 5th, it was specified that Cornwallis should move with the main army toward King's Mountain at the same time that he gave the order for Tarleton to advance, so that while Tarleton should attack Morgan in front, Cornwallis with the main force should be in Morgan's rear and intercept the retreat. Cornwallis accordingly moved on the 7th, but so slowly that at the end of eleven days he had only marched thirty miles, and was twenty-five miles away from Morgan. He was moving leisurely so as to give time for Leslie to join him, which, as Tarleton justly observes, formed no part of the original plan, and was, moreover, unnecessary, as Cornwallis's force, even without the addition of Leslie's, largely outnumbered Morgan's. Tarleton's fugitives reached Cornwallis's camp at Turkey Creek on the evening of the 17th, but Cornwallis still waited another day for Leslie to join him. On the 19th he advanced, but instead of moving north through Yorkville to intercept Morgan at the fords of the Catawba, which were as near to him as to Morgan, he moved northwest toward King's Mountain, according to the original plan, and apparently with the idea that Morgan would remain on the Broad River after his victory. When he reached the Little Broad on the 21st, he learned that Morgan had passed it on his retreat three days before. Cornwallis therefore turned east in pursuit of Morgan,

THE RETREAT TO THE DAN.

but still moved so slowly that he was four days in covering the twenty-five miles to Ramsour's Mill on the west fork of the Catawba. He then decided that his army had too much baggage for the rapid movements that would be required of it, and he stopped two days on the banks of the west fork to burn up his own baggage and that of his men, and all his wagons except those which were loaded with hospital stores, salt, and ammunition, and four which were reserved empty for the use of the sick and wounded. On the 28th he cautiously resumed his march, and on the 29th arrived on the west bank of the Catawba opposite Morgan. His conduct during the three weeks of this tardy pursuit was not up to his reputation, and was far different from the energy which he had displayed in his march from New Brunswick to Trenton in the Christmas week of 1776. He lost the chance which was easily within his grasp of crushing Morgan and placing himself across Greene's line of retreat at the very beginning of the campaign.

In the meantime Greene had heard of the victory at the Cowpens by a brief note from Morgan, received at his camp at Cheraw, on the Pedee, on the evening of the 24th. Greene's first idea was that he could utilize this victory to act on the offensive in the western part of South Carolina, and on the 25th he wrote to Marion to ask his opinion on the feasibility of crossing the Santee and making a raid with three hundred or four hundred horsemen around Cornwallis's rear, rejoining him at Ninety-Six. On the 26th he wrote to Lee that he intended to start for Charlotte and consult with Morgan, Davidson, Sumter, and Pickens in regard to assembling all his force and moving against Ninety-Six. But, on further reflection, he seems to have abandoned these ideas and determined to limit his plans to a junction of his main body with Morgan, and resisting, if possible, Cornwallis's advance toward Virginia. He therefore wrote to the governors of North Carolina and Virginia appealing for militia to join him on the Catawba, ordered Huger to break camp immediately and march up the Yadkin toward Salisbury, sent instructions to Colonel Lee to rejoin Huger as soon as possible, and then taking his aid, Major Burnett, a sergeant, and three mounted militiamen, he started on the 28th to ride across the country ninety miles to Charlotte and then join Morgan wherever he should find him on the Catawba. He reached Morgan's camp at Beatty's ford on the 30th, and learned that Cornwallis was only a few miles away, across the river. During the 27th and 28th it had rained very heavily, and the Catawba had risen during the 29th so that the fords were impassable. The water was at its height during the night of the 29th, but on the 30th, when Greene arrived, it had already begun to subside. It was evident that the fords would be passable on the following day, and Morgan's force was insufficient to prevent the passage by Cornwallis. Greene therefore determined at once to send Morgan in retreat toward Salisbury and there join Huger and the main body of Continentals, reserving the militia under Davidson as a rear guard to protect the fords and delay Cornwallis's crossing as long as possible. It is said that Morgan did not approve this plan, but preferred a divergent retreat, his own force going westward over the mountains; and he insisted on this so urgently, that he told

THE RETREAT TO THE DAN.

Greene he would not be answerable for the consequences if his plan was not followed. But Greene quickly asserted his authority by replying: "Neither will you, for I shall take the measure upon myself." And Morgan cheerfully complied with his orders.

The river continuing to fall during the next two days, on the evening of January 31st Cornwallis determined to force a passage. He divided his force into two bodies, sending Lieutenant-Colonel Webster with the Thirty-third Regiment, the second battalion of the Seventy-first, Hamilton's corps of militia, the Yagers, the six-pounders, and all the wagons—about nine hundred men in all—to make a feint at Beatty's ford, where he supposed the main body to be; while with the balance of his force, about fifteen hundred and fifty men, consisting of the Brigade of the Guards, the Twenty-third Regiment, the regiment of Bose, and what was left of Tarleton's Legion, he moved against McGowan's ford, six miles lower down the river, which he supposed to be unguarded. In fact, however, Morgan had been stationed at Beatty's ford, and had left it that morning to march to Salisbury; and McGowan's ford was guarded by the North Carolina militia under Davidson, numbering about five hundred men.

Both detachments marched during the night, and just before dawn Cornwallis arrived at McGowan's ford. It was beginning to rain, and he feared another rise in the river; so the Guards were ordered to lead across the ford, and not to fire until they reached the opposite bank. The river was about five hundred yards wide, the bottom rocky and the current swift. When the Guards were about half way across they were discovered by the militia, who promptly opened fire on them. Lieutenant-Colonel Hall, of the Guards, was killed, and Cornwallis's horse was shot under him and only lived long enough to reach the bank. The Guards pressed on in spite of the fire and without returning it, but the guide became frightened and managed to escape. Instead of following the ford, which inclined down the stream, the column then moved straight across the river; the men got into very deep water, but they reached the bank in safety. The escape of the guide was fortunate for the British and equally unfortunate for the militia. The latter were posted behind rocks and trees at the end of the ford, where they could pick off the British as they approached the shore; but as the British did not follow the ford, they reached the bank some distance above the militia. This made it necessary for the latter to leave their chosen position and form to meet a flank attack from the British. In attempting to do so, Davidson and several of his men were killed, whereupon the rest fled and dispersed. On the British side, in addition to Lieutenant-Colonel Hall, three men had been killed and thirty-six wounded.

During the previous day Morgan had marched from Beatty's ford to Salisbury, and Greene had followed him on February 1st to Mr. David Carr's house, about five miles from Salisbury, which had been appointed as the rendezvous of the militia of the adjoining counties, which Greene had endeavored to call out as soon as he reached Morgan's camp. As soon as Cornwallis established himself on the east bank of the river, he sent Tarleton with the Legion and the Twenty-third Regiment to attack the rear of the American camp at Beatty's ford; but on

THE RETREAT TO THE DAN.

arriving there they found the camp deserted, and Tarleton began scouting toward Salisbury. He soon learned that some of Davidson's men, who had fled from the river, and some of the militia from the county, were to meet during the afternoon at Tarrant's tavern, about ten miles from the Catawba. He rode forward to disperse them, and did so after a short skirmish in which he lost seven men and twenty horses. He then returned to Cornwallis's camp. Had he continued his scouting five miles farther toward Salisbury he would have captured Greene, who was waiting at Carr's house for the militia to assemble. He was attended only by his staff. The militia did not assemble, but about midnight, in the midst of a drenching rain, a few of those who had been dispersed at Tarrant's tavern came to Carr's house and told Greene that Davidson was killed, the militia dispersed, and Cornwallis over the Catawba. It was bad news, and as Greene rode on in the rain toward Salisbury the outlook for his campaign was as dark as the night itself. Two days before, he had written to Lee to make a forced march to join him, and in exuberant spirits had added, " Here is a fine field and great glory ahead." But now, when at the close of this night of February 1st he dismounted at the tavern in Salisbury, and some one expressed surprise at his being alone, he truthfully and sadly answered, " Yes, tired, hungry, alone, and penniless."

On that same morning of February 2d Cornwallis pushed forward in pursuit, and he pushed actively. There was no more of that delay which had characterized him at the time of the battle of the Cowpens. During the chase from the Catawba to the Dan he acted with his old-time vigor and energy. He entered Salisbury on the morning of February 3d, and found it already evacuated, not only by Morgan's troops but by a large portion of its inhabitants, who had packed their household goods on horses or in wagons and preferred to take their chance with Morgan in his retreat rather than remain in their homes during the occupation by the British.

On entering Salisbury, Cornwallis was informed that Morgan was only a few miles ahead of him at the Trading ford on the Yadkin, and that he had not yet crossed. Cornwallis therefore sent forward an advance guard under General O'Hara, consisting of the Guards, the regiment of Bose, and the cavalry. But they did not reach the ford until after dark, and then learned that Morgan had crossed on the previous day and night in boats, and had kept all these boats on the north shore. Owing to heavy rains the river was not fordable, and O'Hara could only sit down on the bank opposite Morgan, with his infantry, and send Tarleton and the cavalry back to report the facts to Cornwallis. Tarleton was then ordered to reconnoiter up the stream and, if possible, find a crossing place. He reported that the upper fords above the forks of the Yadkin were passable and unoccupied. O'Hara was therefore brought back to Salisbury, and on the 7th the entire force moved up to the Shallow fords, crossed there, and continued their march to Salem, where Cornwallis arrived on the 10th. On the previous day Greene's army was united at Guilford, twenty-five miles east of Salem.

Before leaving the Catawba, on the morning of February 1st, Greene had written to Huger, who was marching toward Salisbury, telling him that Cornwallis had just crossed the Catawba and would doubtless press vigorously to Salisbury and soon be there. Huger was therefore directed to push for Salisbury, if he was in condition to make a forced march, and arrive before Cornwallis; otherwise to move north to Guilford, where Morgan would join him; in any event, the baggage and stores were to go to Guilford, and horses were to be impressed in order to hasten the march. On the 2d, Greene wrote Huger from Salisbury, telling him to move direct to Guilford, as there was no chance of his reaching Salisbury before Cornwallis. Greene then went on to the Trading ford with Morgan, crossed with him on the evening of the 2d or morning of the 3d, and saw O'Hara arrive there on the evening of the 3d. The river began falling on the 4th, and it was evident that Cornwallis would soon be able to cross either at the Trading ford or the fords above. Morgan's force was entirely too small to meet him alone, and Greene therefore resumed his march on the night of the 4th, drawing Morgan back about twenty-five miles to the vicinity of Salem and waiting there to see what Cornwallis would do. On the 7th he learned that Cornwallis was marching toward the Shallow ford, and Greene thereupon moved over to Guilford, where Huger and Lee joined him on the 9th. At the same time Morgan was compelled by ill health to leave the army.

Greene's returns at this date show a total force of 2,036, of whom 1,426 were Continentals. Cornwallis's return of February 1st shows 2,440, and March 1st, 2,213 "present and fit for duty." At this date the numbers were probably about 2,300, and nearly the whole force was of British regulars, the best troops in the army, with the two battalions of the Guards at their head.

Greene was anxious to give battle. He feared that the effect of his retreat would discourage the people of the Carolinas and Virginia, and he had no intention of retreating forever before Cornwallis. He had hoped that by the time the two divisions of his army were united he would be joined by twelve hundred or fifteen hundred militia, and, if so, he was determined to fight. But, in spite of his appeals in every direction, not a man had appeared. He therefore felt obliged to submit the question to a council of war, and the members of this promptly and unanimously decided against a battle and in favor of continuing the retreat to Virginia.

Cornwallis, on the other hand, was using every effort to force Greene to battle. He was already one hundred and fifty miles from his base of supplies at Winnsborough and Camden, and every day was increasing the distance. He had destroyed his baggage and wagons, and although he might subsist on the country, he had no means of replenishing his ammunition. He knew that he was superior to Greene in numbers and much more in the quality of his men, and he felt confident that if he could force him to battle he could inflict such a defeat as would dispose of all armed resistance in the Carolinas and open the way unobstructed to Virginia. When he succeeded in getting across the Yadkin, on February 7th, he debated between two plans. If he pushed rapidly between Morgan and Huger he might succeed in beating each in succession before they effected a junction. But, on the other hand, if he got between Greene's two detachments and the Dan

THE RETREAT TO THE DAN.

River, he could cut Greene off from the fords of the upper Dan and force him to the lower part of the river, where it was not fordable. He felt sure that Greene could not collect enough boats to carry his force across the river, and his retreat to Virginia would thus be completely cut off and he would be at Cornwallis's mercy. Cornwallis decided on the second plan, and his decision was based on correct principles. It was a perfectly fair and proper presumption that Greene could not collect the boats. Nevertheless, Greene did collect the boats, and so Cornwallis's plan came to grief.

Having made his decision, Cornwallis moved out from Salem on the 11th, marched nearly due north till he came close to the Dan, and then followed along its southern bank to the eastward.

On the 10th Greene began his march straight for Boyd's Ferry, on the Dan River, eighty miles away. Carrington had joined him the day before, and reported that the boats had all been collected in the vicinity of the ferry, in accordance with Greene's order given six weeks before, when Carrington was appointed quartermaster general. Before starting, Greene sent orders to Sumter to collect his followers in South Carolina and threaten the posts at Ninety-Six and Camden. He also sent Pickens, who had just returned after conducting the prisoners taken at the Cowpens to Virginia, to Charlotte, to raise the militia in that vicinity and hang upon Cornwallis's rear, break up his communications with South Carolina, and pick up any bodies of stragglers. Finally he formed a detachment of seven hundred men, and gave the command of it to his young adjutant general, Colonel Otho H. Williams. It consisted of a body of picked infantry under Lieutenant-Colonel Howard, of Washington's Cavalry, and Lee's Legion. Greene sent this detachment off on his left flank, toward the upper fords of the Dan, with instructions to get in front of Cornwallis, delay his march as much as possible, and keep always between Cornwallis and the main body of Greene's army. Williams performed this duty with marked ability. His rear guard under Lee was in sight of Cornwallis's advance guard under O'Hara all the time during the next four days, and most of the time was skirmishing with it.

Greene made good time with the main body, and covered the eighty miles to Boyd's Ferry in a little over three days. On the morning of the 13th he arrived at the river bank and was ferried over, establishing himself under cover of the partially completed earthworks which Kosciusko had been sent back to build a week before. Williams arrived the next afternoon, and, leaving Lee to hold the rear against O'Hara, ferried his infantry over before dark. Lee skirmished with O'Hara till after nightfall, and then silently withdrew. As he reached the river bank the boats were there to carry over his men, and the horses were forced to swim. Before midnight all were safe on the northern bank. Cornwallis came up the next day and saw Greene's force on the other side of the river. He had no means of crossing, and was forced to encamp on the south side of the Dan River.

Thus ended this memorable retreat of two hundred and thirty miles, made by a half-clad army, over miry roads, in the dead of winter, " several hundreds of the soldiers tracking the ground with their bloody

THE RETREAT TO THE DAN.

feet." It elicited the admiration of friend and foe at that time, and it has since called forth the praise of every student who has examined it. In a burst of generous enthusiasm for his own commander, Harry Lee said: "Happily for these States, a soldier of consummate talents guided the destiny of the South." And Tarleton, in calmer but not less complimentary language, wrote: "Every measure of the Americans, during their march from the Catawba to Virginia, was judiciously designed and vigorously executed." Washington wrote to Greene: "You may be assured that your retreat before Lord Cornwallis is highly applauded by all ranks, and reflects much honor on your military abilities."

Cornwallis had reached the border of Virginia, but there his progress was blocked. He could only retreat to the fords of the upper Dan, and, crossing these and the head waters of the Roanoke, make a long and circuitous march, with Greene on his flank, to join Arnold on the James, or else retire into North Carolina and give up the offensive. Having destroyed all his baggage, the former plan was out of the question, and he chose the latter. By easy marches he returned to Hillsborough, in North Carolina, and there "raised the royal standard" on February 20th, and issued his proclamation inviting the King's "faithful and loyal subjects to repair, without loss of time, with their arms and ten days' provisions, to the royal standard now erected at Hillsborough, where they will meet with the most friendly reception." Pending the acceptance of this invitation, he did what he could to refit his army, which was exhausted by its long and arduous march.

Greene had made a masterly retreat, but to his

mind that was not the whole of generalship. He meant to resume the offensive at the earliest possible moment, and no sooner did Cornwallis withdraw from the Dan than Williams and Lee were sent in pursuit, to hang upon his flanks and rear and keep in close contact with him. Pickens had also collected a few hundred militia about Charlotte, and, marching along the route over which the two armies had just passed, he was already nearly at Guilford. Greene intended to cross the Dan with his main body just as soon as re-enforcements, which were expected from Virginia, should arrive. It has been contended that Greene's retreat was part of a deep-laid plan to draw Cornwallis away from his base, while Greene constantly approached his. There is no evidence of this. The retreat was forced upon Greene by Cornwallis, and Greene accepted it reluctantly. Nevertheless, the result was the same as if it had been Greene's own plan. Every day Cornwallis had been getting farther away from his supplies of clothing and ammunition, and he was now in need of both; and every day Greene had been coming nearer Virginia, from which alone he could hope for re-enforcements, clothing, and arms. All Virginia was now thoroughly alarmed at Cornwallis's approach, and the militia were finally beginning to turn out in force.

During the two months that Steuben had been in Virginia he had done everything in his power to call out the military resources of the State, and Governor Jefferson had spared no effort to assist him. Steuben's main purpose had been to collect men and supplies and forward them to Greene, but he had only been able to send forward one detachment in December, when Arnold landed at the mouth of the James with a force from New York, and advanced toward Richmond. The month of January was consumed in a campaign against Arnold, driving him back to Portsmouth, and during this month not a man could be sent South. Steuben worked at the problem with indefatigable energy, but his irascible temper was sorely tried by the difference between the way in which military affairs were conducted in Virginia and in Prussia. Jefferson issued his orders calling out the militia in every county, and making requisitions to fill the Continental quota; but he declined to take any steps for procuring clothing, arms, or equipment, claiming that this was the duty of the Continental authorities. As Congress had no power to enforce its requisitions, and neither Congress nor Virginia had any ready money, when the men arrived at the rendezvous nothing could be done to organize or equip them. Interest in the war had died out, and advantage was taken of every defect in the militia law to escape service. Boys and dwarfs were sent to fill requisitions, and if the militia had been called out once during the year they refused to assemble a second time; if the militia was in service the counties refused to fill the Continental quota. No longer service than eighteen months was talked of, and in most cases this was reduced to two. Large bounties in paper money were promised, but as the currency was depreciated to 140 for 1, the actual amount was small, and only a portion of this was paid, whereupon the recruits deserted.

By reason of these various obstacles Steuben was unable to send Greene more than four hundred men, who left Chesterfield Court House under command of Colonel Campbell on February 25th; but the approach of Cornwallis had so alarmed the border counties of Virginia that the militia from these counties turned out in considerable force. Jefferson had sent an aid-de-camp to Greene's headquarters to learn the exact situation, and this officer reported on March 2d that seven hundred men under General Stevens and four hundred from Botetourt had already arrived; Colonel Campbell was daily expected with four hundred, and Colonel Lynch with three hundred from Bedford. In all, this made eighteen hundred from Virginia. A small number of recruits were on their way for the Maryland line, and Pickens's force was being daily increased by fresh accessions of North Carolina militia.

On the other hand, the loyalists of North Carolina at first began to rally around the King's standard at Hillsborough, but the misfortune which overtook the largest of these bodies, under Colonel Pyle (as will presently be narrated), put an effectual damper on the loyalist ardor, and the King's supporters returned to their homes instead of joining his army. Cornwallis was bitterly disappointed at this desertion, and characterized the loyalists as "dastardly and pusillanimous."

Cornwallis, as we have seen, remained only a day on the banks of the Dan. He arrived on the afternoon of February 15th and left early on the 17th, arriving at Hillsborough on the 20th. Greene followed him closely. On the 17th he issued orders for Pickens and Lee to cross the Dan, get in front of Cornwallis, keep watch of his movements, and prevent any body of loyalists from joining him. Pickens and Lee crossed the river on the morning

THE RETREAT TO THE DAN. 207

of the 18th, and marched about twenty-five miles on the road to Guilford. During the night Greene made a hurried visit to their camp to explain still further his instructions, and to notify them that he would cross the Dan with the main body just as soon as the expected re-enforcements from Virginia arrived. The next day Pickens and Lee continued their march to the southward, leaving the Guilford road and moving through the broken country so as to strike the highroad from Hillsborough to Salisbury, along which, as they learned from their reconnoitering parties, Tarleton was advancing to meet a party of Tories and escort them back to Hillsborough. After several days of cautious manœuvring, on February 25th Pickens and Lee came up with this party, which proved to be a body of four hundred loyalists under Colonel Pyle. They were moving through a lane in a southerly direction in the hope of meeting Tarleton on the road from Hillsborough to Salisbury. Tarleton was on this road a few miles south of them, and was just going into camp for the night. Pickens and Lee had formed their detachment for the purpose of attacking Tarleton, but as they advanced they learned from two prisoners that Colonel Pyle was between them and Tarleton. Lee instantly formed the plan of capturing this detachment bodily. The uniform of his men closely resembled that of Tarleton's Legion. He therefore compelled the two prisoners, under pain of instant death, to act as if his legion was a re-enforcement moving to Tarleton's assistance, and with the two prisoners at the head of the column he moved along the lane toward Pyle. Presently two well-mounted young countrymen were met and cordially received by Lee, who assumed his part so well that they were completely deceived, and rode back to Pyle with a request that he form his men on the right of the road so as to allow this reenforcement, tired with their march, to pass. Pyle did so, and Lee with his legion passed along their entire front. Lee had just shaken hands with Pyle, who was on the right of his line, and was about to explain his true character and demand his surrender, when some of Pyle's men on the extreme left saw Pickens's men in rear of the Legion, and, recognizing their uniform as that of Americans, opened fire on them. The stratagem being thus exposed, there was nothing for the Legion to do but return their fire; they faced to the right and did so at arms' length. The result was that ninety of Pyle's force were killed outright, nearly all the rest, including Pyle himself, were wounded, and those who were able to run instantly dispersed. Lee did not lose a man. Cornwallis, having heard on the previous day that Greene had crossed the Dan, sent three messengers in succession to Tarleton with orders to return to Hillsborough at once. Pickens and Lee were at first disposed to attack Tarleton that same afternoon, but, on account of the long march and fatigue of the men, they decided to postpone it until morning. Tarleton on his side was equally determined to attack Lee in the morning; but during the night the three couriers arrived from Cornwallis, and he had no option but to retreat. He did so promptly, and by morning had passed Lee and was at the fords on the Haw River. Pickens and Lee followed them, but as they anticipated that Cornwallis had sent a re-enforcement to Tarleton, it was deemed imprudent to attack him, and Tarleton effected his retreat without molestation.

Meanwhile Greene, having received a portion of the re-enforcements expected from Virginia, had recrossed the Dan on February 23d, and was marching up the same road to Guilford, over which he had retreated two weeks before. On the 28th he crossed the head waters of the Haw at High Rock ford, about fifteen miles from Guilford; and on the following day he moved forward a few miles in the country between Troublesome and Reedy Forks, two branches of the Haw.

Cornwallis had given the loyalists ten days from February 20th to assemble at Hillsborough, but none came, and the country in that vicinity was destitute of provisions. On February 26th, the day after Pyle's detachment was cut to pieces, he broke up his camp at Hillsborough, marched on the road to Salisbury until he had crossed the Haw, and then turned to the right and went into camp on the banks of Allemance Creek, on February 28th. Two days later he sent Tarleton with the cavalry of his Legion and about two hundred and fifty infantry to reconnoiter in the direction of Greene's army; on the previous day Greene had sent out a similar force for the purpose of reconnoitering Cornwallis's position. It was under command of Colonel Williams, and consisted of Pickens's militia, Lee's Legion, and a body of mountaineers under Colonel Preston, who had joined Lee the evening after Pyle's defeat. The two bodies met on the afternoon of March 2d, about three miles from Cornwallis's camp, and a sharp skirmish resulted, after which Williams retreated toward the main body.

The two armies were thus in contact. Cornwallis was anxious to bring Greene to battle at once. Greene was equally anxious to fight, but not till his militia had all arrived. In following Cornwallis so closely when the latter retired from the Dan, and before his own re-enforcements had arrived, Greene took great risk. But he had a most important object in view, in which he was entirely successful—viz., to prevent the uprising of the royalists in support of Cornwallis; and as Lee well says, he assumed the risk, "depending on the resources of his fertile mind and the tried skill and courage of his faithful though inferior army." It was now imperative, however, that Cornwallis should not force him to battle until the militia had arrived. For the next ten days both sides sparred for position, Cornwallis trying to bring on an engagement and Greene determined to avoid one. Every night Greene changed his position, and every day his troops were in motion, until Cornwallis was equally bewildered as to his position and his strength, and came finally to believe that he had between nine thousand and ten thousand men. The gallant Earl, however, was nothing daunted, though he had but two thousand men; he knew their good quality, and was determined to force a battle at the earliest moment. His camp on the Allemance Creek was well chosen, for it was at the meeting point of roads leading to Salisbury, Guilford, High Rock ford, and Hillsborough. He could strike in any one of these directions if the favorable opportunity offered. On the 6th he learned that the Virginia reenforcements, which should have followed the direct road from Boyd's Ferry to Guilford, had turned off to Hillsborough. They had heard that Cornwallis had left Hillsborough and was moving down toward

THE RETREAT TO THE DAN. 211

the Cape Fear River. Presuming that Greene would be following him, they marched toward Hillsborough instead of continuing on the road to Guilford. Greene heard of it and sent them instructions to march west from Hillsborough. But Cornwallis heard of it too, and he determined to strike a blow before they arrived, and in a direction which would prevent their junction. On the 6th of March, therefore, in a heavy fog, he crossed Allemance Creek and moved rapidly toward High Rock ford. Williams with his detachment of light troops was a few miles in front of him and to his left, and Greene was in rear of Williams at Boyd's Mills on the Reedy Fork. Tarleton and his Legion, and Webster with his brigade (Twenty-third, Thirty-third, and Seventy-first Regiments), were in the lead of Cornwallis's army, and their road led to a crossing of Reedy Fork at Wetzell's Mill, and thence to the High Rock ford on the Haw. If Cornwallis could gain and hold this point, the Virginia re-enforcements would be completely cut off before they could join Greene. Webster and Tarleton on one road, and Williams with Pickens and Lee on the other, thus raced for the crossing at Wetzell's Mill. Greene with the main body moved back to the fords on the Haw some miles above High Rock ford, and then marched down the north bank to that point. He thus avoided the risk of being cut off by Cornwallis before he could cross the river.

Williams reached the river first, got his men safely across, and retreated about five miles to a place he had picked out for a camp for the night. Webster was close behind him at the mill, and there was skirmishing there and on the north side of the creek between Tarleton and Lee all the afternoon. But the losses were slight, and Cornwallis's main body was not near enough to make a vigorous assault upon Williams. Just as Williams was going into camp at dusk, Major Burnett, Greene's aid-de-camp, rode up with instructions to cross the Haw. Williams did so, and the next morning joined Greene just above the High Rock ford.

This move of Cornwallis's was a brilliant one, and if it had been as vigorously executed as it was skillfully conceived, it is hard to see how Greene could have escaped. If Cornwallis had had his entire force in hand, he must have crushed Williams and reached and crossed High Rock ford before Greene could get there; he would then have cut off the re-enforcements coming from Virginia *via* Hillsborough; and Greene, with one third of his best troops gone, would have been forced to retreat to Virginia with all haste. But Greene was quicker than Cornwallis; Williams and Lee made a skillful defense, and Greene reunited his whole force on the north of the Haw before Cornwallis got there. The latter knew it would be useless to attempt to force a passage in the face of Greene, and he did not attempt it. Thus, for the fourth time—first at the Catawba, then at the Yadkin, then at the Dan, and now at the Haw—Greene, by his literally sleepless energy and the celerity of his movements, put a river between himself and his foe, and saved his little army from destruction. Cornwallis saw that he had been outmanœuvred, and on the following day retreated about twenty miles to Deep River, partly, as he says, to attempt to raise the loyalists, and partly to approach the Cape Fear River with a view to opening up communications with the coast. Tarleton blames Cornwallis for not continuing the movement and vigorously attacking Greene after Williams had joined him. He claims that if this had been done it "would probably have averted many of the subsequent calamities." But the criticism is not warranted. Cornwallis had lost in this particular manœuvre, and was now in an unfavorable position for attack; he was quite right in retreating a few miles and manœuvring for a more favorable position.

Three days later (March 10th) the long-expected re-enforcements joined Greene at the Iron Works on the Haw, just above High Rock ford. He spent two days in organizing and arranging them, and then moved forward to Guilford to fight. His army now numbered more than at any other time during the Southern campaign—forty-four hundred and forty-four men in all, organized as follows:

Virginia Brigade, Brigadier General Huger, two regiments.....................................	778	
Maryland Brigade and one company of Delaware Battalion, Colonel Williams, two regiments......	630	
Washington's Cavalry, two companies.............	86	
Lee's Legion, one battalion of infantry, one company of cavalry....................................	157	
Total regulars...........................		1,651
First Brigade, Virginia militia, General Stevens..		
Second Brigade, Virginia militia, General Lawson	1,693	
Two rifle regiments, Virginia militia, Colonels Lynch and Campbell......................		
First Brigade, North Carolina militia, General Butler...............................		
Second Brigade, North Carolina militia, General Eaton................................	1,060	
One company of cavalry, Major Bretagne..........	40	
Total militia............................		2,793
Aggregate.............................		4,444

The artillery consisted of two detachments of two guns each, commanded by Lieutenants Singleton and Furey, and numbering sixty gunners—or, as they were then called, matrosses. They were attached to the Maryland and Virginia brigades, and are included in the numbers given above.

There was much difference in the quality of these troops. The Maryland brigade had fought with great gallantry at Long Island, Trenton, Brandywine, Germantown, Camden, and Cowpens. The First Regiment still contained a large number of veterans, but the Second had been cut to pieces at Camden and was now almost wholly composed of recruits. The Virginia brigade had served under Greene's own command in the Pennsylvania battles, but the old men had nearly all been discharged at the expiration of three years' service, and this brigade also was now principally made up of recruits. In the Virginia militia, Stevens's brigade was partly composed of men who had served their time in the Continental line and partly of substitutes and drafted men; Lawson's Brigade was made up of fresh levies without discipline or experience, and both the North Carolina brigades were of the same character. Washington's Cavalry and Lee's Legion were picked veterans, as fine troops as ever fought, and commanded by officers of unsurpassed merit. Greene's opinions concerning the relative value of regulars and militia were to have in this memorable battle a sad but complete vindication. Had his force, or even half of it, been composed of troops like the First Maryland or Lee's Legion, he would have destroyed Cornwallis's army and terminated the Southern campaign at one blow.

Cornwallis reported to Clinton, under date of

April 10th, that his force at Guilford numbered thirteen hundred and sixty infantry and about two hundred cavalry. But Clinton asked how it was possible that his strength was reduced to such a small figure, and Cornwallis's own returns disprove it. His force was probably in excess of twenty-five hundred, and the exact numbers of "rank and file, *present and fit for duty*," are given in his return of March 1st as follows:

Brigade of Guards, First and Second Battalions, and Grenadiers, Brigadier General O'Hara....................	605
General Leslie's Brigade:	
Seventy-first Foot (Fraser's Highlanders).............	212
Regiment of Bose, Major Du Buy...................	313
Lieutenant Colonel Webster's Brigade:	
Twenty-third Foot...............................	258
Thirty-third Foot................................	322
British Legion, Lieutenant Colonel Tarleton.............	174
Battalion of Yagers.....................................	97
Hamilton's North Carolina Regiment and other provincials.	232
Total...	2,213

There was, in addition, a detachment of the Royal Artillery, under Lieutenant McLeod, numbering about one hundred men, with four guns.

The quality of these troops was of the very best. Most of them had been in America since 1776, and had fought at all the battles around New York and Philadelphia, at Charleston and at Camden. In this campaign Cornwallis proudly says of them: "Their persevering intrepidity in action, their invincible patience in the hardships and fatigues of a march of above six hundred miles, in which they have forded several large rivers and numberless creeks, many of which would be numbered large rivers in any other country in the world, without tents or covering against the climate, and often without provisions, will sufficiently manifest their ardent zeal for the honor and interests of their sovereign and their country."

On the 12th of March Greene put his army in motion from High Rock ford, and on the 14th reached Guilford. On the same day Cornwallis sent his baggage down the Deep River, under escort of Hamilton's North Carolina Regiment, and marched toward Guilford. Both were anxious for battle, and, as Greene said in his letter to Washington, "when both parties are agreed in a matter all obstacles are soon removed." On the morning of the 15th, Lee and Tarleton, who were reconnoitering in front of their respective armies, came together on the Salisbury road, about four miles south of Guilford, and there was a sharp skirmish, in which Tarleton was wounded in the hand. Greene immediately sent his baggage back to the Iron Works on the Haw, which was designated as the rallying place in case of defeat, and began posting his men. His position was along the Salisbury road, just south of the courthouse at Guilford. Both Tarleton and Lee, as well as subsequent historians, unite in saying that the position was admirably chosen and the troops judiciously posted.

Guilford Court House was situated on a hill from which the ground sloped gradually for half a mile to the southward, ending in a small rivulet. The surrounding country was mostly a wilderness, with cleared fields here and there. Around the courthouse was such a clearing of old fields about three hundred yards in extent. In the middle of this a branch road from Reedy Fork united with the highroad to Salisbury. This latter wound down the gentle slope through tall woods with dense underbrush; and at a distance of about half a mile, just before reaching the brook, there were fields on either side of the road about two hundred yards in extent, which had been planted the previous summer in corn. Beyond the field, on the east of the road, was a strip of woods, and then another field about one hundred yards in extent.

Greene placed his army in three lines. In the first were the two brigades of North Carolina militia, under Generals Butler and Eaton. They were posted on both sides of the road, in the edge of the wood, behind a fence which surrounded the fields. On their right flank were the Delaware battalion, under Kirkwood, and Lynch's Virginia Riflemen, and on the left the infantry of Lee's Legion and Campbell's Riflemen. The second line was composed of the Virginia militia, under Generals Stevens and Lawson; they were posted about three hundred yards in rear of the first line, in the woods on either side of the road. The Continental regiments, the best troops, were naturally posted in the third line, or reserve, about four hundred yards in rear of the second. They were on the edge of the hill, in the clearing just south of the courthouse—the Virginia Brigade on the right and the Maryland on the left. Between the two were two guns, under Lieutenant Furey; the other two guns were in the center of the first line. Washington's Cavalry was in rear of the right flank, and Lee's in rear of the left.

After crossing the brook, Cornwallis deployed in the following order: General Leslie on the right, with the regiment of Bose and the Seventy-first Highlanders; Lieutenant-Colonel Webster, with the

Twenty-third and Thirty-third Regiments in the center, on either side of the road; the Yagers and Light Infantry of the Guard on the left. The Guards were in reserve close behind the main line—the first battalion in rear of Leslie, the second in rear of the Twenty-third Regiment, and the Grenadiers in rear of the Thirty-third. The artillery was in the road, between the Twenty-third and Thirty-third, and Tarleton's Cavalry was in rear of the whole line.

The battle opened at half past one o'clock in the afternoon by a cannonade from the British guns, which lasted twenty minutes. Then the infantry advanced. The position of the North Carolina militia was so advantageous—in the edge of a wood behind a fence, and with open fields in front, the flanks protected by riflemen so posted as to enfilade the British line as it advanced—that it was anticipated that very serious and possibly successful resistance could be made to the British advance at this point. But, to the dismay of the Americans, when the militia saw the redcoats advance in a steady line across the field, then discharge their pieces and start to charge with a loud yell, they threw away their guns and scattered in every direction through the woods without firing a shot. The riflemen on either flank stood their ground, and this caused Leslie to gain ground to the right and Webster to the left; the three battalions of guards were brought up to fill the gaps in the line— the First Battalion between the regiment of Bose and the Seventy-first, and the Second Battalion and Grenadiers between the Twenty-third and Thirty-third. The riflemen on each flank held their own so well that it became necessary for Leslie to order the regiment of Bose to change front in order

THE RETREAT TO THE DAN.

to meet Lee's infantry; and Webster did the same on the left, with the Thirty-third Regiment to oppose Lynch and Kirkwood. The main body then pushed forward to attack the Virginia militia. These made an excellent defense, and held the British in check for some time; every man of the latter was brought into action, and Tarleton says that "at this period the event of the action was doubtful, and victory alternately presided over each army." Gradually, however, Webster with the Thirty-third began to push back Lynch and Kirkwood's Riflemen, and O'Hara, with the Second Battalion of the Guards and the Seventy-first, caused Lawson to give way; Stevens was badly wounded and had to be carried off the field, which had a demoralizing effect upon the Virginians. But the infantry of the Legion and Campbell's Riflemen, on the American left, would not yield a foot to the Hessians and the First Battalion of the Guards. Thus the success of the British on their left and center caused them to execute a rightwheel in advancing, O'Hara passing across the Salisbury road and Webster coming into it. The road being thus opened, McLeod brought up two three-pounders and put them in position on a slight eminence at the southern side of the open ground, about two hundred and fifty yards from the courthouse, where, half an hour later, they did great service, and saved the British army from defeat. As the British continued to advance, gradually wheeling to the right, the Virginia militia finally gave way and retreated in fairly good order—part of them through the woods to the northeast and part through the open ground, passing around the left flank of the Continentals to the courthouse. The riflemen under

Lynch and Kirkwood, and the cavalry under Washington, fell back straight to the position of the Continentals, and passed through the gap between the Virginia and Maryland regiments. Webster followed up this advantage closely with the Thirty-third, but when he came in front of the Continental line the First Maryland received him with such a deadly fire that his men fell back somewhat precipitately to his left and rear across a ravine, where they rallied—Webster himself, a most gallant and able officer, being killed.

The Virginia militia having been driven off into the woods on the right, there was nothing left between O'Hara and the Continental troops in front of the courthouse. He therefore sent the Second Battalion of the Guards, commanded by the Honorable Lieutenant-Colonel Stewart, closely followed by the Grenadiers and the Seventy-first, along the Salisbury road against this position. Their advance led them against the Second Maryland, and Williams, who commanded the Maryland Brigade, hastened to this regiment expecting to give the Guards as warm a reception as the First Maryland had given to the Thirty-third. But the Second Regiment was made up of new recruits, and was a far different body from that First Maryland which had done such splendid service in nearly every important battle of the last five years. To the intense mortification of Williams, the Second Regiment broke and ran. Stewart pressed on and carried the position, capturing the two guns which Singleton had originally placed in the line of the North Carolina militia, and after their flight had brought back and planted on the flank of the Second Maryland. Stewart's advantage, however, was of short duration. Williams rushed back to the First Maryland, wheeled them to the left, and struck Stewart full in the flank. His men retreated hastily, carrying back with them the Grenadiers and Seventy-first Regiment, who were hastening to their assistance, and losing the two pieces which they had captured. Washington's Cavalry was now brought forward in a fine charge, which still further accelerated the retreat of the British.

The battle was now at its most critical stage. Greene and Cornwallis were both personally in the thick of it, and each in quick succession narrowly escaped capture. O'Hara was dangerously wounded, and Stewart was instantly killed in a hand-to-hand encounter with Captain Smith, of the First Maryland. Had Greene thrown forward the two Virginia regiments, both of which were still fresh and unengaged, he might possibly have completed the rout of Cornwallis's army. But he had seen not only the North Carolina militia run at the first fire and the Virginia militia driven off after a stubborn contest, but also the Second Maryland leave the field without any serious resistance. The two Virginia regiments were Continentals, but they were both composed entirely of recruits. If they failed him as the Second Maryland had done, his army was annihilated. He was not willing to take the risk of total destruction, and, instead of sending the two Virginia regiments after the retreating Guards, he placed the better of them, the First Virginia, under Colonel Greene, in reserve in rear of the position which the Maryland Brigade had formerly occupied. Cornwallis, on his side, seeing the retreat of the Guards, concluded that if it could not be stopped the day was lost. He therefore rode rapidly to the little hill where McLeod had posted his two three-pounders, and ordered him immediately to open fire with grape. O'Hara, dismounted and badly wounded, remonstrated against the order, because the First Maryland was so close upon the Guards in their retreat that the fire would do as much damage to his own men as to the enemy. But Cornwallis peremptorily insisted on the execution of the order. Though a number of his men were killed and wounded by it, yet it had the desired effect. The assault of the First Maryland and Washington's Cavalry was arrested, and they soon returned to their original position in front of the courthouse.

There was now a short lull in the fight. While the contest had been going on in front, the struggle, now far in the rear, between the Hessians and the First Battalion of the Guards on one side, and the infantry of Lee's Legion and Campbell's Virginia Riflemen on the other, had still been going on, and the latter were in the same position as at the beginning. But Lee finally saw that he was completely separated from the rest of the army, and therefore withdrew though the woods, making a circuit with the intention of joining the left flank of the Continentals near the courthouse. This left the Hessians and the First Battalion of the Guards with no enemy in their front, and they moved by the left to rejoin the rest of the British force. Cornwallis then reformed his line on the edge of the clearing south of the courthouse, and prepared for a final assault.

Greene had nothing that he could depend on except the First Maryland, two hundred and eighty-five strong, and Washington's cavalry, eighty-six in number. Lee and Campbell had not yet come up from the left, and, in fact, did not join him until the next day. The militia were all broken, as well as the Second Maryland, and the two Virginia regiments were composed of recruits who had never been under fire. Cornwallis had still fifteen hundred trained, well-disciplined soldiers; they had been roughly handled, but they were full of determination, and were now being reformed under his eyes for a final effort. Greene had the alternative of receiving their assault—which, if unsuccessful, would give him the victory, and if successful, would completely destroy his army and lose the Southern States forever—or of retreating while retreat was still possible. He chose the latter, and at half past three, after two hours of as hard fighting as the Revolution saw, he withdrew his army in good order, Colonel Greene with the First Virginia covering the retreat. The artillery horses had all been killed, and his four guns and two ammunition wagons had to be left on the field. He moved out to the west by the Reedy Fork road, and after a march of three miles he reached that stream and halted to reform his men. Cornwallis attempted a feeble pursuit with the Twenty-third and Seventy-first Regiments, but it was quickly abandoned.

The day had been cloudless, with a sharp, frosty air. As night fell, a cold drizzle set in, and later this turned into a pouring rain. Through this and the deep mud of the clay road Greene's army pursued its retreat, crossing the Haw at the Iron Works just before daybreak. Here the troops were posted in a defensive position before they lay down to sleep, and were ready to receive Cornwallis in case he continued the attack. But Cornwallis was in no condition for further offensive movements. He had fought his last battle in the Carolinas.

The British loss was about one fourth of their total strength—ninety-three killed, four hundred and thirteen wounded, and twenty-six missing; total, five hundred and thirty-two. The loss in officers was appalling—Webster, Stewart, and nine others killed; O'Hara, Tarleton, and seventeen more wounded. On the American side the losses were seventy-eight killed, one hundred and eighty-three wounded, and ten hundred and forty-six missing; total, thirteen hundred and seven. The missing were nearly all in the militia, which had broken at the beginning of the engagement. Major Anderson, of the First Maryland, was killed; General Huger slightly and General Stevens severely wounded.

Stedman, the British historian, compares this battle of Guilford with Crecy, Poictiers, and Agincourt, the most glorious feats of British arms; and he is fully justified. The British general had attacked a force of double his strength, advantageously posted in a strong position of the enemy's choosing; and he had won the day after as hard fighting and as heavy losses, in proportion to his strength, as in any battle which the English had until then fought. It was a splendid victory for the British soldier. As Lee says, "On no occasion, in any part of the world, was British valor more heroically displayed."

On the other hand, Greene, although apparently superior in force, had only three hundred and seventy-one veterans in his command—viz., the First Maryland, Lee's Legion, and Washington's Cavalry. Opposed to him was the flower of the British army, over two thousand strong, well disciplined, and all veterans of nearly five years' incessant fighting in America. The rest of Greene's force was militia or recruits now for the first time under fire. Part of these ran at the first shot, but another part made a stout resistance against the British Guards. As for the few veterans that Greene had, their conduct even excelled that of the British. Greene chose his position skillfully, posted his men to the best possible advantage, and handled them well during the course of the fight. He had two opportunities—one just after the charge of the First Maryland, and the other when Cornwallis prepared for a final assault, when, by a vigorous charge, he might perhaps have put Cornwallis to rout. But had he failed—and the chances were in favor of failure—his army would have been destroyed. He had previously expressed his firm determination never to put his army in a position where its total destruction was possible; and, though the temptation was great, he rigidly adhered to his decision. As for the final result, all the advantages were on Greene's side. He lost the battle but gained the campaign. He retreated a few miles and took up another defensive position, ready to accept battle again if Cornwallis offered it. But three days later Cornwallis began a precipitate and long retreat to the seaboard.

The news of this little battle, fought in the backwoods of America with a few thousand men on each side, created a sensation in England. Fox declared that "another such victory will ruin the British army. . . . In the disproportion between the two armies, a victory was highly to the honor of our troops; but had our army been vanquished, what course could they have taken? Certainly they would have abandoned the field of action, and flown for refuge to the seaside—precisely the measures the victorious army was obliged to adopt." He moved that measures be taken immediately for concluding a peace. Pitt supported the motion, and affirmed that it was "a most accursed war, barbarous, cruel, and unnatural," full of "ineffective victories and severe defeats." Fox added that "we can lose nothing by a vote declaring America independent," for "America is lost, irretrievably lost, to this country."

As for Greene himself, he was so worn out that he did not realize how well he had done. In his letters to Washington and Congress he claimed but little for himself; he simply recited the facts, regretted that he had lost the day, and expressed his unabated determination to continue the struggle, and his "hope, by little and little, to reduce him [Cornwallis] in time." In truth, he had nearly reached the limit of physical endurance. For six weeks, since he left his camp on the Pedee to join Morgan on the Catawba, he had not taken off his clothes. During the four days' retreat from Guilford to the Dan he had not slept over four hours, and in the ten days' manœuvring prior to the battle of the 15th he had hardly done better. While making the rounds one night during this time he found the colonel in command of a large outpost asleep, and asked him how he could sleep when he was in contact with the enemy, and might be attacked at any time. The ready answer was, "Why, General, we all knew you would be awake." But now the nervous strain and loss of sleep began to tell upon him,

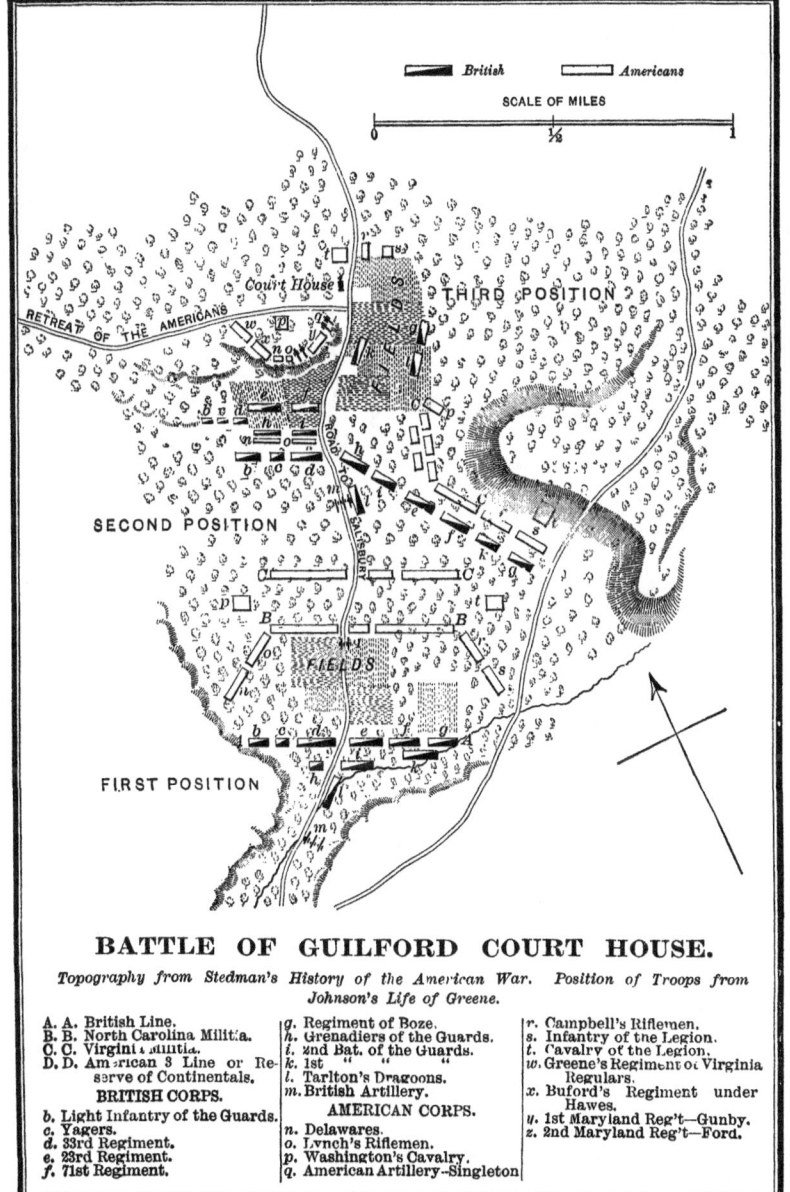

BATTLE OF GUILFORD COURT HOUSE.

Topography from Stedman's History of the American War. Position of Troops from Johnson's Life of Greene.

A. A. British Line.
B. B. North Carolina Militia.
C. C. Virginia militia.
D. D. American 3 Line or Reserve of Continentals.

BRITISH CORPS.

b. Light Infantry of the Guards.
c. Yagers.
d. 33rd Regiment.
e. 23rd Regiment.
f. 71st Regiment.
g. Regiment of Boze.
h. Grenadiers of the Guards.
i. 2nd Bat. of the Guards.
k. 1st "   "   "
l. Tarlton's Dragoons.
m. British Artillery.

AMERICAN CORPS.

n. Delawares.
o. Lynch's Riflemen.
p. Washington's Cavalry.
q. American Artillery–Singleton
r. Campbell's Riflemen.
s. Infantry of the Legion.
t. Cavalry of the Legion.
w. Greene's Regiment of Virginia Regulars.
x. Buford's Regiment under Hawes.
y. 1st Maryland Reg't—Gunby.
z. 2nd Maryland Reg't—Ford.

and the day after Guilford he fell over in a fainting fit of dizziness; and this was repeated on the following days, so that he was compelled to take some rest; this, with his robust constitution, quickly restored him to health.

CHAPTER XII.

THE BATTLE OF HOBKIRK'S HILL AND THE SIEGE OF NINETY-SIX—1781.

ON the 18th of March Cornwallis issued a proclamation boasting of "the compleat victory obtained over the Rebel forces on the 15th inst.," offering a pardon to all the rebels who would surrender themselves with their arms and ammunition, and promising them protection in their persons and properties. This proceeding subjected him to considerable ridicule, for on the same day he abandoned his wounded in hospital and began a rapid retreat.

In truth, Cornwallis had spent his force at Guilford. He was too weak to think of renewing the battle, and his army was so much in need of supplies of all kinds that he could not remain where he was. Retreat was inevitable, and his only alternative was between going back to South Carolina or turning toward the seacoast. At the outset of the campaign he had given orders for supplies to be sent to Wilmington, and he had recently given instructions to have these sent up the Cape Fear River to Cross Creek, or Fayetteville. His nearest post in South Carolina was at Camden, and the distance was about the same as to Wilmington—one hundred and forty miles; but the distance to Cross Creek was only

THE BATTLE OF HOBKIRK'S HILL. 229

about half as much, and he hoped (though he had no positive information) that his supplies had been sent up to that point. The idea of going back to South Carolina was intolerable to him; it would be to acknowledge the complete failure of the campaign. If he went to the seacoast perhaps Greene would follow him; at all events, he would save appearances, and, after refitting his army, he could resume the offensive. He therefore decided to march to Cross Creek, and he put his army in motion on the afternoon of the 18th. Greene started in pursuit the following day, sending the indefatigable Lee again in advance with his Legion and Campbell's Virginia Riflemen, and telling Lee: "I mean to fight the enemy again, and wish you to have your Legion and Riflemen ready for action on the shortest notice. If in the meantime you can attempt anything which promises an advantage, put it in execution. Lord Cornwallis must be soundly beaten before he will relinquish his hold." Greene could not move as rapidly as he wished, for there were " provisions to draw, cartridges to make, and several other matters to attend to, which will oblige us to halt a little earlier than common" at the end of each day's march. Moreover, Cornwallis had a full day's start of him and was losing no time. Greene did not, therefore, come up with Cornwallis until the 28th, when he reached the Cape Fear River at Ramsay's Mills, a few hours after Cornwallis had crossed on a temporary bridge of his own construction. Lee was so close on Cornwallis's heels that the latter was unable to destroy the bridge. But Greene did not cross, for he had other plans. Cornwallis then hurried along unmolested, reaching Cross Creek a few days later. Here he found no provisions or signs of his orders having been received, and he was obliged to continue his march to Wilmington, arriving there on April 7th.

Greene decided not to pursue Cornwallis any further. During the retreat to the Dan, Cornwallis had had the benefit of the initiative, but since then Greene had possessed this advantage and had kept the control of the campaign in his own hand—pursuing Cornwallis only so far as he thought best, fighting only on ground of his own choice and at his own time. He did not purpose to give up this control by following Cornwallis off to one side of the theatre of campaign. He stopped pursuit at Ramsay's Mills, and determined to carry the war into South Carolina. On the following day (March 29th) he wrote to Washington explaining his reasons for this course. He was " remote from re-enforcements, inferior to the enemy in numbers," and had "no prospect of support." By going to South Carolina he would force Cornwallis to follow him, and thus give up the contest in North Carolina, or else lose his posts in South Carolina. He considered the movement warranted by the soundest reasons, both political and military; and while it would be critical and dangerous, and subject the troops to every hardship, yet, as he shared this with them, he hoped they would "bear up under it with that magnanimity which has already supported them, and for which they deserve everything of their country." He wrote to Sumter to the same effect on March 30th, and to Steuben and Lafayette on April 2d.

There is no doubt that his resolution was as sound as it was bold, and it resulted in the brilliant success which it deserved.* Having made his decision, Greene at once undertook the necessary preparations to carry it into effect. First of all, he had to send off all the Virginia militia. These men had enlisted for six weeks, and they claimed that their time should count from the day of enlistment at their homes to the date of discharge, also at their homes. They insisted, during his march to Ramsay's Mills, on being sent back at once, so as to reach Virginia before their time was up. Greene had managed to hold them, as he hoped every day to overtake Cornwallis and bring him to battle, but when he gave up the pursuit this was no longer possible. He therefore sent them off on April 2d. They had joined him on March 10th, and were present with the army only twenty-three days. The North Carolina militia had fled at the battle of Guilford, and only a small part of them had since returned. Greene's army was thus reduced to the four Continental regiments, two of Virginia and two of Maryland, Lee's Legion, Washington's Cavalry, and Campbell's Riflemen, numbering in all fourteen hundred and fifty men. With these he intended to move as rapidly and secretly as possible on Camden, which was at the center of the British line of posts in South Carolina. At the same time he planned to secure the co-operation of the

---

* Greene consulted Lee concerning his plan of operations, and probably referred to the Second Punic War and the famous "carrying the war into Africa." Lee replied on April 2d: "I am decidedly of opinion with you that nothing is left for you but to imitate the example of Scipio Africanus" In his funeral eulogy on Greene, Hamilton says: "This was one of those strokes that denote superior genius and constitute the sublime of war. 'Twas Scipio leaving Hannibal in Italy to overcome him at Carthage."

partisan corps of Marion, Pickens, and Sumter in his effort to reconquer South Carolina. Sumter had been disabled by a wound in an engagement with Tarleton in the previous month of November. But he had recovered in January, and during Greene's retreat to the Dan he had been collecting his followers on the Broad River. Greene directed him to be prepared to join the main body at Camden. Pickens, as we have seen, had been with Lee when Pyle's detachment was destroyed on February 25th, but a few days later he had been detached, and had returned to his old recruiting ground in the western part of South Carolina. He was now directed to advance against Ninety-Six, and either attack that post, or at least prevent its garrison from marching to the relief of Camden. Marion, assisted by Lee, had been engaged in an expedition against Georgetown in January, when Greene began his retreat. It then became necessary to recall Lee, and Marion's own followers were not sufficient to keep up the contest alone. They were therefore forced to retreat into their hiding places in the swamps along the Black River, where they had since remained. Marion was now instructed to attack the posts along the Santee between Camden and Charleston.

In brief, then, Greene was to attack the center of the line of posts with his main body of four small Continental regiments; to threaten the left flank at Ninety-Six with Pickens's partisans, and the right flank between Camden and Charleston with those of Marion. The campaign was planned as accurately and elaborately, and the issue at stake was as great, as if the contending forces were great armies; yet Greene had less than fifteen hundred men in his main

THE BATTLE OF HOBKIRK'S HILL.

body, and his partisans on either flank were numbered only by hundreds. It is true that he had hopes of re-enforcements. He had written to Governor Jefferson, of Virginia, asking for fifteen hundred militia to take the place of those who had fought so well at Guilford, but had made so short a stay in his army; he had heard also that General Gist was on his way southward with recruits for the Delaware and Maryland line. Lafayette had recently come to Virginia with twelve hundred men, and he, as well as Steuben, was under Greene's orders. But it was more difficult for them to communicate with Greene than with the Northern headquarters, and they received their orders direct from Washington, or acted on their own responsibility. Wayne was now on his way with the Pennsylvania line to re-enforce Lafayette. The possibility of all these troops joining Greene was discussed in his letters to Lafayette and Steuben, and both were personally anxious to march southward. But it was necessary at all hazards to preserve intact his line of communications through Virginia, against which Clinton had just sent his third expedition, under Phillips. Greene therefore had no definite expectations of re-enforcements. He knew that he must rely on his small Continental force, and such assistance as he could derive from the roving bands of partisans and the local militia that could be raised in the two Carolinas.

On the 6th of April he began his march, sending Lee, with the Legion, re-enforced by Oldham's company of the Second Maryland, toward Cross Creek, and marching with the main body almost due west on the road to Charlotte. His instructions to Lee gave that officer great latitude, but their general intent was to use the Legion as a cover between Cornwallis and himself (in the same way that it had been used on the retreat to the Dan) in case Cornwallis followed Greene into South Carolina—a course which Greene expected and somewhat desired that Cornwallis would follow. Lee was therefore to follow the road to Cross Creek so far as he thought proper in order to give Cornwallis the idea that Greene was pursuing him; then he was to turn abruptly to the west, and, keeping on Greene's left flank, to advance with him to the line of the Santee and attack or threaten the post of Fort Watson, about fifty miles below Camden. In case Cornwallis pursued, Lee was to keep close to the main body; otherwise he was to use his own discretion as to the point of crossing the Pedee and approaching the Santee. Cornwallis made no effort at pursuit, and Lee therefore kept well to the eastward, quite out of communication with Greene, crossed the Pedee near its mouth at Georgetown, and put himself in communication with Marion, with whom he effected a junction on the 14th of April, after a march of one hundred and sixty miles accomplished in eight days. Marion had four hundred followers, and Lee brought him about three hundred good troops. Together they laid siege to Fort Watson on the 15th. This was one of a series of small posts extending along the line of the Santee, from Camden to Georgetown, and covering the communications with Charleston, which was the headquarters of the British army in the South. These posts consisted of Camden, garrisoned by nine hundred men, under Lord Rawdon; Fort Motte, at the point where the Congaree and Wateree unite to form the Santee, garrisoned by one hundred and fifty men under Lieutenant McPherson; Fort Watson, about thirty miles below Fort Motte, garrisoned by one hundred and twenty men under Lieutenant McKay; and a small force at Georgetown, at the mouth of the Pedee. On the west of these was another line, consisting of Augusta, occupied by Lieutenant-Colonel Brown with six hundred and thirty men; Ninety-Six, with Lieutenant-Colonel Cruger and five hundred and fifty men; Fort Granby, near the site of the present city of Columbia, where the Broad and Saluda join and become the Congaree, garrisoned by sixty regulars and two hundred and eighty loyalists under Major Maxwell; and Orangeburg, south of Fort Granby and west of Fort Watson, occupied by three hundred and fifty men. In addition to the garrisons of these eight small posts, a large force was stationed in Charleston. The total effective force in South Carolina on May 1, 1781, according to the returns in the British Record Office, was seventy-two hundred and fifty-four. They were spread over a tract one hundred and sixty miles long and fifty miles wide. It was against these that Greene was advancing with his fifteen hundred Continentals and their partisan allies.

Fort Watson consisted of a stockade built on an Indian mound, about thirty-five feet high, on the bluff of the Santee River. It was garrisoned by eighty regulars and forty loyalists under Lieutenant McKay. Neither the garrison nor the assailants had any artillery. Marion summoned McKay to surrender on the 15th, and McKay promptly refused to do so. Marion then cut off his communications with a neighboring lake from which McKay derived his supply of water, and completely surrounded the stockade. But McKay dug a deep well within the fort from which to get a fresh supply of water, and he was well stocked with provisions. As Marion had no artillery, he was at a loss to see how to make any impression on the garrison. Whereupon one of his officers, a Colonel Maham, suggested a device similar to those employed in the time of Cæsar. The surrounding country was heavily wooded, and Marion's men were good backwoodsmen. They promptly set to work with the axes which were gathered from neighboring farms, and after they had cut a sufficient amount of timber a large force of the besiegers was employed one night in bringing it up on their shoulders to the immediate vicinity of the stockade; and there a high wooden tower was erected during the night, completely dominating the interior of the stockade. When day broke on the morning of April 23d the garrison was treated to a fusillade fired from the top of this tower by a picked detachment of skilled marksmen selected from Lee's Legion. Under cover of this fire a breach was made in the stockade. McKay saw that resistance was useless, and at once surrendered his entire garrison. Marion had lost only two killed and six wounded.

But he had lost eight important days at this place, and time was precious. On the one hand, Greene must now be approaching Camden, and Marion was anxious to join him. On the other hand, Colonel Watson with five hundred men had been detached from Camden a few weeks before and sent down to find and punish Marion in the vicinity of Georgetown. Marion had eluded him by first retiring into the swamps, and then joining Lee and

THE BATTLE OF HOBKIRK'S HILL. 237

marching to Fort Watson. Rawdon, having heard of Greene's approach, had recalled Watson in all haste, and the latter was now moving back from Georgetown toward Camden. Marion had heard of this, and was determined, if possible, to intercept Watson and prevent him from re-enforcing Rawdon. For this purpose he moved to the High Hills of Santee, whence he could throw himself in front of Watson by whatever route he approached. Watson, on the other hand, was equally determined to avoid Marion. Finding the route blocked on the east side of the Santee, he returned nearly to its mouth, crossed, and made a wide detour to the left, reaching the river again at Fort Motte and joining Rawdon on May 7th. In the meantime the battle of Hobkirk's Hill, or Camden, had been fought.

Greene, as before stated, left his camp at Ramsay's Mills, on Deep River, on the same day as Lee—April 6th. He reached the Pedee, at the mouth of the Yadkin, on April 11th. There he was detained three days in getting boats to cross. Then he moved south to Camden, and arrived there on the 20th. He had not overtaxed his men, for he wished to bring them before Camden in good order. Still, he had marched one hundred and forty miles in fourteen days, three of which had been lost in collecting boats. He had hoped to surprise Rawdon, but the inhabitants gave word of his approach, and this was impossible. He reconnoitered the works with a view to making an assault, but he found them too strong, and he therefore fell back to a wooded slope known as Hobkirk's Hill, about two miles north of the town, and there selected a defensive position. He was in hopes that Rawdon would come out to attack him; if not, he would observe the place and attack any troops moving into or out of it.

Camden had now been occupied by the British for nearly a year, and during that time they had constructed fortifications of considerable importance. The village lay in open ground, about two miles wide, inclosed on the east and south by Pine Tree Creek, and on the south and west by the Wateree River. In the center was a large stockade, and outside of this was a line of strong independent redoubts curving around from river to creek. The garrison (after Watson had been detached) consisted of nine hundred men, under Lord Rawdon, and some loyalist militia, which came in just before Greene arrived.

Greene had sent over three hundred men with Lee, and had lost a few by sickness on the march; so that the force which he brought to Camden numbered only eleven hundred and seventy-four Continentals and two hundred and fifty-four North Carolina militia, who had just joined him. He sent orders to Sumter to collect all his adherents along the Broad River and its branches and be ready to join him at Camden. But Sumter was less fond of complying with orders than of conducting an independent raid. Instead of coming to Camden, he moved independently against Fort Granby, and, far from aiding Greene, the result of his movements was to increase Rawdon's strength at Camden by driving the loyalist militia to that point.

On the evening of April 21st, the day after Greene arrived in front of Camden, he heard a rumor that Watson was returning to join Rawdon, and he therefore moved a few miles to the eastward in order to intercept Watson. As he had to cross a marshy

THE BATTLE OF HOBKIRK'S HILL.   239

creek, the two pieces of artillery which he had recently received from Virginia, and his baggage, were sent under charge of Colonel Carrington and the North Carolina militia to get around this marsh by making a detour of twenty miles to the north. On the 23d he received more accurate information, and returned to his position in front of Camden, sending word to Carrington to rejoin him at once. His force was posted in a defensive position on the brow of Hobkirk's Hill, the two Virginia regiments on the right of the Charlotte road, the two Maryland regiments on the left, and the two guns in the center. The North Carolina militia was in rear, and Washington's Cavalry supported the right flank. Kirkwood's Delaware battalion formed the outpost stationed at the foot of the hill, about five hundred yards in advance of the line. In this position the men camped and slept, ready to take arms at a moment's notice. On the night of the 24th one of the men deserted, and told Rawdon that Greene's artillery and militia had been sent to the rear. Rawdon thought it a judicious moment to attack, especially as he feared that Marion and Lee might join Greene any day. At nine o'clock on the morning of the 25th, therefore, he sallied out with every man in the garrison that could carry a musket—about nine hundred in all. He moved through the woods along the swamps of Pine Tree Creek, as the approach to Hobkirk's Hill was easiest from that direction. About ten o'clock he came upon Kirkwood's pickets, who fell back on the main body of the outpost and retreated skirmishing up the hill.

Greene's men had received some supplies that morning. These were being issued, and the men were washing their clothes, when the alarm was given by the firing of the pickets. The men were called in and quickly formed in position, so that they were ready to receive Rawdon by the time he reached the hill—about 11 A. M. After driving Kirkwood back, Rawdon deployed his force in line, the Sixty-third Foot, supported by the Volunteers of Ireland (Rawdon's own regiment) on the right; the King's American Regiment, supported by Captain Robertson's detachment, on the left; and the New York Volunteers in the center. The South Carolina regiment and a detachment of cavalry was in the rear. In this formation he advanced slowly up the slope. Greene watched the formation, and, thinking that it presented a narrow front, he determined not to wait on the defensive, but to make a counter attack instantly. He therefore directed Campbell, with the First Virginia, on his right, to wheel to the left, so as to envelop Rawdon's left flank, and Ford, with the Second Maryland, to make a similar movement on his left; he also ordered the two remaining regiments in the center to advance with the bayonet, and Washington's Cavalry to make a charge around Campbell's right. The artillery meanwhile opened with grape. These manœuvres were somewhat complicated for troops most of whom had had so little experience. Still, they were executed with tolerable precision, and a vigorous engagement was soon brought on. It resulted in Rawdon's left flank beginning to retire, and his center to waver. Washington's charge was most successful, and he penetrated to Rawdon's rear and took two hundred prisoners, including all the surgeons in the army. Everything was tending to a brilliant victory for Greene, when

THE BATTLE OF HOBKIRK'S HILL.   241

Captain Beatty, of the famous First Maryland, was killed. This caused his company to halt and then to fall back in disorder. In order to retrieve this, Colonel Gunby ordered the entire regiment to fall back with the intention of reforming their line. But once the retreat began it was impossible to stop it, and this regiment, which was the pride and boast of the army, and had done such splendid service on so many fields, now broke and ran. The panic was communicated to the Second Maryland, and leaving its commander, Colonel Ford, mortally wounded, it also left the field in disorder. Seeing this, Rawdon's line quickly rallied and pushed forward in pursuit, turning the left flank of the Second Regiment under Hawes. Greene saw that there was no hope of saving the day, and bent his whole energy to making an orderly retreat and saving his artillery. This was accomplished by Washington's cavalry, which returned from its charge, and, abandoning its prisoners, rushed into the *mêlée* which was in progress around the guns, and stayed the advance of the British long enough for the guns to be withdrawn and the army to effect its retreat under cover of Hawes's regiment. Greene retreated in good order for about five miles, and took up a new position in which to receive an attack. But Rawdon did not attempt any pursuit.

The losses on the American side were nineteen killed, one hundred and fifteen wounded, and one hundred and thirty-six missing—total, two hundred and seventy; on the British side, two hundred and fifty-eight, of whom thirty-eight were killed.

Greene took his defeat much to heart. It seemed as if he were fated never to win a battle. But he had no idea of giving up the struggle. To the French Minister (Luzerne) he wrote: "We fight, get beat, rise, and fight again";* and in his orders for the day following the battle the parole was "Persevere," and the countersign was "Fortitude."

Greene attributed his defeat to the action of Colonel Gunby, and time only confirmed him in this opinion. Months afterward he wrote, in a personal letter to his friend Reed, of Pennsylvania, that Rawdon and his whole command would have been made prisoners in three minutes more if Gunby had not ordered his regiment to retire; and he added: "I was almost frantic with vexation at the disappointment." In his order to the army the day after the battle he complimented several organizations, and then added: "Our loss is so inconsiderable that it is only to be lamented that the troops were not unanimous of a disposition to embrace so excellent an opportunity of gaining a victory." This pointed allusion caused Gunby to apply immediately for a court of inquiry. It made its report on May 2d, and, after reciting the facts, stated that "it appears from the above report that Colonel Gunby's spirit and activity were unexceptionable. But his order for the regiment to retire, which broke the line, was ex-

---

* Greene's main object, in his correspondence with Luzerne, was to persuade him to put into active service the French army of five thousand men which now for nearly a year had been cooped up in Newport, doing nothing. If these joined Washington, doubtless a re-enforcement could be spared for Greene. Luzerne wrote a flattering reply to the letter from which the above extract is made, but it contained nothing more definite than this: "Be assured that his Majesty will think his troops well employed in co-operating with a general who has effected such great things with such inferior means."

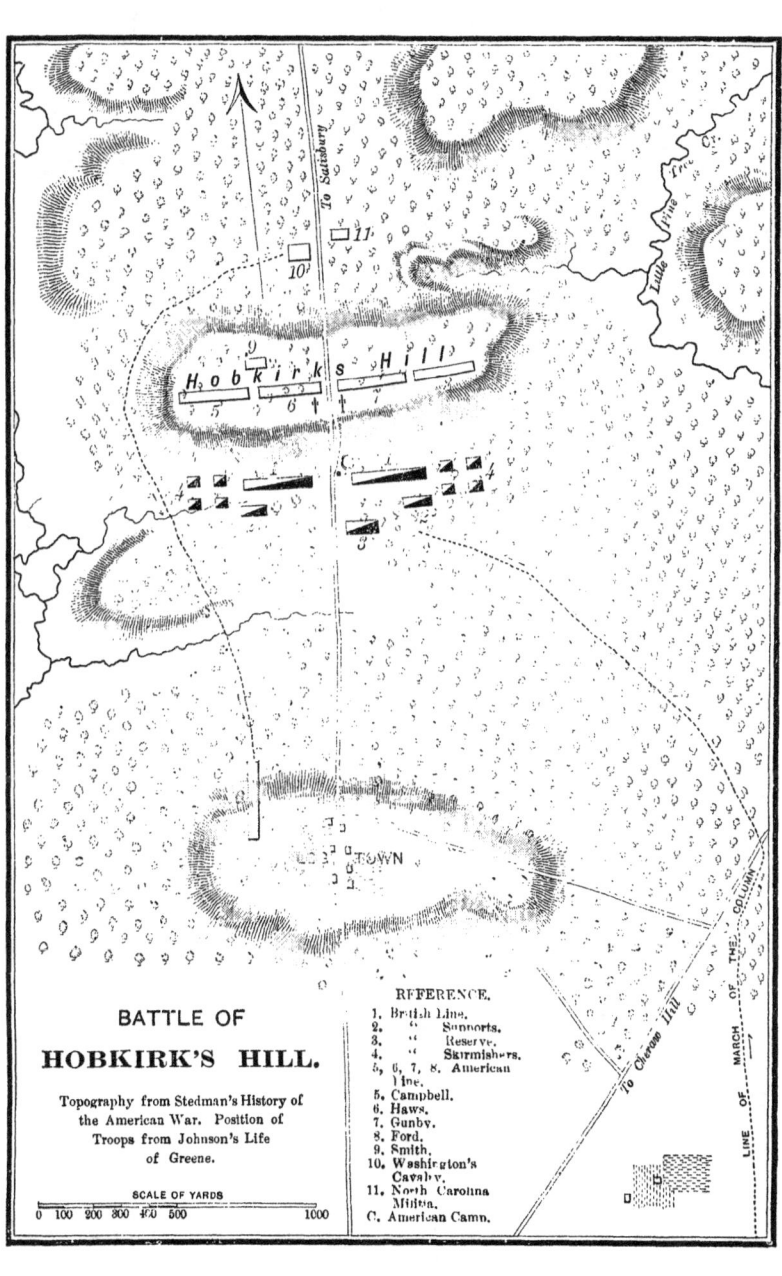

THE BATTLE OF HOBKIRK'S HILL 243

tremely improper and unmilitary, and in all probability the only cause why we did not obtain a complete victory."

Greene remained for two days in the position he had chosen just after the battle, and then retired ten miles farther north to Rugely's Mill. On the 7th of May, Watson succeeded in making his way into Camden, and with this large re-enforcement Rawdon again moved out to attack Greene; but the latter marched to the west side of the Wateree and manœuvred for two days until he occupied a position where he was willing to fight. Rawdon reconnoitered this position and deemed it too strong for attack; he therefore returned to Camden. In the meantime Marion and Lee had been sent to besiege Fort Motte, and Sumter was operating against Fort Granby and Orangeburg. Rawdon at Camden was completely surrounded, his communications with Charleston were interrupted, and his supply trains were being captured. It was difficult to obtain provisions in the neighboring country, and he saw that he would soon be cut off and starved out. On the 10th, therefore, he abandoned Camden, burned such stores as he could not carry, and began his retreat to Charleston. On the 11th Sumter captured Orangeburg; on the 12th Marion took Fort Motte; on the 15th Fort Granby surrendered to Lee. Early in June Marion entered Georgetown, the garrison escaping to Charleston. The whole eastern line of posts thus went down with a crash within a month from the time that Greene crossed the South Carolina line. He had captured four posts with their garrisons, amounting to over eight hundred men, and had driven the British back to the vicinity of Charleston. He had lost the principal battle, but his movements were so well planned that again, as at Guilford, he had gained all the objects of the campaign.

Meanwhile, where was Cornwallis? As already stated, he reached Wilmington on April 7th. On his retreat he had feared that possibly Greene might go into South Carolina, and he had therefore sent messages to Rawdon from Cross Creek to be on the lookout for him. On the 22d a small vessel arrived from Charleston, bringing him news which confirmed his worst fears. Greene had marched into South Carolina, was already approaching Camden, and the upper posts were all in danger on account of the uprising of the people. There is something almost comical in the way in which Cornwallis complained of being outmanœuvred. To Phillips, in Virginia, he wrote, April 24th: " My situation here is very distressing. Greene took the advantage of my being obliged to come to this place, and has marched to South Carolina." Greene had indeed taken advantage of the misfortunes of his adversary, as skillful generals usually do; he had manœuvred him out of the theatre of operations, and had then quickly gone to attack his posts. The question with Cornwallis was, What should he do? Should he follow Greene into South Carolina? or should he march north to join the British troops at the mouth of the Chesapeake? He decided to march north.

This decision had a most important bearing on the termination of the war, and it gave rise in after years to an elaborate and acrimonious discussion between Clinton and Cornwallis. Clinton maintained that his written instructions of June 1st and November 6, 1780, positively enjoined upon Cornwallis the

THE BATTLE OF HOBKIRK'S HILL. 245

protection of Charleston, and forbade any movement to the north until the two Carolinas were entirely subjugated; and then the movement, if any, was to be by vessel to the Chesapeake, there to act in concert with Clinton on the Delaware in an expedition against Philadelphia. He contended that Cornwallis by his first move into North Carolina, and still more by his march to Virginia, violated the letter and spirit of his orders, and in so doing brought about the disaster at Yorktown and the ruin of British affairs in America. In Clinton's opinion, Cornwallis should have retreated to Camden immediately after the battle of Guilford; having failed to do so then, he should have done so from Wilmington, when he heard that Greene was approaching Camden.

Cornwallis does not seem to have taken his instructions so literally, but rather to have considered himself as having more latitude in his separate command, hundreds of miles away from the commander in chief, and unable to communicate with him and get a reply in less than two to three months. He contended that it was necessary for him to act on his own judgment; that he was compelled to fall back to Wilmington to refit his army; that it was impossible for him to reach Rawdon in time to be of any assistance; and that he thought he could be of most service in uniting his force, now reduced to fifteen hundred men, with that which had recently been sent to the Chesapeake under Phillips. This was the position he maintained in the pamphlets with which he and Clinton pelted each other on their return to England after the close of the war.

It is out of place in a biography of Greene to go into the details of this interesting controversy. It may be remarked, however, that one of the reasons which Cornwallis gives for not marching back to South Carolina was as follows: "I did not think that I could, with thirteen hundred infantry and two hundred cavalry, undertake such a march, and the passage of two such rivers as the Pedee and Santee, without exposing the corps under my command to the utmost hazard of disgrace and ruin." Yet Greene made just such a march, with a smaller force, not so well equipped, and at the end of it attacked and broke up a line of posts garrisoned by nearly twice his numbers. Cornwallis would not have hesitated to attempt this march, or one even more hazardous, had it followed the line of glory instead of that of disgrace. To go back to South Carolina was to acknowledge himself beaten and his campaign a failure; and this was doubtless the main reason why he marched north. Nevertheless, there was a fair chance of success in Virginia; and had he beaten Washington at Yorktown, he would have overrun Virginia and cut off all Greene's communications with the north, thus strangling his Southern campaign. Greene saw this clearly. He expected and hoped that Cornwallis would follow him; and when he learned that he had gone to Virginia he seriously meditated on two separate occasions—the first, after the battle of Hobkirk's Hill, and the second after the siege of Ninety-Six—leaving Huger in command in South Carolina to hold his own on the defensive as best he could, while he [Greene] went to Virginia to take command in person of the troops under Lafayette and Steuben, and with them fight Cornwallis.*

---

* His instructions from Congress and from Washington, both at the beginning of the campaign and subsequently, fully author-

THE BATTLE OF HOBKIRK'S HILL. 247

So important did Greene consider his line of communications through Virginia. Without aid from the North—as he was now writing incessantly to Washington, Lafayette, Luzerne, the President of Congress, Governor Reed, and others—he felt that his little army could not much longer sustain itself; and if that failed, the partisans and militia would soon disband and the Southern States be hopelessly lost. Washington entertained the same opinion, and determined to drive the British out of Virginia the moment he succeeded in getting the co-operation of the French army at Newport. It would seem, therefore, that Cornwallis's fault was not so much in marching to Virginia as in being beaten after he got there. Why he was beaten in Virginia, and whether he or Clinton was responsible for it, can not be discussed here.

As soon as Rawdon began his retreat toward Charleston, Greene made his preparations for moving against Ninety-Six. They were slightly delayed by the sensibilities of his partisan chiefs. Sumter made a written protest against the taking of Fort Granby by Lee, asserting that he had been at great pains to reduce the post, that it was in his power to

---

ized this. His command reached from Delaware to Georgia, and all operations in these six States were under his control. As late as April and May, 1781, Washington continued to direct Lafayette and Steuben to act under Greene's orders, and they were in constant communication with him. The delays in this communication, however, were so great that Greene usually left them to act on their own discretion. But early in May, when Greene learned definitely that Cornwallis was marching to Virginia, he sent orders to Lafayette, who was then preparing to march to South Carolina, to remain in Virginia; and also to halt the Pennsylvania line under Wayne when it arrived, and with them to oppose Cornwallis.

do it, and he thought it "for the good of the public to do it without regulars." Greene replied that Lee had acted in accordance with his orders. Whereupon Sumter tendered his resignation, but Greene wrote him a flattering letter and declined to accept it. Marion also was offended. There had been much controversy about the impressment of horses. On the one hand, people in Virginia complained that Greene's officers were carrying off their stallions and brood mares, and the Legislature took up their complaint and directed the return of all such animals, and of all geldings worth more than £5,000 (in paper currency). Greene protested through Jefferson that a horse worth less than £5,000 would be useless to carry a dragoon, and the act was repealed.* On the other hand, Greene had great difficulty in getting mounts for his cavalry, and Lee wrote him that Marion's men were not only all well mounted, but had horses to spare. Greene called upon Marion to furnish them. Marion took offense at the tone of the letter, offered to dismount his own men, and asked leave to retire to Philadelphia, alleging as a reason that his men could never be depended upon. Greene replied in excellent temper, alternately praising Marion's past services and appealing to his patriotism. "It is true your task has been disagreeable, but not more so than others'. It is now going on seven years since the commencement of the war; I have never had leave of absence an hour, or paid the least attention to my own private affairs. Your State is invaded; your all is at stake; what has been done will signify nothing unless we persevere

---

* Tarleton and Simcoe soon afterward raided through Virginia and carried off all the best horses, regardless of their value.

to the end. I left a wife in distress, and everything dear and valuable, to come and afford you all the assistance in my power; and if you leave us in the midst of our difficulties, while you have it so much in your power to promote the service, it must throw a damper on the spirits of the army to find the first men in the State are retiring from the busy scene to indulge themselves in more agreeable amusements." Marion yielded to this appeal, and remained with the army till the last British soldier had left the United States.

Having adjusted these matters, Greene put his little force in motion toward Ninety-Six and Augusta, the only posts in the interior of the State now remaining in British possession. On the 16th of May he sent Lee with the Legion against Augusta, and this officer with his usual energy marched over one hundred miles in four days, and reached the banks of the Savannah River on the 19th. Greene started with the main body on the 17th, and five days later arrived in front of Ninety-Six. Numerous messengers had been sent by Rawdon to Colonel Cruger, at Ninety-Six, directing him to abandon his post and retire to Augusta, there joining his force to that of Colonel Browne, and subsequently acting on his discretion; but these messengers had all been intercepted, and Cruger had no very definite information of what had taken place in and around Camden in the last three weeks except such as he had been able to gain from an American militia officer who had been captured. He therefore remained at Ninety-Six, and employed his entire force in strengthening its fortifications, in the anticipation that Greene would probably besiege it.

On approaching the Savannah River, Lee learned that the annual presents for the Indians were being transported up the river and had reached a point about twelve miles below Augusta, called Fort Galpin, where they were guarded by two companies from the garrison of Augusta. The presents consisted of powder, ball, small arms, rum, salt, blankets, and other articles of which the Americans were much in need. Against this place Lee employed the well-known stratagem of which the first recorded use is by Joshua at the attack of Ai in 1451 B. C. Concealing the greater part of his force in the vicinity of the stockade, he sent a small body to attack it on the opposite side. The defenders rushed out to drive off or capture this small force, and, as it retreated, the main force charged into the stockade and took possession of it. In this manner Lee not only captured all of these valuable stores, but the entire garrison of one hundred and twenty-six men; his own loss was only one man, who was overcome by the heat. After resting only a few hours he pressed on later in the same day (May 21st) toward Augusta, approaching it from the west, and joining on his way the militia of Pickens and Clarke, who had been assembling in this vicinity.

Augusta was then a small village, and its defenses consisted of Fort Cornwallis, a stockade in the middle of the village, garrisoned by five hundred and fifty men, mostly regulars, under Lieutenant-Colonel Browne; and another stockade called Fort Grierson, situated about half a mile up the river, and defended by eighty Tory militia. Lee summoned Browne to surrender, and this being contemptuously refused, he surrounded Fort Grierson.

THE SIEGE OF NINETY-SIX.

The garrison attempted to escape to Fort Cornwallis, and as soon as they came out of their stockade nearly half of them, including Lieutenant-Colonel Grierson and the major, were killed by the Georgia militia, who were exceedingly bitter on account of the cruelties which they and their families had suffered from the Tories. Several of the others were wounded and taken prisoners, and a few only managed to make good their escape.

Lee and Pickens then closed in around Fort Cornwallis; but Browne made a good defense. On three successive nights he made vigorous sallies, and by means of mines he blew up one of the houses which he supposed was occupied by the besiegers. Recourse was then had by Lee to the Maham tower, which had been so successfully used at Fort Watson, and this time it was built strong enough to hold a six-pounder on its top. This completely dominated the fort and dismounted its two guns. A renewed demand being made for surrender, it was finally agreed to, and on June 5th the garrison marched out and laid down its arms. Leaving Pickens to dispose of the stores, Lee set out on the following morning to join Greene at Ninety-Six, arriving there on June 8th. Pickens followed a few days later.

Greene, with his so-called army, consisting of the four Continental regiments, two from Virginia and two from Maryland, the remnants of Kirkwood's Delaware battalion, and one from North Carolina, numbering in all, according to the May returns, nine hundred and eighty-four men, had left the vicinity of Camden on May 17th and arrived in front of Ninety-Six on the 22d. This place derived its name from being ninety-six miles from Keowee, the principal village of the Cherokees. It was a frontier post, consisting originally of a stockade for defense against the Indians; but during the last year additional works had been planned under direction of Lieutenant Haldane, of the Royal Engineers, an aid-de-camp on Cornwallis's staff. These had only been partially completed in the spring of 1781, but when Greene approached Camden, Cruger laid waste the surrounding country, which was one of great fertility, and, calling in all the slaves, set them to work night and day on the defenses. On the west of the village stockade there was a spring and rivulet from which the garrison obtained its supply of water. To protect this, the jail, which stood just within the stockade, was strengthened and put in condition for defense; and on a slight eminence across the rivulet a stockaded fort was built, inclosing two blockhouses. This fort and the jail completely commanded every point from which water was taken. On the east of the village a redoubt was built about seventy yards in diameter, with sixteen salient and re-entrant angles, giving cross-fire on every point of approach. From its shape, this was called the Star. Around this a ditch was dug, the bottom of which was twelve feet below the parapet of the redoubt. This ditch was continued with less depth around the entire village stockade, and it was protected with fraise and abatis. A covered way connected the stockade fort and the village stockade, and this in turn connected with the Star redoubt, so that there was covered communication from one end of the defenses to the other. Three pieces of light artillery, one six-pounder and two four-pounders, were within the Star, and platforms had been built at several points along its para-

THE SIEGE OF NINETY-SIX.

pet, to which the guns could be moved as required. The garrison consisted of one battalion of De Lancey's Loyalists, of New York, the Second Battalion of New Jersey Volunteers, and a body of South Carolina Tories. They numbered five hundred and fifty men in all, and those from New York and New Jersey had been enlisted at the beginning of the war and had been in active service ever since. The commanding officer was Lieutenant-Colonel John H. Cruger, of New York.

During the 22d, Greene, accompanied by Colonel Kosciusko, his chief engineer, made a careful reconnoissance completely around the enemy's works. He found them so strong that, as he wrote to Lafayette the next day, success with his small force was almost impossible. Yet he determined to make a vigorous effort. During the evening his little force was posted at four points, so as practically to surround the garrison and prevent any escape. During the night, which was dark and rainy, Kosciusko broke ground for his first parallels at seventy yards from the Star redoubt. When Cruger saw this in the morning he determined to punish such an insult, and he ordered a sally with one company under Lieutenant Roney, protected by the fire of the three guns and all the infantry of the garrison. It was entirely successful, broke up the intrenching party, captured their tools, destroyed the work which they had done, and escaped back to the redoubt before the supporting parties could come to their assistance. On the following night ground was again broken for the first parallel, but this time at a distance of four hundred yards. The work was continued vigorously night and day, in spite of constant and vigorous but unsuccessful sorties on the part of the garrison. A mine was begun from the end of the first parallel, and a battery built in the second; the second parallel was completed on June 3d, and the garrison was then formally summoned to surrender. Cruger rejected the summons, and the third parallel was begun, its progress being greatly assisted by resorting to the now familiar device of the Maham tower.

While the siege was in progress Marion was operating in the lower districts. He procured the Charleston papers of June 2d, and his messengers covered the two hundred miles to Ninety-Six in four days and placed these papers in Greene's hands on the night of the 6th. They contained the worst possible news. The long-expected re-enforcements from Ireland had arrived, and Greene knew that Rawdon would now soon be marching against him. Rawdon had retreated after the evacuation of Camden and the loss of his other posts to the vicinity of Charleston, and was there awaiting these re-enforcements, which consisted of the Third, Nineteenth, and Thirtieth Regiments of foot, a detachment of the Guards, and a considerable body of recruits. After his arrival in Virginia Cornwallis had sent a dispatch boat to Charleston with orders to Rawdon not to let these re-enforcements cross the bar, but to turn them northward to Virginia the moment they were sighted. Unfortunately for Greene, this dispatch boat was captured by an American privateer, and Rawdon did not receive these orders until after he had marched to the interior with these re-enforcements. On his side, Greene was also expecting the re-enforcements of Virginia militia, which he had asked for in March, when the six weeks' militia had gone home. He had

THE SIEGE OF NINETY-SIX.

asked for fifteen hundred, and Jefferson had ordered out two thousand. After long delays and innumerable difficulties, Steuben had finally collected about five hundred and fifty men, and he was impatient to march with them to Greene's assistance. They were just starting during the latter part of May, when they were recalled by Jefferson in consequence of Cornwallis's operations in Virginia. Greene heard of this a few days after he learned that Rawdon's re-enforcements had arrived at Charleston. In consequence of two unforeseen events, Greene was thus deprived of his own re-enforcements, and his adversary received his.

In order to oppose Rawdon's advance, Greene sent the most explicit instructions, under date of June 10th, to Sumter, to summon Marion to his assistance, and to put himself in front of Rawdon, retard his advance in every way possible, to fall back slowly before him and put himself in communication with Greene, his intention being to fight Rawdon before he reached Ninety-Six. On the 11th Greene received information that Rawdon had begun his march, and on the same day Pickens arrived at Ninety-Six from Augusta. Greene immediately sent him to re-enforce Sumter; but Sumter could not or would not move his men out of their own district. They took post at Fort Granby, thinking that Rawdon would besiege them. But Rawdon naturally pushed past Sumter without noticing him, arriving in the vicinity of Ninety-Six on June 21st. Thus Greene was not only deprived of his re-enforcements, but lost all assistance from his partisan bands through their failure to carry out his instructions.

Meanwhile the siege had been progressing. Lee

had arrived on the 8th, and had immediately broken ground on the left, opposite the stockade fort. On the night of the 9th a sortie was made by two strong parties, who penetrated to the battery in the third parallel, destroyed the mine, and wounded Kosciusko. But they were driven back before they had been able to injure the guns. Lee pushed his works vigorously against the stockade fort, and soon had it so completely under his fire that the defenders could not go out for water during daylight, and were reduced to obtaining it at night by means of slaves, whose black bodies it was supposed would not be seen. On the night of the 12th he attempted to set fire to the abatis, but the result was a disastrous failure, the party sent out for this purpose being all killed or wounded. On the afternoon of the 12th a picturesque incident occurred. A countryman rode into the lines from the south and moved along conversing with the officers and men. This was a daily occurrence, and attracted no attention. But this man, when he reached a favorable point, put spurs to his horse and galloped toward the village stockade. Hundreds of bullets were sent after him, but he escaped unhurt, and as he neared the stockade he turned in his saddle and waved a letter in his hand. It was a dispatch from Rawdon to Cruger, telling him "that he had passed Orangeburg and was in full march to raise the siege."

Greene now knew that he could not hope for a surrender. His only possible chance of success was in a speedy assault, and for this he made preparations. The troops were all anxious to try it. The third parallel was now within thirty yards of the redoubt, and a mine and two trenches, led from it to

THE SIEGE OF NINETY-SIX.

within a few feet of the ditch. The Maham tower commanded the interior of the redoubt, and all efforts of the garrison to destroy it had failed. From its top the riflemen picked off the gunners so that the guns were silent during the day. At night, however, the guns resumed fire, as the besiegers had not succeeded in dismounting them. The parapet had been raised three feet higher, making its total height above the ditch fifteen feet, by means of sandbags, leaving openings through which the field pieces as well as the muskets could fire.

The 18th of June was fixed as the day of the assault. Axes were provided to cut out the abatis, fascines to fill up the ditch, and long poles with hooks at the end to pull down the sandbags. Campbell, with his own regiment, the First Virginia, and a detachment of Marylanders, was to storm the Star redoubt, and Lee, with the Legion, was to attack the stockade fort. The rest of the force was to man the Maham tower, the battery and the third parallel, and cover the assault with their fire. At eleven o'clock in the morning Greene opened the most vigorous cannonade that his four guns could produce, and his riflemen were ready to pick off every head that showed itself above the parapet. At noon the storming parties rushed forward and soon gained the ditch. Here they were subjected to a terrible cross-fire on their flanks from the salient angles of the redoubt, and from above their heads through the loopholes of the sandbags. It was found impossible to pull down these bags, either because the bags were too heavy or the poles were not long enough. Nevertheless, the men continued to work in the ditch for nearly an hour, clearing out the abatis and piling up the fascines; but finally, of their leaders, Captain Armstrong was killed and Lieutenants Seldon and Duval were wounded, and just then two parties of the garrison—one under Campbell, of New Jersey, and the other under French, of De Lancey's battalion—came out through the sallyport of the redoubt, and, entering the ditch at that point, one part on each side, charged the assailants in the flank. Attacked thus on all sides, the storming parties were driven out of the ditch and forced back into the third parallel.

On the left, Lee's attack upon the stockade fort met with much better success. The storming party was led by Captain Rudolph, of the Legion, and it was supported by the rest of the Legion and Kirkwood's Delaware battalion. It captured the stockade fort, and was preparing to assault the jail and then take the Star redoubt in reverse, when Lee was recalled by Greene.

When his storming party found it impossible to make any headway out of the ditch, Greene had the same opportunity that had presented itself to him at the close of the battle of Guilford. He could send every man to the support of the storming party and risk everything on the result, which would be either success or the total destruction of his entire force. Now, as then, he adhered to his resolution never to place his army within the possibility of complete destruction. He therefore withdrew within his own lines and made preparations to raise the siege and begin his retreat toward Charlotte, North Carolina, in the morning. The siege had lasted twenty-eight days. Greene had lost fifty-seven killed, seventy wounded, and twenty missing; the garrison lost twenty-seven killed and fifty-eight wounded.

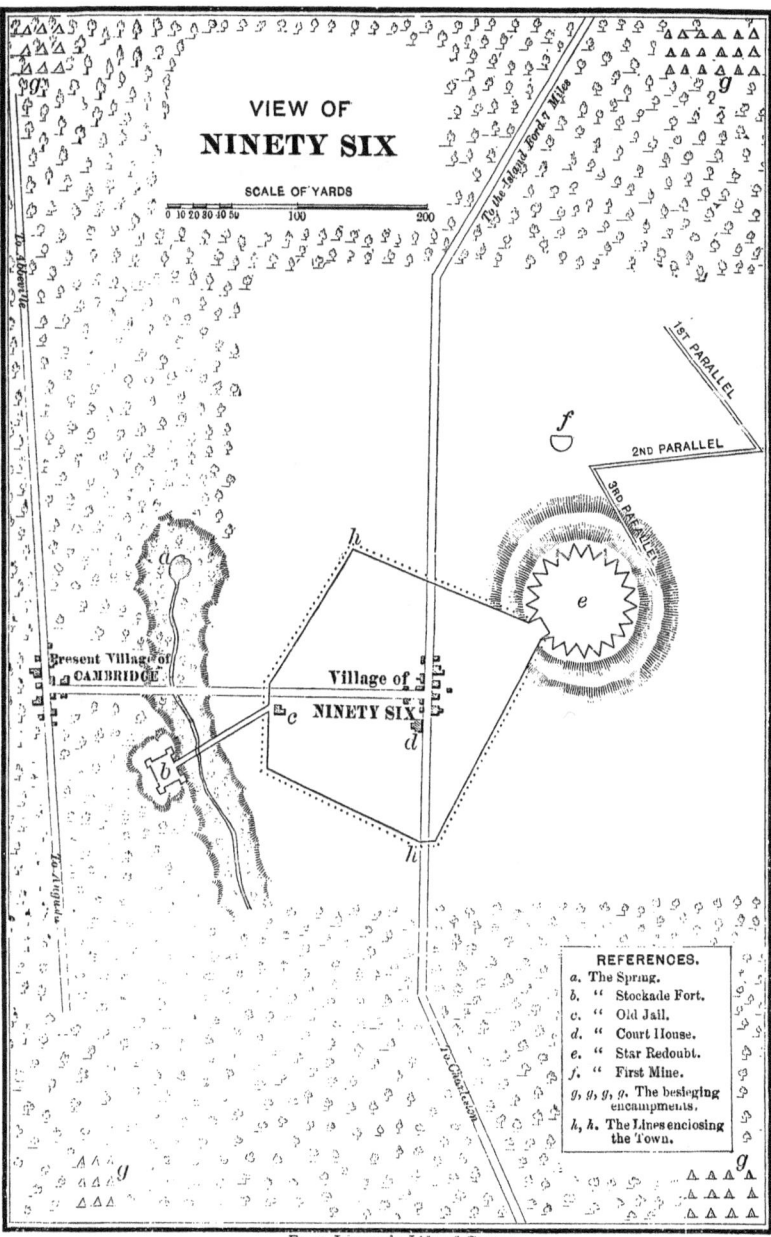

From Johnson's Life of Greene

THE SIEGE OF NINETY-SIX.

Rawdon arrived at Ninety-Six on the 21st of June, bringing with him fresh troops to the number of about eighteen hundred infantry and two hundred cavalry, besides irregular partisans. He was hailed with delight, and Cruger was congratulated on the gallant defense which he had made. Greene had begun his retreat on the morning of the 20th, taking the road toward Charlotte, and sending orders to Sumter to join him. Rawdon wasted no time at Ninety-Six, but marched in pursuit of Greene a few hours after his arrival. On the 23d he came up with the rear guard, under Lee and Washington, on the banks of the Ennoree, Greene with the main body being farther on, behind the Broad River. He had retreated about fifty miles in three days. Rawdon saw that he could accomplish nothing by continuing the pursuit, and he therefore retraced his steps to Ninety-Six, Lee and Washington following him closely all the way.

It was impossible for the British to retain a garrison at Ninety-Six. The distance from Charleston was about one hundred and sixty miles, all the intermediate posts had been broken up, and communications could not be maintained through a country infested with hostile partisans and an active adversary. Rawdon therefore made preparations for its immediate abandonment. Thus, for the third time, the British had won the action, but Greene had gained the object of the campaign.

The entire population of the State being in arms on one or the other side, and both pursuing each other with relentless vigor and cruelty, it was necessary to provide for removing the Tory inhabitants of the district around Ninety-Six at the same time that the post was abandoned. This duty, as well as the removal of the stores, was intrusted to Cruger and considerably more than half of the united force, while Rawdon, with eight hundred infantry and sixty cavalry, began his retreat to Charleston on June 29th. His route lay through Fort Granby, or Friday's Ferry, where he expected to be joined by Lieutenant-Colonel Stuart and the Third Regiment from Charleston. Lee hung close to Rawdon in all his movements and kept Greene fully informed of them. The latter immediately marched to Winnsborough (whence Cornwallis had started on the campaign six months before), and leaving there his baggage, stores, and invalids, with orders to proceed to Camden, he continued his march toward Fort Granby. Sumter and Marion were again urged to join him, and Lee was directed to put himself in front of Rawdon and delay his march as much as possible. Rawdon reached Fort Granby on July 3d, two days before Greene, but Lee was constantly on his flanks, and picked up between forty and fifty of his dragoons who imprudently left the column on a foraging expedition. At Fort Granby Rawdon expected to find Lieutenant-Colonel Stuart and the Third Regiment, who were under orders to march from Charleston and meet him at that point. But he was not there. His march had been delayed, and the letter from Colonel Balfour to Rawdon, informing him of this fact, had been intercepted and placed in Greene's hands. Rawdon therefore continued his retreat to Orangeburg, Lee in front of him and harassing him all the way. On the 8th he reached that point, his men half dead with heat and fatigue; and here he was joined by Stuart and the Third Regiment, or

THE SIEGE OF NINETY-SIX. 261

Buffs. On the same day Cruger, with over thirteen hundred troops and his caravan of emigrants, left Ninety-Six, closely watched by Pickens and Clarke. On the 10th, Sumter and Marion joined Greene at Fort Granby with about one thousand State troops and militia, carrying Greene's total strength to over two thousand men. He immediately marched from Fort Granby to Orangeburg, hoping to fight Rawdon on favorable ground before Cruger could join him. He took up a position in front of Orangeburg, in the expectation that Rawdon would come out to attack him; but Rawdon occupied an excellent position at Orangeburg and declined to leave it. On the other hand, this position was too strong for Greene to attack it. Cruger, having convoyed his refugees well on their way toward Charleston, was now marching across to join Rawdon at Orangeburg, giving him a united force of nearly three thousand regulars. Greene therefore decided, on July 13th, to retreat from Orangeburg and post his Continental troops on the High Hills of Santee, for the purpose of giving them a short but much-needed rest and recuperation,* while the partisan troops and the Legion were sent on a raid against the posts just outside of Charleston. This expedition did not realize all that was expected of it, but it captured or destroyed a considerable amount of stores, horses, and wagons, took one hundred and fifty prisoners, drove the Nineteenth Regiment from Monk's Corners into Charleston and penetrated within five miles of that city, and all without any losses of consequence. They then re-

---

* For the last ten days the army had subsisted almost entirely on rice and frogs.

turned, and on the 22d of July the force was posted as follows: Greene with the main body and Lee's Legion on the High Hills of Santee; Sumter at Friday's Ferry, on the right; Marion at Nelson's Ferry, on the left; and Pickens recruiting on his old ground, in the vicinity of Ninety-Six.

Rawdon returned to Charleston, and thence sailed for New York on leave of absence. His vessel was captured by De Grasse on his way to Yorktown, and he joined Cornwallis as a prisoner at the latter's surrender. Stuart, who was left in command of the troops in the field, advanced slightly from Orangeburg toward Friday's Ferry. In these positions both armies, prostrated with the intense heat and worn out with their prodigious marches and incessant combats, rested for the next six weeks.

CHAPTER XIII.

EUTAW SPRINGS AND THE CLOSE OF THE SOUTHERN
CAMPAIGN—1781-'83.

ON the 2d of December, 1780, Greene had taken command at Charlotte, and early in January the active campaign had begun with the battle of the Cowpens. It was now the last of July, 1781, and during these seven months—through the snows of winter, the mud and rains of spring, and the torrid heat of summer—the campaign had been in progress with hardly a day's intermission. It was a superbly sustained effort. Without assistance from the North, without proper equipment, without money, without any resources except such as his genius called forth from an exhausted country, opposed to an enemy outnumbering him three to one, he had broken up all their posts in the interior, had manœuvred one part of their force into Virginia and driven the rest back toward the seacoast, where their fleet gave them immunity. He had marched nine hundred and fifty miles, fought three battles, carried on a siege, conducted a most skillful retreat and an equally brilliant advance. When the enemy concentrated their army for attack he divided his force for the purpose of distracting their attention; and when they dispersed in order to hold the conquered territory and reintroduce their Government, he assembled his troops to fall upon their posts in quick succession and destroy them. Defeated in every general engagement and losing his principal siege, he yet gained the ultimate object of every movement. His adversaries as well as his companions have united in testifying to his well-merited success. The British historian Steedman says: "Through his own firmness and perseverance . . . he succeeded in the main object of the campaign." And the brilliant and generous Lee, to whom more than to any one else of his subordinates he owed his success, and who, more fortunate than Greene himself, failed in hardly a single one of the enterprises confided to him, wrote that "such results can only be attributed to superior talents, seconded by skill, courage, and fidelity. Fortune often gives victory; but when the weak, destitute of the essential means of war, successfully oppose the strong, it is not chance but sublime genius which guides the intermediate operations and controls the ultimate event." Greene was cheered at the time by a cordial letter from Washington, saying: "It is with the warmest pleasure I express my full approbation of the various movements and operations which your military conduct has lately exhibited, while I confess to you that I am unable to conceive what more could have been done under your circumstances than has been displayed by your little, persevering, and determined army."

The hot and sickly season was now at its height, and it was imperatively necessary to rest and recruit his exhausted force. For this purpose Greene selected the High Hills of Santee, an elevated and comparatively healthy region about ninety miles from Charleston. Here he placed his little force in

CLOSE OF THE SOUTHERN CAMPAIGN. 265

tents, instituted daily drills, parades, and guard duty, and re-established its discipline.

He had now practically abandoned all hope of re-enforcements from the North, and his only resource was to draw fresh men from the two States he had reconquered. He had been so disappointed in regard to the Virginia militia that it seemed useless to ask for any more; but he did ask of the new Governor (Nelson) that recruits might be sent to fill up the quota of the two Continental regiments from Virginia. His appeal was unsuccessful, for all the men that could be raised in Virginia were needed within her own borders. In North Carolina the draft had been ordered. It was feebly enforced, but two hundred recruits were sent to the Continental regiments, and about five hundred militia came forward, imperfectly armed, under General Sumner. In South Carolina the Governor (Rutledge) had just returned from the North and was at Greene's camp. Measures were taken to restore civil government throughout the State. It was not deemed expedient to order a draft, but Sumter was authorized to raise a brigade to fill the State's Continental quota. So far from doing this, however, Sumter, without consulting Greene, retired to his home on the plea of ill health, and did not rejoin the army until four months later. Moreover, he left instructions with the officer to whom he turned over his command that he wished "the troops to have a respite from service until the 1st of October, and as many of them furloughed from time to time as the service will permit of." And he did this in face of a letter from Greene, received only a few days before, saying that "as soon as re-enforcements arrive and the troops have had a little relaxation, we will draw our force to a point and attack the enemy wherever he may be found." Such a flagrant case of insubordination deserved the severest punishment, and Greene's first thought was to bring Sumter to immediate trial. But on reflection he saw that this would introduce dissension in a State where he needed every available assistance. Moreover, he fully appreciated Sumter's brilliant abilities as a partisan leader, and he was perhaps not without hopes that Sumter might soon return to duty. He therefore decided to pass over his dereliction in silence. He had no hesitation, however, in peremptorily rescinding the order for furloughing the men; and he directed their new commander, Colonel Henderson, not only to give no furlough, but to call out every man at home. In this Henderson was only partially successful, and the number of men he brought to the battle of Eutaw Springs was less than two hundred. In the final effort which Greene was about to make to drive the British out of South Carolina the troops of that State numbered barely seven hundred in all.

In Georgia a small force of about one hundred and fifty militia had been raised, but before they could take the field they were smitten with small-pox, and were disbanded.

The six weeks of repose on the High Hills of Santee had thus brought nothing in the way of re-enforcements but about seven hundred raw levies from North Carolina, and these so deficient in arms that only half of them could be brought into action. It had brought nothing in the way of clothing or other equipments. Rutledge had indeed come back with promises of money from Robert Morris, the new Superintendent of Finance. But the promises were

CLOSE OF THE SOUTHERN CAMPAIGN. 267

not cash; only authority to draw drafts on Morris to a limited extent, and these were conditioned upon subscriptions being obtained from Southern planters to shares in the new bank. The idea of expecting planters, in the midst of a civil war, to subscribe to a new-fangled idea of a bank away off in Philadelphia was in the last degree visionary. Rutledge could not secure a subscription for one share along the whole line of his journey from Philadelphia to the Santee. Greene wrote to Morris telling him of the result; and thinking that Morris could not possibly comprehend his situation, he endeavored to paint it for him in unmistakable colors. "When I tell you that I am in distress, don't imagine that I mean little difficulties, but suppose my situation to be like a ship's crew in a storm, where the vessel is ready to sink and the water gains ground in the hold with every exertion to prevent it. It is a maxim in republican governments never to despair of the commonwealth; nor do I. But I foresee more difficulties than I can readily see how to conquer. I wish to discharge my duty, but events will depend upon the means and upon the hand of Providence. If I have any opportunity of obtaining money and drawing bills on you, I shall embrace it. But 'tis a very uncertain source, and therefore I leave you to judge of the prudence of exposing an army to such contingencies." For the present he found no one ready to buy drafts on Morris. But the Governor discovered a small source of revenue in seizing indigo, of which a considerable amount was raised in the State, and this was sold for cash, with which the wants of the army in the matter of clothing were slightly relieved.

For food the army depended now, as it always

had, on forced impressment from the surrounding country. The necessity for this was a constant incentive to plunder, and the intense hatred between Whig and Tory still further increased this tendency. This disposition was naturally more noticeable among the partisan troops of the State than among the Continentals. Greene repressed it with a heavy hand, several marauders being hanged. The same punishment had to be meted out to deserters, and one sergeant was shot for inciting to mutiny. While Greene did not shirk the responsibility for these acts, yet his kindly nature was sickened at the sight of them and of the miseries of the people around him. In writing to his wife he could not repress his longing "for a peaceful retirement, where love and softer pleasures are to be found. Here, turn what way you will, you have nothing but the mournful widow and the plaints of the fatherless child, and behold nothing but houses desolated and plantations laid waste. Ruin is in every form and misery in every shape." It was more than six years since he had left his home, and nearly two years since the last glimpse of his wife at the winter camp at Morristown. The activity and excitement of the campaign had absorbed his attention, and it was doubtless not lacking in that pleasure which a vigorous man always feels in the accomplishment of important deeds; yet, in the temporary inaction of camp, surrounded by misery, and with a still uncertain future before him, there must have been many a long, sad, and weary hour, in which his thoughts turned to home and wife and children.

But these six weeks, though they brought but a handful of re-enforcements and a pittance in money,

CLOSE OF THE SOUTHERN CAMPAIGN. 269

had refreshed and invigorated his army, restored its discipline, and raised its hopes. It was in good spirits in spite of its almost incredible hardships, and nothing was to be gained by further inaction. He therefore sallied forth from his camp to fight the British army once more, hoping to inflict a disastrous defeat upon it and drive the remnants into Charleston, where, as he more than once suggested to Washington, he hoped that the French fleet would come to capture them.

On the 23d of August he broke camp at daybreak and marched up the Wateree toward Camden. Stuart, with a force slightly larger than his own, was encamped nearly opposite to him and about sixteen miles distant, at the junction of the Congaree and Wateree. It was open to Greene to march down the river to Nelson's Ferry, about two miles from Eutaw Springs, and, crossing there, place himself between Stuart and Charleston; but to this there were manifold objections. The rivers were enormously swollen by recent rains, and Greene did not possess enough boats to insure his crossing; if Stuart reached Nelson's Ferry before him, his army was not sufficiently numerous to force a passage across the river. Moreover, throughout the whole campaign he always manœuvred so as to keep as near as possible to the headwaters of the streams, and never to allow the enemy to get between him and the base of the mountains, along which in case of necessity lay his line of retreat to Virginia. Finally, the militia of Pickens and Henderson (formerly Sumter's) were in the vicinity of Fort Granby, and he wished to unite with them before making an attack. The plan of moving down the river was therefore renounced in favor of a circuitous march through Camden and Howell's Ferry, thus approaching Stuart from the north and west, and on the same side of the river that he was.

Owing to the intense heat, Greene moved slowly, and on the 28th reached Fort Motte. Stuart, as soon as he heard that Greene was at Camden, began his retreat toward Charleston, and established himself at Eutaw Springs. Sending all his heavy baggage back to Howell's Ferry, and keeping only two wagons loaded with hospital stores and rum, Greene moved slowly forward in pursuit. On the 5th he learned of a successful encounter between Marion (who with his own partisans and Washington's Dragoons was raiding the lower country toward Charleston) and a party of British and Hessians at Parker's Ferry on the Edisto, in which Marion killed and wounded about one hundred of his opponents, with only a trifling loss on his own side. Marion joined him on the evening of September 7th, about seven miles from Eutaw Springs.

On the morning of the 8th Greene formed his army in two columns, each ready for instant deployment. In the first were four small battalions of militia—two from North Carolina, under Colonel Malmedy, and two from South Carolina, under Pickens and Marion; in the second were three small brigades of Continentals, from North Carolina, Virginia, and Maryland, under Sumner, Campbell, and Williams respectively. Lee with his legion covered the right flank, Henderson with the South Carolina partisans the left flank, and Washington's Cavalry with the remnants of Kirkwood's Delaware Battalion formed the rear. Two three-pounders were with the first column and two six-pounders with the second.

CLOSE OF THE SOUTHERN CAMPAIGN. 271

In this order Greene moved forward at daylight toward Eutaw Springs. His total strength was about twenty-three hundred, of whom twelve hundred and fifty-six were Continentals and the rest militia. Stuart's force was almost exactly equal in strength, and consisted of the Third Regiment or "Buffs," lately arrived from Ireland, the Sixty-third and Sixty-fourth Regiments, which had served through the whole war, a battalion of Grenadiers, and the New York and New Jersey Volunteers under Cruger. They were camped in a clearing about two hundred yards west of Eutaw Springs, on the main road along the Congaree. Except in this clearing the surrounding country was heavily wooded. They do not seem to have kept a very good watch, for although Greene had passed the night within less than seven miles of them, they had no knowledge of his approach, and on the morning of the 8th the usual detachment of "rooting parties" was sent out from each regiment, unarmed and accompanied only by a small escort, to dig for sweet potatoes. Two deserters came into Stuart's camp during the night telling of Greene's approach, but their story was not credited; they were thought to be spies, and were sent to the guard house. Nevertheless, a detachment of cavalry under Captain Coffin was sent out after the "rooting parties" to reconnoiter. This detachment met Greene's advance guard about 8 A. M., four miles from Eutaw. Supposing it to be a party of militia, Coffin charged impetuously. He soon learned his mistake, and his men broke and fled, leaving forty prisoners and a number of dead and wounded on the field. The "rooting parties" who were in the fields near the river, hearing this firing, came through the woods to the road, where they were all captured.

The sound of Coffin's skirmish told Stuart that the enemy was near him, and he quickly put his force in position across the road, about two hundred yards in front of his camp. The Third Regiment was placed on the right, the Volunteers under Cruger in the center, and the Sixty-third and Sixty-fourth on the left. A battalion of light infantry under Major Marjoribanks protected his right flank, extending from the Third Regiment to the steep bank of Eutaw Creek. His three pieces of artillery were placed in the center, on the road.

Greene moved forward quickly in pursuit of Coffin, deploying his two columns into lines as rapidly as the ground would permit, and sending his artillery in advance to open the engagement. In this manner he continued to move forward until he came upon the enemy's main line. Here a very hot fight took place. The militia, under the lead of Pickens and Marion, fought with great determination and held their ground for a long time, but they were finally forced back in the center, and Sumner was ordered from the second into the first line. Thus reenforced, the first line renewed the battle and again gained ground, but after a while it was again forced back. Greene then sent Williams and Campbell forward with orders not to fire, but to use their bayonets; at the same time Washington's Cavalry was advanced against the British right under Marjoribanks, and Lee with the infantry of the Legion against their left. A most determined assault was then made on all sides; the men came to close quarters and the bayonet was freely used. On the left Washington

CLOSE OF THE SOUTHERN CAMPAIGN. 273

met with disaster. Marjoribanks made a stubborn defense, and the ground was much too densely wooded to allow the cavalry to operate with advantage. Washington's horse was shot under him, he was bayoneted, and would have been killed but for the intervention of a British officer, who made him prisoner.. All of his officers but two were killed or wounded, and nearly half of his men met the same fate. The remnants were withdrawn by the two surviving officers, and their retreat was covered by Colonel Wade Hampton and the South Carolina partisans. In the center and on the right the Americans met with complete success. In the desperate struggle Campbell was killed, Howard and Henderson were wounded, the gallant Duval, who had led the storming party into the ditch at Ninety-Six, was killed, and many others were wounded; but the line pressed on, greatly assisted by the fire of the Legion upon the British left flank. Two of the three British guns were captured and three hundred prisoners were taken; and finally their whole line gave way and fled in confusion through their camp. Marjoribanks from the right followed and covered their retreat.

The greater part of the British force ran until they reached the two roads some distance in rear of their camp. Here Stuart succeeded in rallying them. But a portion of the New York Volunteers under Major Sheridan rushed into a strongly built brick house on the edge of a garden surrounded by a stout fence. Marjoribanks halted in the garden on the right of this house. Sheridan was pursued so closely by the infantry of Lee's Legion that both reached the brick house at the same moment, and for a time there was a struggle for the possession of the door. But the British finally held it and closed it, and then began a vigorous fire from the windows. Unfortunately, the line of the American advance led directly through the British camp, and it was filled with an abundance of good things to eat and drink. The Americans could not resist the temptation to stop and enjoy these luxuries, to which they had so long been strangers; they considered the battle won, and no efforts of their officers could induce them to continue the pursuit. Thus the Legion, alone and unsupported, reached the house. It could not maintain itself against the fire from the windows and was forced to retreat. It did so, protecting itself from the fire by means of the prisoners which it took. Seeing their retreat, Coffin with his cavalry, which was in the woods on the British left and had not been carried away in their retreat, emerged and made a vigorous charge against the American right, and Marjoribanks resumed the offensive against Kirkwood on their left. Coffin was met by Hampton in a desperate encounter, in which the former was routed. The two six-pounders from the American second line, together with the two which had been captured from the British, were then brought up for the purpose of demolishing the house. Hampton was so successful that both he and the artillery pushed on too far and without proper support, the bulk of the American force still being in complete disorder, eating and drinking in the British camp. Seeing this, Marjoribanks made a bold and successful flank attack, inflicting great loss on Hampton, driving him back, and capturing three out of the four pieces of artillery. This put an end to the action. The American force was in such confusion that their only safety was in re-

CLOSE OF THE SOUTHERN CAMPAIGN. 275

treat, which Greene now ordered. It was nearly noon, the battle had lasted between three and four hours, the heat was now intense, and there was no water available. Collecting his wounded, Greene fell back seven miles to Burdell's plantation, whence he had marched in the morning. Hampton brought up the rear, but the British attempted no pursuit beyond the line of their camp. On the following evening Stuart destroyed such stores as he could not carry away, and, leaving seventy-two of his wounded and one thousand stand of arms, began a hasty retreat toward Charleston. Greene thereupon moved forward as far as Eutaw Springs with his main body, and sent Marion and Lee in pursuit. They skirmished with Stuart's rear guard, but were not strong enough to accomplish anything. Greene followed them with his entire force to Ferguson's Swamp, fourteen miles from Eutaw; but here Stuart was joined by a considerable re-enforcement from Charleston, and Greene was not in condition to attack this increased force; he therefore retreated slowly through Eutaw Springs, across Nelson's Ferry, and up the east bank of the river to his former camp on the High Hills of Santee.

The battle of Eutaw Springs was the most hotly contested engagement of the war. Greene, who had been in nearly all the battles at the North, wrote to Washington that it was "a most bloody battle—by far the most obstinate fight I ever saw." The numbers were small—only twenty-three hundred on each side—but the losses were proportionately very great. On the American side eighteen officers and one hundred and two men were killed, forty-three officers and three hundred and thirty-two men wounded, and eight missing; a total of five hundred and twenty-two, or about one fourth of their entire strength—the proportion in officers being still greater. The British, according to their own account, lost three officers and eighty-two men killed, sixteen officers and three hundred and thirty-five men wounded, and ten officers and two hundred and forty-seven men missing; a total of six hundred and nine y, or nearly one third of their strength. But these figures were inaccurate, at least in the number missing, for Greene carried off the field four hundred and thirty prisoners, in addition to seventy-two wounded who were abandoned by Stuart on the day after the battle. Their loss was thus at least nine hundred men out of a force of twenty-three hundred. The gallant Marjoribanks, who had contributed so much to save their army from complete capture, died on the retreat to Charleston.

Greene claimed a victory because, although he retreated from the field, he regained it the second day afterward, and pursued the enemy more than fourteen miles beyond it. It was in reality a drawn battle, but it was remarkable not only on account of the fierceness of the fighting, but as being the only case during the war in which the British regulars were driven headlong in an open fight; it was the second case—Stony Point being the first—in which the Americans freely and successfully used the bayonet. It was still more remarkable for the unflinching stubbornness with which the militia fought. The substantial results of victory were all on Greene's side, and were so recognized by Washington, Congress, and the people generally. Congress passed a highly eulogistic vote of thanks to Greene for his "most

BATTLE OF EUTAW SPRINGS.

1st VIEW.
Showing the Armies drawn up in the wood.

2nd VIEW.
Showing their situation after the British were driven into the old field.

REFERENCE.

1. American Reserve.
2. Maryland Line.
3. Virginia Line.
4. N. Carolina Line.
5. S. Carolina Militia.
6. N. Carolina Militia.
7. Lee's Legion.
8, 9. Henderson's Command.
10. Marjoribanks.
11. The British Line.
12. British Reserve.
13. Kirkwood.
14. Lee's Infantry.
15. Hampton.
16. Capt. Coffin.
17. Cavalry of the Legion after un Enemy's defeat.
△ British Encampment.

From Johnson's Life of Greene

signal victory," and ordered a gold medal and a British standard to be presented to him; and Washington wrote him a most flattering letter, saying: "How happy am I, having it in my power to congratulate you upon a victory as splendid as I hope it will prove important! Fortune must have been coy, indeed, had she not yielded at last to so persevering a pursuer as you have been."

The battle of Eutaw Springs was fought on the 8th of September, 1781, and Yorktown with Cornwallis's army surrendered on the 19th of October. The two events practically terminated the war, although Charleston was not evacuated until December 14, 1782, and New York till November 25, 1783. De Grasse, with his fleet and the troops he had brought with him, sailed back to the West Indies; Rochambeau wintered his army in Virginia; Washington divided the American troops at Yorktown into two bodies, sending one under Lincoln back to the Hudson, and the other under St. Clair to re-enforce Greene.

This scattering of the force which had taken Yorktown was a grievous disappointment to Greene and Governor Rutledge. When the latter arrived at Greene's camp on the Santee at the beginning of August, he brought the news that De Grasse's fleet would be on the coast by the latter part of the month. Greene thereupon wrote to Washington, under date of August 6th, a long letter, giving an exact account of the situation in the South and his own suggestions as to the way in which the French fleet might be utilized. Washington had written for just such a report on July 30th, but his letter was not received until six weeks after Greene had sent his. In this letter Greene expressed confidence in the success of the intended operations against New York, of which Washington had informed him in June. When this should be accomplished, he suggested as follows: "Twenty-five hundred regular forces, to be added to the Marquis's army, besides what may be expected from Pennsylvania and Virginia, would oblige Cornwallis to take a position and fortify himself; and if the supplies to his army could be cut off by water, which the fleet may easily effect after the reduction of New York, he would be obliged to surrender in a fortnight, or three weeks at most, for want of provisions." This letter outlined with remarkable accuracy the subsequent result at Yorktown. Washington did not receive it till he was on his way thither, and the suggestion had no special influence on his plans, which were already formed before he received it; but the letter is interesting as showing how completely Greene understood the situation, and how fully his mind was in accord with Washington's. He then goes on to state that the most important point in the South is Charleston, and urges that, as soon as Yorktown is taken, a force of ten thousand men be sent to reduce that place "with certainty and dispatch"; or, if so many can not be sent, that the attempt be made with a smaller force, provided the French naval force be strong enough to maintain absolute control on the sea.

Washington was too busy at Yorktown to make any immediate reply to this letter, and on September 17th Greene, having received word from Lafayette of the march toward Yorktown, wrote again to Washington, expressing the fullest confidence in the capture of Cornwallis's army, and urging once more the advisability of the entire force moving against Charleston as soon as this should be accomplished. "Charleston itself may be easily reduced if you will bend your forces this way. And it will afford me great pleasure to join your Excellency in the attempt; for I shall be equally happy, whether as principal or subordinate, so that the public good be promoted."

Governor Rutledge was at Greene's camp on the Santee after the battle of Eutaw and in daily communication with him. Greene doubtless impressed upon him the importance of these views, and on October 5th Rutledge wrote a long letter to Washington of the same tenor. Washington on his part had already come to the same conclusions, and although De Grasse before leaving the West Indies had written him that he could not remain longer than October 15th, yet in his first interview with him after his arrival Washington had ventured to suggest the desirability of an expedition against Charleston as soon as Yorktown should fall. De Grasse did not think favorably of it, and replied that he could not remain longer than November 1st at the very latest. Nevertheless, when Yorktown fell, on October 19th, Washington on the very next day wrote at length to De Grasse urging the project in the strongest possible language, proving conclusively that it would be successful, and telling De Grasse that it was in his power " to terminate the war and enable the allies to dictate the law in a treaty." De Grasse replied that he " would be happy to be able to make the expedition to Charleston, all the advantages of which he feels; but the orders of his court, ulterior projects, and his engagements with the Spaniards render it impossible to remain here the necessary time for this operation." In his letter he stated that he would be very happy to co-operate in the campaign of the next year, if not incompatible with the orders of his court. Washington eagerly grasped at this, and wrote back that it could not be decided until spring whether the expedition should be against New York or Charleston; but he urged upon him the "indispensable necessity of a maritime force capable of giving an absolute ascendency in these seas," and requested that his fleet rendezvous in Chesapeake Bay in May. De Grasse said that he would lay the proposition before the French court; and then, on the 4th of November, with his fleet and his troops, he sailed away to the West Indies, to meet destruction and capture at the hands of Rodney in the following April.

Thus, by the French making their co-operation with the Americans secondary to their "ulterior projects," was lost the chance of putting a summary end to the war, which was to continue in a sputtering fashion for more than a year longer. Washington made one effort toward terminating it by considering the plan of marching overland to the siege of Charleston. Lincoln, having been besieged and captured in Charleston, and being thus familiar with the locality, was asked to give his views in writing on this project. He did so, and showed conclusively that it was impracticable, because the siege material alone would weigh twenty-five hundred tons, and there was no possibility of obtaining the necessary transportation for such an amount. He advised that a part of the American army be sent to re-enforce Greene so as to enable him to confine the

CLOSE OF THE SOUTHERN CAMPAIGN. 281

British in Charleston; the rest to go back to the Hudson, and Rochambeau to winter his troops in Virginia, where they could give assistance in either direction as might be necessary. Washington adopted his recommendations, issued the necessary orders, and the troops were put in motion on the 1st of November. Those destined for the South consisted of the Pennsylvania, Maryland, and Virginia lines. St. Clair commanded the whole, and Wayne those from Pennsylvania. But the Virginia troops refused to march unless they received their arrears of pay, and as there was no money to pay them they were left behind. The others came on, consuming more than two months in the march of over five hundred miles from Yorktown to Charleston, and joining Greene before the latter place on the 5th of January. Greene had meanwhile been resting his troops at the High Hills of Santee. He had an enormous number of wounded to care for, and his hospitals extended from the Santee back to Charlotte. Unfortunately, the hospital stores destined for his army had been captured in passing through Virginia, by Tarleton and Simcoe. There were none to be had in the South, even if he had possessed the means to buy them. There was thus great suffering among the wounded, and the exposure to which his troops had so long been subjected, combined with insufficient food, lack of clothing, and a sickly climate, had produced the usual result of a great amount of sickness. Nevertheless, when the cool season came on in November, and he finally learned that there was no hope of the French co-operating in a determined effort against Charleston, Greene broke up his camp on the Santee for the last time and marched into the low country, partly to obtain supplies for his army and partly to hem the enemy in at Charleston. No re-enforcements had reached him except five hundred militia from the mountains of North Carolina, who deserted in a body a few days after his movement had begun; his losses at Eutaw and by sickness had reduced his force to about 1,500 men, including militia. It is astounding to learn from the official returns in the British Record Office that their force in South Carolina at this time (and they occupied no other point than Charleston) consisted of no less than 9,775 effectives—viz., 5,024 British regulars, 1,596 Hessians, and 3,155 Provincials. That Greene should be able, with the handful of men which by courtesy was called his army, to shut this force up in Charleston and hold them there for the remaining year of the war without any further attempt on their part to resume the offensive, is hardly less than incredible. It leads one to think that there was truth as well as rhetoric in the remark of Dr. Ramsay, the historian, that when Congress sent Greene to the Southern States they sent "a general whose military talents were equal to a re-enforcement"; and the similar remark of Morris, the Superintendent of Finance, giving his "fullest applause to an officer who finds in his own genius an ample resource for the want of men, money, clothes, arms, and supplies." The lessons of Guilford, Hobkirk's Hill, Ninety-Six, and Eutaw Springs must have made a profound impression upon the British commanders, when they allowed themselves to be reduced to impotence by a ragged and half-starved force less than one fifth their own in numbers.

CLOSE OF THE SOUTHERN CAMPAIGN. 283

That Greene had succeeded in overawing the British is evident from their behavior as he approached Charleston. He had left the Santee on November 18th, following the familiar route across the Congaree and Wateree to Orangeburg, and thence down the Edisto toward Charleston. Placing Williams in command of the main body with instructions to continue the advance slowly, Greene took four hundred men, selected from the Legion, Washington's Cavalry, and Sumter's partisans, and with them he pushed rapidly to the front. Stuart was then at Goose Creek Bridge, about fifteen miles north of Charleston, with about two thousand men ; and eight miles on his left, at the village of Dorchester, on the Ashley River, was another post with one thousand men, of whom eight hundred and fifty were infantry and one hundred and fifty cavalry. Greene made a dash at Dorchester on the morning of December 1st. There was a short but sharp skirmish between Hampton's "State Horse" and the British cavalry, in which the latter were defeated. Then throwing his cannon into the river and destroying his stores, the British commander retired with great haste toward Charleston, Stuart doing the same from Goose Creek Bridge. The two roads on which they were retreating united at the Quarter House, a few miles out of Charleston, and here they made their first stand. So great was the alarm that the entire garrison of Charleston was ordered out, and even the negroes were called to arms and enrolled. As Williams wrote to Greene, " Your success at Dorchester would make your enemies hate themselves if all the circumstances were generally known."

Having thus driven the enemy into the city limits

of Charleston by a mere feint, Greene rejoined the main body and stationed them at a camp which Kosciusko had selected at a place called the Round O, about forty miles northwest of Charleston, in a district of great fertility, where good crops had been raised, as it had seen no campaigning since 1779. Here he established his main body on December 9th, with Lee's Legion and the partisans spread out fan-shape over a wide territory thirty miles in front of him. His "main body" contained only about eight hundred effective men, and after supplying the detachments with ammunition it had only four rounds per man left; but Greene relied upon the detachments in his front to keep these disagreeable facts from being known to General Leslie, who had now taken command in Charleston.

On the 4th of January St. Clair at last arrived from Yorktown with numbers largely reduced by his long march. At the same time the term of service of the Virginia line expired, and they were sent home. St. Clair's re-enforcement barely brought Greene's strength up to what it had been before the battle of Eutaw. It was necessary to retain all the infantry with him in South Carolina, but part of the cavalry which had arrived was united with detachments from the State troops to form a command for Wayne, with which he was dispatched to the conquest of Georgia. He started on January 9th, and reached the Savannah River, about thirty miles above the city of Savannah, on the 16th. The British forces in Georgia at that time numbered about one thousand men, composed of a small body of regulars, some Tory militia and Creek and Choctaw Indians. General Clarke was in command, and next in rank to

CLOSE OF THE SOUTHERN CAMPAIGN. 285

him was Colonel Browne, who had been captured and paroled at Augusta, and subsequently exchanged. At Wayne's approach Clarke retired into Savannah and Browne retreated toward the interior. Wayne's force was so small—never exceeding four hundred in all, and fluctuating from time to time as the militia came and went—that he was unable to undertake any serious movements. He kept his little force between Savannah and Browne's detachment, constantly manœuvring, destroying the enemy's stores with small raiding parties, and never placing himself in a position where he could be advantageously attacked. He had two skirmishes with Browne's militia and Indians, one on May 21st and the other on June 23d, in both of which he was successful. The Indians then retired to the mountains, and the Tory militia under Browne retreated to Florida. Clarke evacuated Savannah on July 11th and took its garrison to Charleston. The State was thus completely freed from British occupation, and the Assembly convened at Savannah to restore civil order. Wayne rejoined Greene.

There were no further movements of any military importance. During the year 1782 and the first half of 1783 Greene's attention was absorbed in assisting the civil authorities to restore the State governments, in confining the British to the limits of Charleston, and in finding food and clothing for his army. Expeditions were undertaken from time to time, under Pickens, Marion, and Lee, against the islands north and south of Charleston, but none of them were of permanent importance, except one in August, in which young John Laurens—one of the most gifted men of his time, with a future of great usefulness before him—lost his life. Greene moved his camp from one place to another in front of Charleston, in order to afford protection to the Legislature and to find provisions for his men.

The Legislature of South Carolina convened, for the first time in two years, on January 18, 1782, at the village of Jacksonborough, about thirty-five miles northwest of Charleston. Rutledge was Governor, and he fully appreciated how much the State owed to Greene. The greater part of his address was taken up with a eulogy of him. He spoke of the "wisdom, prudence, address, and bravery of the great and gallant General Greene, and the intrepidity of the officers and men under his command. . . . A general who is justly entitled, from his many signal services, to honorable and singular marks of your approbation and gratitude." The Legislature replied in a similar strain, and a few days later, putting their thoughts into deeds, they passed a bill "for vesting in General Nathanael Greene, in consideration of his important services, the sum of ten thousand guineas." As soon as the Legislature of Georgia heard of this it took similar action, making him a grant of five thousand guineas. And this was followed by North Carolina, which gave him twenty-four thousand acres of the best lands in the western part of the State, which subsequently became Tennessee. The two former grants were not paid in money, but in confiscated lands. South Carolina allotted him a plantation known as Boone's Barony, to the south of the Edisto, together with the slaves that were attached to the land. Georgia gave him a beautiful and highly improved estate belonging to the late Tory

CLOSE OF THE SOUTHERN CAMPAIGN. 287

Governor Graham; it was called Mulberry Grove, and was situated on the south bank of the Savannah River, about fourteen miles above Savannah. The adjoining estate was presented to his friend and fellow-soldier, Wayne. These valuable gifts would have made Greene independent in fortune if they had not been swept away by the obligations he had assumed in the effort to find clothing and food for his men, as will be afterward explained.

As has already been stated, it was fifteen months after hostilities practically ceased with the battle of Eutaw Springs before Charleston was finally evacuated, and it was twenty-one months before the troops were discharged and sent home. Nothing is more trying to the discipline of an army than the period of inaction between the close of hostilities and the declaration of peace. At the North, Washington barely succeeded in preventing a mutiny at Newburg, and in the South, Greene had an equally difficult problem. Several hundred of his men had no other clothing than the remnants of a coat or blanket, which they pinned around the waist with a thorn. They were so ragged that they could not in decency leave their tents. They had received no pay for more than a year, some of them for longer periods. They had subsisted by means of forced impressments of food, but now the Legislature passed a law forbidding this method. They were camped in a sickly country, and large numbers were sick with dysentery and fever. They had suffered hardships and privations beyond description, and now, when the war seemed practically over, the longing to return to their homes was almost irresistible. Many of the officers succeeded in getting away. St. Clair obtained a leave of absence; Carrington, Williams, and others went North on public business, in the hope of securing supplies or money for the army; Lee pleaded ill health and unrequited services, and went to Virginia to marry his beautiful and rich cousin, Mildred Lee. The officers of the Legion were dissatisfied with their new commander, and other officers were restive under the enforcement of proper regulations regarding public property. Finally the men became mutinous. Wayne's division had mutinied at Morristown two years before, and, as Lafayette said, "had been well paid and well clothed in consequence of it." These men were now in Greene's army, and among them was a sergeant named Gornell, who had commanded one of the regiments in the New Jersey mutiny. He put himself in communication with the enemy and concocted a scheme to seize Greene in the night and deliver him to the enemy. This was to be followed by a general mutiny of the Pennsylvania and Maryland troops

The difficulties connected with holding his troops together during the last eighteen months of their service were among the most serious that Greene ever had to contend with; but he faced them manfully. As for the mutiny, he put it down with a heavy hand. Having gained satisfactory proofs of the conspiracy, he caused Gornell to be arrested, tried, and hanged, on April 22d. Four other sergeants were sent into the interior under guard, and the other ringleaders succeeded in escaping that night to the enemy. There were no further overt acts on the part of the men. In dealing with the officers he used firmness mingled with patience. The

CLOSE OF THE SOUTHERN CAMPAIGN. 289

officers of the Legion resigned in a body because their requests, presented in respectful language, in regard to their commanding officer and the method of reorganizing the corps, were not approved. To their astonishment, Greene accepted their resignations. Seeing that they were in the wrong, they pleaded to have their commissions restored, and to be allowed to present their grievances to Congress. Greene somewhat reluctantly acceded to this. As soon as the matter came before Congress his orders were confirmed.

Another trouble with the officers arose from their appropriating public horses to their private use and selling or exchanging them. A flagrant offender was a certain Captain Gunn. Greene brought him before a court of inquiry, when, to his surprise, the court acquitted him and justified the transaction. Greene disapproved the finding in general orders, required the horse to be restored, and referred the matter to Congress, by whom he was fully sustained.

The greatest difficulty of all, however, was to keep his army from starving to death and to secure enough clothing to cover its nakedness. For supplying the Northern army the Superintendent of Finance had entered into contracts payable at the Treasury of the United States, but he left the Southern army to be supported by the Southern States. Virginia and North Carolina repudiated this arrangement and refused to contribute anything. The entire expense of supporting the Southern army thus fell upon South Carolina. Its Legislature passed a law to stop the method of impressment, by which the army had hitherto obtained food, and appointed its own agent to collect supplies and turn them over to the army. The system worked well for a time, but during the summer, through the lack of energy of the agent or from other causes, it began to work very badly. Greene addressed urgent letters to the Governor on the subject, but, in spite of every disposition on the latter's part to aid him, there was no improvement. Finally he had to take the matter into his own hands. On the 24th of October he addressed a letter to the agent in which he said: " The army have had but a few days' rice for more than a month. Our prospects of beef are not less alarming than our supplies of rice have been deficient. The discipline and temper of the army have been ruined from the irregular manner in which they are subsisted; and a continuance, not to say an increase, of the difficulties on this head will soon reduce things to a state of desperation. My duty obliges me, therefore, to call on you to give me a decisive answer, whether you can by the present mode afford certain and effectual supplies for the army or not. If you can not, some other measures must be adopted." The agent referred the letter to the Governor and Council, and, no answer being returned, four days later Greene issued orders for resuming the method of impressment, taking care to provide strict rules in regard to it, and cautioning his men that it " should be conducted with the greatest prudence, delicacy, and equality among the people." In taking this step, he acted in disregard of the State law, but his soldiers were starving, and their safety was to him the supreme law.

In the matter of clothing, the situation was equally bad, but different measures had to be adopted. There was abundance of it in Charleston, and the British garrison was short of food. A contraband trade to a limited extent was therefore permitted under the supervision of Lee and Laurens—rice going into the city, and shirts and other articles coming out. But this could not be permitted to any large extent, and in the spring Greene employed Mr. John Waties, afterward Chancellor of North Carolina, to obtain supplies of rum, blankets, hospital stores, and salt from Georgetown, paying for them in bills drawn on the Superintendent of Finance, which the people were now persuaded to take, though with some hesitation and at a considerable discount. These means, however, afforded only a partial relief. In the month of May Leslie proposed to Greene a cessation of hostilities and the opening of a trade between Charleston and the interior. Greene was too good a soldier to enter into any negotiations relating to peace, and merely referred the offer to Congress, by whom it was promptly rejected. In regard to permitting trade, he consulted with the Governor and Council, and at their request he declined it. This possible source of supply was thus cut off, and the suffering for lack of clothes continued to increase. In August some of the clothing which had been nearly nine months on the way from Yorktown arrived, just as the condition of the army was growing desperate. At this time Greene wrote: "For upward of two months more than one third of our men were entirely naked, with nothing but a breech-clout about them, and never came out of their tents, and the rest were as ragged as wolves." Soon after this the army was reorganized and consolidated in pursuance of a resolution of Congress, and a considerable number of men whose term was about expiring were sent home. The Yorktown clothing had to be issued to them to fit them for their long march, and those who remained were as badly off as ever. Finally, in October, winter was coming on and some arrangements had to be made. At this time appeared in camp a man named John Banks, of the firm of Hunter & Banks, of Fredericksburg, Va. They were merchants of a speculative turn, and had lately been engaged in privateering. Banks had met Mr. Waties at Georgetown in the previous spring, and had then made a proposition for supplying the army which was favorably received; but before getting a reply he had obtained permission from the local commandant to visit Charleston. He now came forward with a proposition to supply the army with clothing, taking his pay in bills on the Superintendent of Finance at par, provided he could be paid twelve hundred guineas in hard cash. An agent of Mr. Morris was present at Greene's headquarters with a small amount of ready money which he was authorized to dole out when Greene's difficulties became finally insurmountable. With some difficulty Greene persuaded this agent to part with the twelve hundred guineas; the bargain with Banks was carried out, and the army was clothed—"better clothed," said Wayne, "than I ever saw an American army before."

The long months of inaction thus dragged slowly along, beset with petty difficulties of army housekeeping and devoid of any military operations of importance. As early as August Leslie had announced a speedy evacuation of Charleston, but from week to week it was postponed. Finally, on the 14th of December, the British filed through the streets and went on boards their ships, and Wayne, at the head of

CLOSE OF THE SOUTHERN CAMPAIGN. 293

the American army, closely followed them. Greene and Governor Matthews rode into town at three o'clock in the afternoon, the entire population lining the streets to shout their welcome.

The evacuation of Charleston did not, however, put an end to Greene's difficulties. Three months before, Congress had passed a resolution directing him to remain in the Southern States until further orders, to employ his troops offensively or defensively as he might think proper, and saying that it was indispensably necessary to keep a regular force in that department. When the evacuation of Charleston was arranged, Greene wrote to Washington asking for instructions as to the disposition of the troops. Washington replied, giving him authority to march his troops to the northward, but leaving the time and manner almost wholly to his discretion. Greene was much in doubt what course to pursue. Peace was not yet signed, and he hesitated to leave the State defenseless in case hostilities should be resumed; on the other hand, he wished to save further expense, and also to gratify the natural desire of the men to return home. Finally, on the 20th of April, he received news of the ratification of the preliminary articles between Great Britain and the United States.

Greene's first act was to write to Washington, from whom he had recently received a most cordial letter, written on receipt of the news that Charleston was evacuated. The two letters are worth quoting somewhat at length, as showing the relations between the commander in chief and his principal subordinate after nearly eight years of service. Washington's was dated at Newburg on February 6th, and

Greene's at Charleston on April 20, 1783. Washington writes: "It is with a pleasure which friendship only is susceptible of that I congratulate you on the glorious end you have put to hostilities in the Southern States. The honor and advantage of it I hope you will long live to enjoy. . . . If historiographers should be hardy enough to fill the page of history with the advantages that have been gained with unequal numbers on the part of America in the course of this contest, and attempt to relate the distressing circumstances under which they have been obtained, it is more than probable that posterity will bestow on their labors the epithet and marks of fiction; for it will not be believed that such a force as Great Britain has employed for eight years in this country could be baffled in their plan of subjugating it by numbers infinitely less, composed of men oftentimes half-starved, always in rags, and experiencing at times every species of distress which human nature is capable of undergoing. . . . I let no opportunity slip to inquire after your son George at Princeton, and it is with pleasure I hear he enjoys good health and is a fine, promising boy. With great truth and sincerity and every sentiment of friendship, I am, etc."

Greene's letter reads thus: "I beg leave to congratulate your Excellency upon the returning smiles of peace and the happy establishment of our independence. This important event must be doubly welcome to you, who have so successfully conducted the war, through such a variety of difficulties, to so happy a close. If universal respect and the general affections of a grateful country can compensate for the many painful hours which you have experienced in your country's cause, you are richly rewarded.

Every heart feels and every tongue confesses the merit and importance of your services. The polite attention which I have experienced since I have had the honor to serve under your command claims my particular acknowledgment; and I feel a singular satisfaction in having preserved your confidence and esteem through the whole progress of the war, notwithstanding many jarring interests. . . . I have the honor to be, with great respect and esteem, your Excellency's most obedient, humble servant."

These two letters bring to mind those which passed between Grant and Sherman just eighty-one years later, when Grant left the West to assume command of all the armies in the civil war. In fact, the relations between Washington and Greene were very similar to those which existed between Grant and Sherman; and there are no more pleasing facts in all our history than these. The two chief soldiers in our two principal wars were constant friends from their first acquaintance till death separated them. No intrigue—and many were tried in both cases—could break or mar this friendship, or stir up jealousy or discord. Each time there was a faithful, loyal subordinate, and a grateful, generous chief—both striving in harmony to achieve objects of surpassing importance, and both succeeding in conferring priceless benefits on their countrymen and their descendants.

Peace being now definitely assured, Greene no longer hesitated about sending his troops to their homes. As the march would be a long and fatiguing one, he arranged to get transports to take the Pennsylvania and Maryland divisions, now reduced by battle and sickness to such small numbers that they were consolidated into one regiment each, by sea to Philadelphia. The Virginia and North Carolina troops marched home. The Delaware battalion had gone home in December. The South Carolina partisans were disbanded, and there were none from Georgia in service. The arrangements for the march and the vessels consumed much time, and it was not until July that the troops were all started to their destinations. As they left, Greene wrote a parting letter to the Governors of each of the six States within his command, commending the returning soldiers to their care and gratitude, and saying: " Often in the worst of times have I assured them that their country would not be unmindful of their suffering and services; and humbly, yet confidently, do I hope that their just claims will not be forgotten."

While Greene was in Charleston, after its evacuation by the British, occurred an event which caused him the deepest mortification, clouded the rest of his life, subjected him to the most unjust and unmerited insinuations, and ended in the ruin of his pecuniary fortune. As we have seen, he had been compelled in October to disregard the State law and resort to impressment to obtain food for his starving army. But the State authorities were as much opposed to the practice as ever; and when the new Legislature assembled in January, Greene was notified that the civil power of the State would be fully exercised to stop the practice. At that time Banks, who had succeeded in clothing the army, came forward and offered to take a contract to feed it at eleven pence per ration, and take his pay in bills on Morris. Though his price was considered high, yet no one else would undertake the contract on any terms, in spite

CLOSE OF THE SOUTHERN CAMPAIGN. 297

of the fact that an advertisement inviting bidders had been published for more than three months. Banks's proposition was therefore accepted. This man had many schemes on hand besides feeding and clothing the army. He was speculating in various directions in anticipation of the change in prices that would result from a declaration of peace, and he soon became deeply involved. Distrust of the value of the bills on Morris also began to spread, and Banks's creditors refused to advance him anything further. No one else would take the contract, and the only alternative was to resort again to impressment, which would have brought on a most deplorable conflict between the civil and military authorities. The former were tired of seeing the soldiers remain, now that peace seemed assured, and they were for the moment ill-disposed toward Greene, because he had insisted on having certain engagements carried out which he had made with loyalists prior to the evacuation, and also because he was opposed to the harsh legislation which was proposed for confiscating their property and otherwise maltreating them. At this juncture the merchants proposed that if Greene would guarantee Banks's debts they would furnish the latter further credit, and would surrender the interest which Banks had assigned to them in the bills on Morris. For the purpose of keeping his men from starvation Greene agreed to this, and executed a bond of surety guaranteeing the debts of Banks. For his security Banks pledged all the bills he had received, both for the clothing and the feeding contracts; the merchants executed a release of their interest in them, and an agent was sent on to Philadelphia during the latter part of May with an order for them on Mr. Pettit (formerly associated with Greene in the Quartermaster General's Department), in whose hands they were reported to be. Before he could return, Greene started North, and, traveling leisurely, did not reach Philadelphia until the autumn. Then, to his dismay, he learned that Banks had previously disposed of the bills in Pettit's hands, and that his security was lost. Banks meantime had gone into bankruptcy, with liabilities of over thirty thousand pounds. In the following summer (1784) Greene returned to South Carolina, and Banks's creditors demanded that Greene pay Banks's debts, according to his bond. They acknowledged that Greene had no interest in the matter except a desire to keep his men from starving, but nevertheless they demanded their money. Banks, hearing of Greene's arrival, immediately left for the interior of the State; and Greene, mounting his horse and putting his pistols in his holsters, started in pursuit. He followed him for more than four hundred miles, mainly over the route of his own marches in 1781, only to overtake him on his death-bed in a raging fever and to see him expire. He then returned to Charleston, and endeavored to raise money in England by a mortgage on his estates in South Carolina and Georgia, but in this he failed; and he was obliged to sell his South Carolina plantation at a ruinous sacrifice, in order to get means to satisfy in part the claims of Banks's creditors. In the summer of 1785, on the advice of his friends, he laid the whole matter before Congress and asked for relief. But before action was taken Greene died. His widow was then left to prosecute the claim, warmly assisted by Hamilton and opposed by Sumter, who was then in Congress,

CLOSE OF THE SOUTHERN CAMPAIGN. 299

and it was not until June, 1796, that relief was finally granted.

Thus an act of kindness, imprudent in a business sense, but inspired by the generous motive of relieving his suffering soldiers, led to endless trouble and pecuniary ruin. Lafayette had done the same thing on a small scale in purchasing clothing for his men when he went through Baltimore in 1781. His act led only to applause, and he was promptly reimbursed by Congress. But in the confusion and weariness at the end of the war Greene's generosity was overlooked.

Worse than this, his motives were impugned, and it was insinuated that he was a silent partner of Banks. To a man of Greene's temperament, conscious of his own integrity, this was a blow tenfold heavier than the loss of fortune. What gave currency to these rumors was the fact that two of Greene's own aids-de-camp, Majors Burnet and Forsyth, had entered into partnership with Banks; not specially with reference to the clothing and feeding contracts, but in his general speculations. Peace was approaching, and they had to look for some occupation in private business. Without consulting Greene and without his knowledge, regardless of propriety, their own dignity and the reputation of their chief, they formed a business connection with the man who had received from their chief what was considered a lucrative contract. Finally, to complete the chain of unfortunate circumstances, Banks had written to a friend at the North, in a letter which was opened by the bearer, " I find General Greene an exceedingly agreeable man; and, from hints dropped already, expect his proposals for an interest in a house we may establish in Charleston." Greene's independent character had made him many enemies, as well as stanch friends, and when this letter of Banks's was made public, and it became known that two of Greene's aids-de-camp were interested in Banks's speculations, his enemies asserted that Greene had become surety for Banks's debts because he was his partner, and not because he wanted to keep the army from starving. What made the matter all the more galling to Greene was the evident fact that he could not treat these rumors with silent contempt, but must notice and answer them. As he afterward said in laying the matter before Congress, "I despise popular prejudices and disdain vulgar suspicions"; but this was a case which must be met. Banks therefore published a card in which he declared that his only reason for imagining that General Greene desired a business connection with him arose from Major Burnet's negotiations with reference to himself; that he regretted having taken an improper liberty with General Greene's name, and that he had already declared "under the solemnity of an oath that he neither has, nor ever had, any commercial connection with me of a private nature, or intimated a wish or desire of the kind; and also that he never granted me a flag in his life, or any other privilege or indulgence for commercial purposes." Greene also placed in the hands of Wayne and Carrington all the papers in the matter, including authority from the Secretary of War to procure clothing from Charleston, his acknowledgment of Greene's full reports of the transaction and his approval thereof, and the satisfaction of the Superintendent of Finance, who was prepared to pay the drafts on presentation. Greene asked Wayne and Carrington to examine the whole matter and state their conclusions. They did so, and fully approved of all his acts, and exonerated him from the slightest suspicion of wrongdoing.

Further than this, there was nothing for Greene to do. His conduct throughout this humiliating incident was dignified and proper, with one single exception. He should have instantly dismissed his aids-de-camp. They had compromised his reputation in a manner wholly without justification. But they had served him faithfully and gallantly through five years of war; they had been with him in battle, and had suffered in common with him every possible hardship. One of them was now absent, carrying to Washington the news of the evacuation of Charleston. Both of them were soon to be thrown on the world to earn their livelihood as best they could. Greene could not bring himself to punish them, or even to treat them harshly.

The subject may well be dismissed by quoting what Washington thought of it, from a letter written to Jeremiah Wadsworth, of Connecticut, soon after Greene's death: "Persuaded as I always have been of General Greene's integrity and worth, I spurned those reports which tended to calumniate his conduct in the connection with Banks, being perfectly convinced that, whenever the matter should be investigated, his motives for entering into it would appear pure and unimpeachable. I was not without my fears, though, that he might suffer in a pecuniary way by his engagement with that man. I would fain hope, however, that the case ultimately may be otherwise; and that upon a final settlement of his affairs there will be a handsome competency for Mrs. Greene and the children. But, should it turn out differently, and Mrs. Greene, yourself, and Mr. Rutledge should think proper to intrust my namesake, G. W. Greene, to my care, I will give him as good an education as this country (I mean North America) will afford; and will bring him up to either of the genteel professions that his friends may choose, or his own inclination shall lead him to pursue, at my own cost and charge."

Washington's generous intentions with reference to his namesake were not carried out, as Lafayette had previously made a similar offer, which was accepted. The lad went abroad and was educated under Lafayette's care, until the troubles of the French Revolution caused his mother such anxiety as to induce her to recall him in 1794. Just after his return, at the age of nineteen, he was drowned in an accident in the Savannah River.

CHAPTER XIV.

CLOSING YEARS AND DEATH—1783-'86.

By the middle of July, 1783, all the arrangements had been completed for sending the troops to their homes. Greene then spent a short time in examining the estates which had been given to him in South Carolina and Georgia, and on August 15th he began his long horseback ride of more than a thousand miles to Rhode Island. His wife had been with him during the last year of the war, having joined him in front of Charleston in March, 1782; but the journey overland was far too long for her, and she had gone North by water in the spring of 1783. Greene's route lay along the coast through Wilmington, Tarborough, Halifax, Petersburg, Richmond, Fredericksburg, Mount Vernon, Alexandria, Arlington, and Annapolis to Baltimore; thence over the battle grounds of 1777 to Philadelphia and on to Trenton, where, at the house of his old friend Colonel Cox, he met Washington and rode with him to Princeton, where Congress was in session. Here he parted from Washington for the last time, and, traveling through New York and Connecticut, reached Rhode Island at the close of November. At nearly every town he entered on his journey of fifteen weeks he was met by the local authorities and a delegation of citizens to present him an address of welcome and ask him to stop and accept their hospitality. At the capitals of Virginia and Maryland he was specially received by the Legislature and given a vote of thanks for his distinguished services. When he reached Princeton he addressed a letter to the President of Congress stating that it was going on nine years since he had had an opportunity to visit his family or friends, and asking permission to return to Rhode Island, having already obtained the permission of the Commander in Chief. A committee was appointed to prepare a suitable resolution, and on their report Congress resolved that he have permission to visit his family in Rhode Island; and that two pieces of field ordnance, taken from the British army at Cowpens, Augusta, or Eutaw, be presented to him " as a public testimonial of the wisdom, fortitude, and military skill which distinguished his command in the Southern Department, and of the eminent services which, amid complicated difficulties and dangers and against an enemy greatly superior in numbers, he has successfully performed for his country." The pieces were ordered to be suitably engraved, expressive of the substance of the resolution. When he reached Rhode Island, the towns of Newport and Providence and the State Legislature voted him addresses and thanks. But probably even more gratifying was the reception he met on his arrival at his old home in Warwick, where the Kentish Guards turned out to cordially welcome him and to claim the honor of having given him his first military instruction.

During his long absence he had lost all connection with the business of the forge at Coventry. He had sold his interest to his brothers, asking them to

CLOSING YEARS AND DEATH. 305

use the proceeds in such manner as they saw fit. They had invested it in privateers and had lost it all. Having nothing to keep him in Coventry, he fixed his residence at Newport, and there passed the winter with his wife and four children, whom now for the first time he saw together. He took a house on Mill Street, nearly opposite the old stone mill, and it was his intention to pass the summer months here and the rest of the year on his plantation in South Carolina. But early in the summer of 1784 he was obliged to go South, as we have already seen, in connection with the obligations he had assumed for Banks. These led to the sacrifice of his South Carolina estate, and the necessity of his living in a much more restricted manner than he had planned. He gave up his Newport home and decided to live on his Georgia plantation, Mulberry Grove, where he took his family in the autumn of 1785.

Immediately after his arrival he received a challenge to a duel with Captain Gunn. This officer, as already stated, had made improper use of public horses in 1782, and Greene had brought him to trial. The Court having acquitted him, Greene disapproved the proceedings and referred the matter to Congress. This body not only confirmed his action, but passed a special resolution expressing its satisfaction therewith, approving the principles laid down in his orders, condemning the action of the Court, directing Captain Gunn to replace the horse he had sold, and announcing that any officer convicted of a similar offense hereafter should be deemed guilty of a breach of the Twelfth Article of War—i. e., be guilty of embezzlement and be dismissed from the service. Gunn had nursed his wrath for three years, during which time he had married a lady of fortune, settled in Georgia, and gone prominently into politics. He now demanded personal satisfaction for Greene's official acts. Such a proceeding in these days would seem preposterous. But at that time the views about dueling were such that, no matter what might be the cause of the challenge, a public man could only reject a challenge at the peril of his reputation. Hamilton sacrificed his life in deference to this prejudice. Greene was not insensible to the prejudice, but after mature deliberation he determined to disregarded it. He declined the challenge, stating his reasons in a courteous letter to Colonel Jackson, who was Gunn's second. Jackson then withdrew from the affair; but Gunn sent a second challenge through another officer. To this Greene declined any answer further than a reference to his letter to Colonel Jackson. Gunn then sent him word that he should attack him wherever he met him. Greene merely remarked that he should always carry pistols. The matter then dropped, and, fortunately, the two men never met.

Greene, in this as in every important act of his since the beginning of the war, wished to feel sure of Washington's approbation. He therefore wrote to him a full account of the affair, and said: "If a commanding officer is bound to give satisfaction to every officer who may pretend to be injured (and this pretense would not be wanting to try to wipe off the stain of public trial and condemnation), it places him in a more disagreeable situation than had ever occurred to me before. But as I may have mistaken the line of responsibility of a commanding officer, I wish for your sentiments upon the subject. It is possible

CLOSING YEARS AND DEATH. 307

you may be placed, by the ignorance of some or the imprudence of others, in the same predicament, though I believe few will be hardy enough to try such an experiment. If I thought my honor or reputation would suffer in the opinion of the world, and more especially with the military gentlemen, I value life too little to hesitate a moment to answer the challenge. But when I consider the nature of the precedent, and the extent of the mischief it may produce, I have felt a necessity to reject it."

Washington replied: "I give it as my decided opinion that your honor and reputation will stand not only perfectly acquitted for the nonacceptance of the challenge, but that your prudence and judgment would have been condemned for accepting it, because, if a commanding officer is amenable to private calls for the discharge of his public duty, he has a dagger always at his breast, and can turn neither to the right hand nor the left without meeting its point. In a word, he is no longer a free agent in office, as there are few military decisions which are not offensive to one party or the other. . . . A precedent of the sort once established in the army would no doubt have been followed up, and in that case would unquestionably have produced a revolution, but of a very different kind from that which, happily for America, has prevailed."

During the few years which intervened between the close of the war and Greene's death public office of different kinds was offered to him. His name was suggested for Secretary of War when Lincoln resigned in 1784; in the same year he was appointed by Congress a commissioner to negotiate a general peace with the Indians; and on his settling in Georgia he was appointed County Judge. But he declined each in succession, being firmly determined to lead the life of a private gentleman. Even the Society of the Cincinnati failed to interest him. He was made president of the Rhode Island Branch, but he never attended a meeting. In the spring of 1784 Washington wrote urging him to attend the meeting which was to be held, to meet the opposition which had been aroused against the hereditary principle of the society. He was suffering at the time from a relapse of the fever which he had had in each year of his service in the South, and was thus unable to attend. But his reply to Washington showed that he took little interest in the matter. It is possible that he did not fully approve the rules of the society. Gordon asserts that, in conversation with him, Greene intimated that such was the case.

In spite of his indisposition to enter public life, however, he could not remain wholly indifferent to the important public questions which arose immediately after the war. His correspondence with Robert Morris, Hamilton, Governor Reed, of Pennsylvania, and finally with Washington, was now almost entirely devoted to questions of politics. The correspondence with Morris had in fact begun in 1780, and one of the first letters from Greene shows such a remarkable grasp of the situation, and outlines so plainly the history of the next seven years, that it is well to give somewhat lengthy extracts from it. After arguing in favor of a regular army enlisted for the war, and showing that public credit had been ruined by sporting with the national faith and trying to redeem the currency at forty for one, he says: "What is to be done? I will tell you in a few words:

Call a convention of the States and establish a Congress upon a constitutional footing. Give them full powers to govern the empire, and make them accountable for their conduct; and oblige them to establish boards for all executive business, independent of their body. . . . Congress, upon their present footing, have not powers to govern the empire; nor will the people ever have confidence in this body of men upon the present Constitution. It is my opinion that, unless we have some supreme power to govern the empire, and that have authority to bring the force and resources of the States all to one point, we can never support the contest." Many people thought that the solution of the difficulty was in appointing a dictator; but Greene had no such idea. He was "in great doubt whether there would be as prompt obedience from the people at large under a dictator as under a congress vested with ample power to command the resources of the country." He was very clear, however, that Congress should be limited solely to legislative functions. "I would advise the appointment of a minister of war and a minister of finance; and let merit, and not family and fortune, direct the choice of these persons. The business of Congress should be merely legislative, and not executive." Here was the essence of the ideas which were finally adopted seven years later. In the following spring the idea of ministers of war and finance was accepted in Congress, and a few days later the Articles of Confederation, which had been under consideration for nearly four years, were at last ratified by all the States. But they contained the fatal defect of leaving the revenues to be raised by the Legislatures of the several States and by them paid over to Congress. The States failed to comply with their obligation. Congress therefore, in February, 1781, recommended to the several States, "as indispensably necessary, that they vest a power in Congress to levy for the use of the United States a duty of five per cent *ad valorem*" upon imports. But this plan never went into effect. To Greene's mortification, Rhode Island was always obstinately opposed to it. Georgia also failed to give its assent, and Virginia and South Carolina, which had at first adopted it, subsequently repealed the acts. Greene saw clearly that without power to raise its own revenues the Confederation was a rope of sand, and for the last two years of his life his correspondence about political affairs almost always turned on this question. He did his utmost, both at the South and at the North, to secure its adoption by the State Legislatures, but without success. He feared that, unless a stronger central government was formed, the Confederation would dissolve; and in writing to Washington from Charleston, in the summer of 1784, he says: "Many people secretly wish that every State should be completely independent, and that, as soon as our public debts are liquidated, Congress should be no more—a plan that would be as fatal to our happiness at home as it would be ruinous to our interest abroad." As in 1775 he had recommended a declaration of independence, so in 1785 he advocated a union of the States into one nation, with a central government endowed with sufficient power to collect its own revenues and make itself respected.

But at the latter date his thoughts were mainly turned to the establishment of his Southern home

CLOSING YEARS AND DEATH.

and the pleasures which he anticipated therein. He was charmed with Mulberry Grove, and found it in a much less injured condition than he expected. "The prospect is delightful and the house magnificent. We have a coach house and stables, a large out-kitchen, and a poultry house, . . . with a pigeon house on the top which will contain not less than a thousand pigeons. Besides these are several other buildings convenient for a family, and among the rest a fine smokehouse. The garden is in ruins, but there are still a great variety of shrubs and flowers in it." Here he expected to live and enjoy life. Anthony Wayne was on the adjoining plantation, and another of his intimate friends, Governor Reed, of Pennsylvania, was proposing to move South the following year and settle in his neighborhood. Captain Pendleton, of Virginia, one of his aids-de-camp, had established himself in Savannah, only fourteen miles down the river. Greene had a large, comfortable house, with plenty of books in the library, and horses in the stable, both his wife and himself being very fond of horseback riding. His children were about him. He seemed to have everything he wished for, and, but for the cloud of the Banks trouble, his happiness was complete. With the opening of spring the farmer was full of business. "This is a busy time with us, and I can afford but a small portion of time to write. We are planting. We have got upward of sixty acres of corn planted, and expect to plant one hundred and thirty of rice. The garden is delightful. The fruit trees and flowering shrubs form a pleasing variety. We have green peas almost fit to eat, and as fine lettuce as you ever saw. The weather is mild, and the vegetable kingdom progressing to perfection. . . . We have in the same orchard apples, pears, peaches, apricots, nectarines, plums of different kinds, figs, pomegranates, and oranges. And we have strawberries which measure three inches around." What more charming picture could there be than this, after eight years of war and anxiety and privation? All his energy and enthusiasm were now enlisted in his new occupation of planter, and he bade fair to be as famous a farmer as soldier. But the Southern sun produces not only figs and pomegranates and nectarines, but deadly diseases as well; and two months after writing this joyous letter Greene's dead body was in the vault at Savannah.

On the 12th of June he was called to Savannah to meet one of Banks's creditors. His wife drove into town with him, and they passed the night at Captain Pendleton's house. They started home in the cool of the morning, but Greene's enthusiasm as a planter led him to stop at a neighbor's plantation on the way and examine his rice fields. They were extensive, and Greene spent several hours in the middle of the day examining them. His neighbor (Mr. Williams) carried an umbrella, but Greene had campaigned so long that he neglected this precaution. Driving home in the afternoon, his head began to ache; the next day the pains in his head were intense, and there was a swelling of the forehead. Captain Pendleton came, and two physicians were summoned. Cupping and blisters were about the limit of their science. Wayne came over from his plantation and watched by his bedside day and night. The pains and inflammation increased, until finally relief came in a stupor from which he never

CLOSING YEARS AND DEATH. 313

roused. A little after daybreak on June 19, 1786, he ceased breathing. "Mad Anthony" Wayne, the same who had stormed Stony Point, sat down, overwhelmed with grief, to write a few words to Colonel Jackson, asking him to make arrangements for the funeral. "My dear friend General Greene is no more. . . . He was great as a soldier, greater as a citizen, immaculate as a friend. . . . Pardon this scrawl; my feelings are but too much affected, because I have seen a great and good man die."

The next morning his body was taken down the river in a boat to Savannah. The militia of the adjoining counties turned out, the artillery at Fort Wayne fired minute guns, the shipping in the harbor hung their flags at half mast, all business in the town was suspended, and the citizens in mass attended the funeral of the man who had reconquered the South from the British.

The news of his death traveled northward as fast as the means of communication of that day permitted, and everywhere produced profound sorrow and surprise. Lee, then in Congress, was the first to convey the intelligence to Washington. "Your friend and second, the patriot and noble Greene, is no more. Universal grief reigns here. How hard is the fate of the United States to lose such a man in the middle of life! Irreparable loss!"

Lee was also chairman of a committee upon whose report, on August 8, 1786, Congress passed a resolution in these words:

"*Resolved*, That a monument be erected to the memory of Nathanael Greene, Esq., at the seat of the Federal Government, with the following inscription: Sacred to the memory of Nathanael Greene, Esq., a native of the State of Rhode Island, who died on the 19th of June, 1786; late Major General in the service of the United States, and commander of their army in the Southern Department.

"The United States in Congress assembled, in honor of his patriotism, valor, and ability, have erected this monument.

"*Resolved*, That the Board of Treasury take order for the due execution of the foregoing resolution."

The order remained unexecuted for ninety years, but in 1875, at the instance of the senators from Rhode Island, the necessary money was appropriated, and two years later an admirable equestrian statue in bronze, by Henry K. Brown, was erected on the public square at the intersection of Massachusetts and Maryland Avenues, in Washington.

Thus died, at the early age of not quite forty-four, the man of whom Sparks said that "he may justly be regarded as the most extraordinary man in the Army of the Revolution." The words are carefully chosen. He was not the greatest man of the Revolution, for Washington, by common consent, had no rival. But when we consider Greene's early education, the suddenness with which he leaped from obscurity to high military command, the great services he rendered in organizing the Quartermaster General's Department, his unflagging devotion to the service (Washington and himself being the only ones of the generals at Boston who served continuously through the eight years of the war), the skill with which he conducted the military operations at the South, and the solidity of the results which

CLOSING YEARS AND DEATH. 315

he accomplished there—when we consider these, and remember his youth and his total lack of experience at the outbreak of the war, we see that he was indeed the most remarkable man among the soldiers of the Revolution, and that there was "no one whose reputation and advancement can with more justice be attributed exclusively to personal merit."

His fame rests upon his military achievements, for his short service in the Rhode Island Assembly was unimportant. What the future would have brought him had he lived to the age he had reason to expect, is mere conjecture. And yet such conjecture is not wholly idle. With his vigorous constitution, outdoor life and temperate habits, he had fairly thirty years more to look forward to. This period would have carried him through Washington's administration, the quarrel between Hamilton and Jefferson, the threatened war with France, the defeat of the Federalists, the long bickering with England, and finally the war of 1812. In all of these events, so important in determining the future of the Republic, he would necessarily have been a prominent factor. Of his talents for civil administration we have no very positive proofs, yet such experience as he had had before the war broke out had been in the direction of civil rather than military affairs. Of his military genius there is no question, and there is reason to believe that he would have developed equally great powers as a statesman. Hamilton was fully convinced of this, and in his eulogy on Greene, already quoted, he speaks of "the vast, I had almost said the enormous, powers of his mind. . . . The sudden termination of his life cut him off from those scenes which the progress of a new, immense, and unsettled empire could not fail to open to the complete exertion of that universal and pervading genius which qualified him not less for the Senate than for the field." And Washington, writing soon after his death, speaks of "the loss [that] the public has sustained by the death of this valuable character, especially at this crisis, *when the political machine seems to portend the most awful events.*" We have glimpses of what induced these opinions in Greene's correspondence about political affairs. He was a close student, and thought much on them, though he had no part in them. His shrewd reasoning while at Boston concerning the probability of a French alliance; his clear ideas as to the advisability of a declaration of independence and the proper military means for carrying on the war; his prompt appreciation of the weakness of Congress, the evils which this would produce, and the necessity for a more perfect union; his sound views about currency and finance expressed in his letters to Robert Morris—all tend to show that with the responsibility and experience arising from active participation in public affairs he would have come to prominence in politics as quickly as he did in war. His name was twice suggested for the office of Secretary of War—once when the office was established, in 1781, and again when Benjamin Lincoln resigned, in 1784. In each case he positively declined to consider the appointment. After so many years of war and separation, his one thought was a quiet home, surrounded by his wife, to whom he was devotedly attached, and his children of whom he had seen so little, and of whom he wrote with unaffected simplicity, "I have a family whom I dearly love." But after a few years of rest he would have felt the longing for action, and there is little doubt that, had he been living in 1789, he would have been called to the Cabinet by Washington in a manner that would have admitted of no refusal. Once there, his natural inclinations would have led him into the Federal party, as a warm and vigorous ally of Hamilton, bringing him additional strength in his struggle with Jefferson. It is not impossible that his good judgment and tact in dealing with men might have averted the disaster to which John Adams led the Federalists in 1800. At all events, he, and not Hamilton, would naturally have been appointed general in chief at the time of Washington's death, when war with France seemed imminent, and at the outbreak of the war with England, in 1812 he would have been the chief military man in the country. It is safe to say that the wretched blunders and defeats of that war would not have taken place under his administration.

But all of these possibilities were cut short by the sunstroke on the banks of the Savannah River in June, 1786. It only remains to consider his actual military career. In studying this we must remember that he was not a trained soldier, commanding part or all of a regular army. He was a self-educated man, who among his studies had included that of the military art simply as a means to an end. He was brought up in an atmosphere where the old-fashioned ideas of militia prevailed. When war came he discarded these ideas instantly, and did all in his power to persuade others to do the same. A force enlisted for the war, ready to go wherever ordered, subject to the orders of one commander in chief, uniformly armed, equipped, and disciplined—this was his conception of the force needed to fight the soldiers of Great Britain. These ideas are commonplace and universal to-day, but in 1775 they were novel and original: to the majority of the colonists they seemed little less than dangerous, and subversive of all liberty. His chief task, therefore, as a brigade and division commander, as quartermaster general, and as commanding general at the South, was to introduce order, discipline, and system in his command, and to keep his men fed, clothed, and armed in the absence of all those resources, without which an army ordinarily can not exist. What he accomplished in these directions seemed then, and still appears now, incredible.

But if he was not a trained soldier, in command of a regular force, he had all the instincts of a soldier of the highest grade. The conditions in other wars were so dissimilar that it is difficult to compare him with other soldiers, with Sherman or Sheridan, or with the famous lieutenants of Napoleon and Frederick. He can, however, be easily compared with his fellow-soldiers of the Revolution, and it is safe to say that in the strictly military domain of strategy and tactics he had no superior among them, not even the immortal Washington himself. He showed these qualities clearly while yet a subordinate, in command of a division at Trenton and Monmouth and Newport, and above all at the Brandywine, when he moved his men for nearly four miles at the double quick toward the sound of the cannon. He had the true military eye for topography and the choice of a position, and he coupled with this a quick decision in the changing events of battle. The formation of his troops for attack or defense was in strict accordance with military principles—the infantry in two or three lines, the cavalry on the flanks, and the artillery in the intervals; the best troops in the second or third line, the action opened by the artillery, and the reserve brought up at the decisive moment; the cavalry well in advance on the march to learn the enemy's movements and in battle threatening the enemy's flanks, leading in pursuit after a victory or covering the retreat after a defeat.

All of these principles were more scientifically applied under his command at the South than at any other time during the war. In spite of this, he was clearly defeated at Guilford and Hobkirk's Hill; he lost the siege of Ninety-Six, and Eutaw Springs was at best a drawn battle. The cause in each case was the inexperience and lack of discipline in a portion of his troops, due not to any defect in the individual qualities of the men, but to their short service and want of training. In each of these battles there was a critical moment when victory might have been secured by a final desperate effort; but if the effort failed, destruction was inevitable. It is an interesting subject of discussion whether he should have made this effort. To a man of his impulsive temperament the temptation to do so must have been great. But in each case he resisted it, and adhered to his deliberate intention never to place his little army within the possibility of destruction. In this he certainly showed great self-control, and it is fair to accept the verdict of his contemporaries, who universally applauded his prudence. But if his battles failed through the imperfection of the tools with which he had to work, he showed the talent of a master workman in that portion of his task which depended on himself alone.

In the rapidity of his retreat to the Dan, the promptness with which he then turned on Cornwallis and pursued him to Guilford, the boldness with which he disregarded Cornwallis and carried the war back into South Carolina, and the skill with which he manœuvred around the head waters of the streams, always keeping his back to the mountains, and finally pushed a much superior force into the fortifications of Charleston and held them there—in all his strategic combinations his plans were so well laid that, in spite of temporary defeat in battle, the ultimate end of each campaign was fully achieved.

His personal character was very attractive. He had a frank, confiding, loyal nature, above petty meanness of any sort. He made strong friendships among those with whom he was associated, and, though a strict disciplinarian, he was respected and beloved by his men. He showed ill temper and a lack of calm judgment in his controversy with Congress while quartermaster general, but it must be admitted that the provocation was very great. On the other hand, when he arrived at chief command, he exhibited rare patience and tact in dealing with the complaints and jealousies of the officers who served under him. He was devoted to his wife and children, and in all his family relations his life was exemplary. He showed proper respect to his superiors, but he never cringed to any man. His loyalty to Washington never failed for one moment, either in deed or thought.

Taken all in all, he was a fine type of that sturdy New England manhood which has been so potent in shaping the destinies of the Western world.

INDEX.

Adams, John, correspondence with Greene, 37, 38, 40, 68, 73, 75.
Alliance with France, 105.
André, Major John, trial and execution of, 154, 157.
Arnold, General Benedict, at Philadelphia, 77; treason at West Point, 154, 157; operations in Virginia, 203, 205.
Augusta, siege of, 250.

Balfour, Colonel Nisbet, 260.
Bancroft, George, historian, criticisms on Greene at Long Island, 38; at Fort Washington, 53; at Trenton, 66; at Germantown, 90.
Banks, John, speculator, receives contract to clothe the Southern army, 292; receives contract for feeding the Southern army, 296; becomes financially embarrassed, and induces Greene to become surety for his debts, 297; fraudulently disposes of the security, 298; flees before Greene, 298; his death, 298; makes statement in regard to his transactions with Greene, 300.
Brandywine, battle of, 81.
British forces in South Carolina, strength of, 178, 190, 199, 215, 282.
British posts in South Carolina, 234, 235.
Brown, John, merchant in Providence, letter from Greene to, 121.
Browne, Lieut.-Colonel Thomas, at siege of Augusta, 235, 250, 251; at Savannah, 285.
Burnet, Major, aide-de-camp to Greene, involved in speculation with Banks, 299, 300; compromises Greene, 301.
Butt's Hill, on Rhode Island, engagement at, 114.

Camden, battle of, 165; occupied and fortified by the British, 180, 234, 238.
Campbell, Colonel Richard, at Guilford, 217, 219, 222; at Hobkirk's Hill, 240; at Ninety-Six, 257; at Eutaw Springs, 270, 272; killed, 273.

Charleston, siege of, 162 ; plans for combined land and naval attack after fall of Yorktown, 277, 279, 280 ; evacuated, 292.

Cincinnati, order of the, Greene's lack of interest in it, 308.

Clinton, General Sir Henry, at Long Island, 41 ; succeeds Howe as commander in chief, 99 ; at Monmouth, 101 ; at Newport, 115, 146 ; defeated at Charleston, 162 ; captures Charleston, 164 ; instructions to Cornwallis, 179 ; sends re-enforcements to the South, 182, 204, 233 ; controversy with Cornwallis, 244, 245.

Cornwallis, Lieutenant-General, Earl, at Long Island, 41 ; at Fort Washington, 56 ; at Fort Lee, 60 ; at Trenton, 61, 64 ; at Princeton, 65 ; at Westfield, 78 ; at Brandywine, 81, 83 ; at Germantown, 89 ; in East Jersey, 91 ; at siege of Charleston, 164 ; in command at the South, 177 ; advances into North Carolina, 181, 183 ; instructions to Tarleton, 186 ; advances to the Dan, 191-203 ; retreats to Hillsborough, 206 ; manœuvres near Guilford, 210 ; gains victory at Guilford, 217 ; retreats to the seacoast, 229 ; marches to Virginia, 244 ; controversy with Clinton, 245.

Cowpens, battle of, 187.

Cruger, Lieutenant-Colonel John H., in South Carolina,
179 ; at Ninety-Six, 235 ; defends Ninety-Six, 249, 252, 253, 259 ; evacuates Ninety-Six, 261 ; at Eutaw Springs, 271, 272.

De Grasse, Admiral, Count, captures Rawdon, 262 ; arrival at Yorktown, 277 ; declines to attack Charleston, 279 ; captured by Rodney, 280.

De Lancey, Colonel Oliver, 179, 258.

D'Estaing, Admiral, Count, at Sandy Hook, 105 ; at Newport, 108, 111 ; at Boston, 114 ; sails to the West Indies, 120.

Du Coudray, General, proposed appointment of, as chief of artillery, 71 ; death of, 75.

Duponceau, Peter Stephen, Steuben's secretary, remarks about Mrs. Greene, 95.

Duval, Lieutenant, leads storming party at Ninety-Six, 258 ; killed at Eutaw Springs, 273.

Eutaw Springs, battle of, 271 ; relation of this battle to Yorktown, 275.

Ferguson, Major Patrick, 181.

Finances, condition of, 118.

Fiske, John, historian, opinion of Greene, 171.

Fort Galpin, capture of, 250.

Fort Granby, 235 ; capture of, 243 ; occupied by Sumter, 255.

INDEX. 323

Fort Lee, headquarters of Greene, 49; evacuated, 60.
Fort Motte, 234; capture of, 243.
Fort Washington, capture of, 49, 56, 59.
Fox, Charles James, comments on the battle of Guilford, 226.

Gates, General Horatio, at Boston, 25; opposition to Washington, 59, 97, 126; appointed to command in the South, 165; defeated at Camden, 153, 159, 165; succeeded by Greene, 167, 171; restored to duty, 172.
Germantown, battle of, 87.
Gornell, Sergeant, ringleader in a mutiny, 288; hanged, 288.
Grant, General U. S., correspondence with Sherman in 1864, 295.
Greene, Catharine Littlefield, wife of General Greene, marriage, 16; at Boston, 28; at Morristown, 68; at Valley Forge, 94; dances with Washington at Middlebrook, 123; starts for West Point, 160; letter from her husband in South Carolina, 268; Washington offers to assist in the education of her children, 302; returns to Rhode Island at the close of the war, 303; herself and family reunited with her husband in their Georgia home, 311, 312.
Greene, Colonel Christopher, 17,
19; defends Red Bank, 91; at Newport, 115.
Greene, John, ancestor of General Greene, 1, 5, 6.
Greene, Nathanael, father of General Greene, 4.
Greene, Nathanael, ancestry, 1; education, 4; member of Assembly, 10; marriage, 16; military studies, 17; in command of Rhode Island troops, 19; at Boston, 23; correspondence with Governor Ward, 30; at Long Island, 35; appointed major general, 35; correspondence with John Adams, 38; at Harlem Heights, 47; at Fort Lee, 49; at Fort Washington, 51, 56, 59; at Trenton, 62, 66; at Morristown, 68; protests against appointment of M. du Coudray as chief of artillery, 71; engagement at Brunswick, 78; at Brandywine, 82; at Germantown, 87; at Valley Forge, 94; appointed quartermaster general, 98; at Monmouth, 101; reproved by Washington, 104; at Newport, 106; at Butt's Hill, 114; at Middlebrook, 123; difficulties of the Quartermaster's Department, 124; . approved by Congress, 130; controversy with Congress, 134; engagement at Springfield, 139; resigns as quartermaster general, 144; action of Congress on his resignation, 147; in

command of the army on the Hudson, 154; president of board to try André, 155; assigned to command at West Point, 159; appointed to command the Southern army, 161; arrival at Charlotte, 171; strength and condition of his army, 173; opens the campaign, 183; retreats to the Dan, 194; pursues Cornwallis, 206; defeated at Guilford, 216; again pursues Cornwallis, 229; carries the war into South Carolina, 230, 237; defeated at Hobkirk's Hill, 239; captures the British posts in South Carolina, 243; advances against Ninety-Six, 247; siege of Ninety-Six, 253; retires from Ninety-Six, 259; pursues Rawdon to Orangeburg, 261; goes into camp at High Hills of Santee, 262, 264; his efforts to secure re-enforcements, money, and supplies for his army, 265, 266, 267; advances against Stuart, 269; fights battle at Eutaw Springs, 270–276; recommends to Washington an attack upon Charleston, 277–280; receives re-enforcements from Yorktown, 281, 284; advances to Charleston, 283; sends Wayne to conquer Georgia, 284; receives resolutions of thanks and awards of land from the Legislatures of Georgia, South Carolina and North Carolina, 286; his difficulties in securing food and clothing for the army, 288–293; takes possession of Charleston and ends hostilities, 292; his correspondence with Washington on the termination of the war, 294; comparison with letters of Grant and Sherman, 295; guarantees the obligations of Banks in regard to feeding the army, 297; loses the bulk of his fortune in consequence thereof, 298; is accused of holding improper relations with Banks, 299; is fully acquitted of the charge, 300, 301; returns to Rhode Island, 303, 305; receives thanks of Congress and State legislatures, 304; challenged to a duel with Captain Gunn, 305; declines all public office, 307; correspondence with Robert Morris concerning political affairs, 308; establishes his home on his Georgia plantation, 311; dies, 312; estimate of his services and character, 315.

Greene, Governor William, 14, 16.

Guilford Court House, battle of, 216.

Gunby, Colonel, conduct at Hobkirk's Hill, 241.

Gunn, Captain, makes improper use of public horses, 289; challenges Greene to a duel, 305.

INDEX.

Hamilton, Alexander, noticed by Greene while drilling his company at New York, 37; appointed secretary to Washington, 66; at Valley Forge, 94; resigns from Washington's staff, 104; advises Greene in his controversy with Congress, 137; informs Greene of André's treason, 154; advocates legislation for the relief of Greene's widow, 298; his opinion of Greene, 66, 231, 316.

Harlem Heights, engagement at, 46, 48.

Hampton, Colonel Wade, at Eutaw Springs, 273, 274; at Dorchester, 283.

Henderson, Colonel, temporarily in command of Sumter's partisans, 266, 270; wounded at Eutaw Springs, 273.

High Hills of Santee, encampment at, 237, 261, 264, 266, 275, 281, 282.

Hobkirk's Hill, battle of, 239.

Howe, Admiral, Lord, at Newport, 110.

Howe, General Sir William, British commander in chief at Boston, 30; at New York, 35; at Long Island, 42; at Kip's Bay, 45; at White Plains, 50; at Fort Washington, 56; manœuvres in New Jersey, 77; moves to the Chesapeake, 77; victory at Brandywine, 82; enters Philadelphia, 85; victory at Germantown, 87; superseded by Clinton, 99.

Huger, General Isaac, commands detachment in Southern army, 184, 194, 198, 200, 246.

Jefferson, Governor Thomas, arrangements for supplying the Southern army, 170, 173, 204–206, 248, 255.

Kentish Guards, organized by Greene and others, 6, 17; marches to Boston, 18.

King's Mountain, battle of, 181.

Kip's Bay, engagement at, 45, 46.

Kirkwood, Major Robert, commands the Delaware battalion at Guilford, 217, 219, 220; at Hobkirk's Hill, 239, 240; at Ninety-Six, 251, 258; at Eutaw Springs, 270, 274.

Knox, General Henry, visit of Greene to his bookstore, 17; chief of artillery at New York, 36; examines defenses at West Point, 67; protests against being superseded by Du Coudray, 71, 72, 74, 75; at Valley Forge, 94; member of board to try André, 155.

Kosciusko, Colonel Thaddeus, engineer of the Southern army, selects camp on the Pedee River, 176; constructs earthworks at the crossing of the Dan, 202; makes reconnoissance at Ninety-Six, 253; wounded in a sortie, 256; selects camp at Round O, 284.

Lafayette, Marquis, joins the army, 79; gallantry at the battle of Brandywine, 83; at Valley Forge, 94; at Monmouth, 100, 101; ordered to Newport, 106; in the operations at Newport, 111-114, 116, 117; returns to France, 120; in operations against New York, 142; member of board to try André, 155; applies to be ordered with Greene, 169; in command in Virginia, 230, 233, 246, 247, 278; his action in purchasing clothing for his soldiers in Baltimore, 299; educates Greene's son in France, 302.

Laurens, Colonel John, aid-de-camp to Washington at Valley Forge, 94, 96; meets D'Estaing at Sandy Hook, 105; applies to be ordered to the South with Greene, 169; in front of Charleston, 285, 291; death of, 285.

Lawson, General Robert, commands brigade of Virginia militia at Guilford, 217.

Lee, General Charles, at Boston, 25; at Long Island, 36; criticisms on the fall of Fort Washington, 58; sends Colonel Malmedy to Rhode Island, 70; rejoins the army at Valley Forge, 99, 100; on the march to Monmouth, 101; his conduct at Monmouth, 102; end of his career, 101, 103.

Lee, Lieutenant-Colonel Henry, remarks about the battle of Germantown, 90; ordered to the Southern army, 169, 179; arrives at Charlotte, 176; in the retreat to the Dan, 194, 197, 199, 202-204; in pursuit of Cornwallis, 205; captures Pyle's detachment, 206, 207; skirmish with Tarleton, 209; at the battle of Guilford, 211, 212, 214, 216, 217, 222, 224; pursues Cornwallis toward the coast, 229; advice concerning carrying the war into South Carolina, 231; advances into South Carolina, 232-234; at the capture of Fort Watson, 236, 239; captures Fort Granby, 243; captures Fort Galphin, 250; captures Augusta, 251; arrives at Ninety-Six, 251; at the siege of Ninety-Six, 256, 258, 259; pursues Rawdon, 260; comments on the Southern campaign, 203, 264; at Eutaw Springs, 270, 272, 273; in front of Charleston, 284, 285, 291; obtains leave of absence and marries, 288; his opinion of Greene, 313.

Leslie, General Alexander, at Harlem Heights, 46; arrives in Virginia, 171; sails to Charleston, 178, 182; marches to join Cornwallis, 186, 192; at Guilford, 215, 217; takes command at Charleston, 284; proposes cessation of hostili-

INDEX.

ties, 291; evacuates Charleston, 292.
Lincoln, General Benjamin, appointed major-general, 76; in command at the South, 130, 163; surrenders at Charleston, 164, 166; ordered to march to the Hudson after the fall of Yorktown, 277; his advice about marching to Charleston, 280.
Luzerne, Minister of France, correspondence with Greene, 242, 247.
Lynch, Colonel Charles, commands Virginia riflemen at Guilford, 217, 219, 220.

Magaw, Colonel Robert, commands at Fort Washington, 53, 57.
Maham Tower, used at Fort Watson, 236; at Fort Cornwallis, 251; at Ninety-Six, 254, 257.
Mahan, Captain Alfred T., comments on the French fleet at Newport, 110.
Marion, General Francis, qualities as a partisan chief, 169, 176; attacks Georgetown, 185; captures Fort Watson, 232, 234-236; marches to Camden, 239; captures Fort Motte, 243; offers to resign, 248, 249; sends couriers to Greene at Ninety-Six, 254; joins Greene at Fort Granby, 261; at Eutaw Springs, 270, 275.
Marjoribanks, Major, at the battle of Eutaw Springs, 272-274, 276.
McGowan's ford, passage of, 195.
Middlebrook, winter camp at, 123.
Monmouth, battle of, 101.
Morgan, General Daniel, joins Greene in East Jersey, 92; at the South, 169, 179; ordered to western South Carolina, 184-186; gains a victory at the Cowpens, 187-190; retreats to North Carolina, 191-196, 198; resigns, 199.
Morris, Robert, Superintendent of Finance, authorizes bills to be drawn on him to provide funds for the support of Southern army, 267; correspondence with Greene, 267; opinion of Greene, 282; leaves the Southern army to be supported by the Southern States, 289; sends agent with small amount of money, 292; approves Greene's arrangements for feeding and clothing the army, 300; correspondence with Greene concerning political questions, 308.
Morristown, winter camp at, 65, 129, 135.

Newport, operations at, 106.
Ninety-Six, siege of, 249.

O'Hara, General Charles, in the pursuit to the Dan, 202; at Guilford, 215, 219, 220; wounded, 221, 222.

Phillips, General William, expedition to Virginia, 233 ; Cornwallis's letter to him, 244.

Pickens, General Andrew, partisan chief, 169, 176, 180 ; sent to raise militia at Charlotte, 201, 204 ; pursues Cornwallis, 206 ; captures Pyle's detachment, 207, 208 ; skirmish with Tarleton, 209 ; at Guilford, 211 ; sent against Ninety-Six, 232 ; captures Augusta, 250, 251 ; at Ninety-Six, 255, 262 ; at Eutaw Springs, 270.

Pitt, William, speech on the battle of Guilford, 226.

Princeton, engagement at, 64.

Putnam, General Israel, appointed major general, 25 ; at New York, 43, 46 ; at Harlem Heights, 48 ; at Peekskill, 91.

Pyle, Colonel, captured with his detachment, 207, 209.

Ramsay, Dr. David, historian, opinion of Greene, 282.

Rawdon, Colonel, Lord, second in command at the South, 177, 178 ; at Camden, 234, 237, 238 ; gains victory at Hobkirk's Hill, 239–242 ; retreats from Camden, 243 ; receives re-enforcements at Charleston, 254, 255 ; marches to Ninety-Six, 256 ; relieves Ninety-Six, 259 ; retreats from Ninety-Six, 260, 261 ; captured by De Grasse, 262.

Reed, Governor Joseph, secretary to Washington at Boston, 24 ; praises condition of Greene's troops, 24 ; conduct at Harlem Heights, 49 ; visits Valley Forge as member of Congress, 96 ; persuades Greene to accept office of Quartermaster General, 97 ; Governor of Pennsylvania, 133 ; correspondence with Greene, 133, 169, 242.

Rochambeau, General, Count, arrives at Newport, 142 ; meets Washington at Hartford, 151, 153 ; proposed as arbitrator in case of André, 156 ; movements of his army after the fall of Yorktown, 277, 281.

Rodney, Admiral Sir George B., destroys De Grasse's fleet, 280.

Rutledge, Governor John, arrives at Greene's camp, 175 ; takes measures to restore civil government in South Carolina, 265 ; fails to secure subscriptions for Morris's bank, 266, 267 ; endeavors to secure re-enforcements from Yorktown, 277, 279 ; convenes Legislature and eulogizes Greene, 280.

St. Clair, General, member of board to try André, 155 ; ordered to re-enforce Greene after fall of Yorktown, 277 ; arrives in front of Charleston,

INDEX. 329

284 ; obtains leave of absence, 288.

Savannah, siege of, 162 ; captured by Wayne, 285.

Schuyler, General Philip, appointed major general, 25 ; sends re-enforcements to Washington, 62 ; member of Congress, 132 ; goes to Washington's camp to consult with him about Quartermaster's Department, 136, 137, 141 ; Greene's letter to him, 143 ; persuades Greene to remain temporarily as quartermaster general, 145 ; his report to Congress, 146.

Sheridan, Major, at the battle of Eutaw Springs, 273.

Sherman, General W. T., correspondence with Grant in 1864, 295.

Smallwood, General William, commands Maryland militia at Germantown, 86.

Spencer, General Joseph, at Boston, 25 ; at Harlem, 43, 45 ; sent to Rhode Island, 70, 106 ; resigns, 106.

Springfield, engagement at, 140.

Stedman, Charles, British historian, comments on the battle of Guilford, 224 ; on the success of Greene's operations in the South, 264.

Stephen, General Adam, appointed major general, 76 ; at Germantown, 86, 87 ; dismissed, 87.

Steuben, General, Baron, arrives at Valley Forge, 95 ; appointed inspector general and drills the squads, 96 ; member of board to try André, 155 ; ordered to the Southern army with Greene, 168, 169 ; stops at Mount Vernon, 170 ; appointed to command in Virginia, 171 ; endeavors to send re-enforcements to Greene, 176, 204, 205 ; letters from Greene, 205, 233, 246.

Stewart, Lieut.-Colonel Alexander, commands the second battalion of Guards at Guilford, 220 ; killed, 221, 224.

Stiles, Rev. Ezra, gives Greene advice about the choice of books, 7.

Stirling, General, Earl of, appointed major general, 76 ; at Germantown, 86 ; at Monmouth, 102 ; member of board to try André, 155.

Stony Point, capture of, 120.

Stuart, Lieutenant-Colonel John, succeeds Rawdon in command at the South, 262 ; defeated at Eutaw Springs, 269 ; retreats toward Charleston, 273 ; at Dorchester, 283.

Sullivan, General John, appointed brigadier general, 25 ; at Boston, 30 ; at Trenton, 62 ; protests against appointment by Du Coudray, 71, 74 ; at Brandywine, 81–83 ; at Germantown, 86–88 ; in command in Rhode Island, 106, 107 ; meets D'Es-

22

taing, 109; advances against Newport, 110, 111; publishes order reflecting on the French, 113; retreats from Newport, 114; fights at Butt's Hill, 115, 117; defeats Indians in New York and Pennsylvania, 120; Greene defends his conduct at Newport, 121, 122.

Sumner, General Jethro, brings re-enforcements from Virginia, 265; at Eutaw Springs, 270, 272.

Sumter, General Thomas, partisan chief, 169, 176; ordered to threaten Ninety-Six, 201; ordered to be prepared to join Greene at Camden, 232; fails to comply with his instructions, 238; captures Orangeburg, 243; protests against capture of Fort Granby by Lee and regular troops, 247, 248; fails to obey instructions for retarding Rawdon's advance, 255; joins Greene at Fort Granby, 261; leaves his command without authority, 265, 266; at Dorchester, 283; opposes legislation for the relief of Greene's widow, 298.

Tarleton, Colonel Banastre, in command of British Legion, 178; ordered to attack Morgan, 185, 186; advances against Morgan, 187; defeated at the Cowpens, 188; pursues Morgan, 195–197; comments on Greene's retreat to the Dan, 203; advances to meet Pyle's detachment, 207; manœuvres near Guilford, 211; wounded in skirmish with Lee, 216; at Guilford, 218, 224; raiding in Virginia, 248, 281.

Trenton, battle of, 62.

Valley Forge, camp at, 94, 100.

Varnum, General James M., friend of Greene in his youth, 14, 15; elected captain in Kentish Guards, 17, 18; appointed Colonel Third Rhode Island Regiment, 19; arrives at Boston, 23; joins Greene in East Jersey, 91; at Valley Forge, 95; ordered to Newport, 106; at Butt's Hill, 115; member of Congress, 184.

Wadsworth, Jeremiah, letter from Washington to him concerning Greene's connection with Banks, 302.

Ward, Governor Samuel, prominence in Rhode Island politics, 13, 16; delegate to Continental Congress, 16; influence in securing Greene's appointment to command Rhode Island troops, 20; correspondence with Greene, 24, 28, 30; death of, 37.

Ward, Major Samuel, Jr., friend of Greene in his youth, 14; elected captain in Rhode Island regiment, 19; volun-

INDEX. 331

teers to join expedition to Quebec and is taken prisoner, 28; at Valley Forge, 95; at Newport, 115.

Washington, General George, takes command at Boston, 24; his first meeting with Greene, 25; captures Boston, 30; marches to New York, 34; his skill in retreating from Long Island, 42; in action at Kip's Bay, 46; fights battle of Harlem Heights, 47; manœuvres toward White Plains and thence to the Hudson, 50; his instructions to Greene concerning Fort Washington, 53; his share of responsibility for the disaster, 58; retreats through New Jersey, 61; his brilliant success at Trenton, 62; arrives at Morristown, 65; protests against appointment of Du Coudray, 71; marches to Delaware, 78; makes reconnoissance with Greene and Lafayette, 80; fights battle of Brandywine, 81; of Germantown, 85; goes into camp at Valley Forge, 94; persuades Greene to accept position of Quartermaster General, 97; fights battle of Monmouth, 101; reproves Greene, 104; sends detachment to Rhode Island, 106; his comments on the failure of the Rhode Island Expedition, 116; goes into winter quarters at Middlebrook, 123;

account of his expenses during the war, 128; his opinion of Greene's service while Quartermaster General, 131, 151, 152, 158; plans an attack on New York, 142; orders Greene to remain as Quartermaster General, 143; writes to Congress giving his opinion of Greene, 149, 151; meets Rochambeau at Hartford, 153; approves sentence against André, 155; orders Greene to West Point, 159; assigns him to command the Southern army, 160; his relations with Greene, 161, 171; his instructions to Greene, 166; writes to Greene approving his operations, 264, 277; corresponds with Greene concerning an attack on Charleston, 278; tries to persuade De Grasse to undertake an expedition against Charleston, 279; orders re-enforcements to Greene, 281; writes to Greene on the close of the Southern campaign, 293; his comments on the charges against Greene in connection with Banks, 302; offers to educate Greene's eldest son, 302; meets Greene for the last time, 303; approves Greene's decision in declining the duel with Captain Gunn, 307; his opinion concerning the loss sustained by Greene's death, 316.

Washington, Martha, joins her husband at Boston, 28; at Morristown, 67; at Valley Forge, 94; at Middlebrook, 123, 128; receives Greene at Mount Vernon, 170.

Washington, Colonel William, cavalry leader, 169; ordered to join Morgan, 183; at the Cowpens, 187-189; in the retreat to the Dan, 202, 204; at Guilford, 211, 213, 214, 217, 221, 222, 224; at Hobkirk's Hill, 239-241; at Eutaw Springs, 270, 272; at Dorchester, 283.

Wayne, General Anthony, at Brandywine, 82; at Germantown, 87, 88; at Monmouth, 100-103; storms Stony Point, 120; marches to Virginia, 233; conquers Georgia, 284, 285; presented with an estate by the Legislature of Georgia, 287; exonerates Greene in his transactions with Banks, 300, 301; settles on a plantation in Georgia, 311; at Greene's deathbed, 312; his opinion of Greene, 313.

Webster, Lieutenant - Colonel James, commands brigade at Guilford, 211, 215, 217-219; killed, 220, 224.

Williams, Colonel Otho H., in command of rear guard during retreat to the Dan, 201, 202; captures Pyle's detachment, 209; at Guilford, 211-213, 220, 221; at Eutaw Springs, 270, 272; at Dorchester, 283; obtains leave of absence, 288.

Williams, Roger, founder of Rhode Island, 1-3, 21.

Yorktown, battle of, 278; its relation to Eutaw Springs and the Southern campaign, 277, 279, 280.

THE END.

www.ingramcontent.com/pod-product-compliance
Lightning Source LLC
Chambersburg PA
CBHW071953220426
43662CB00009B/1115